100 Most Beautiful Museums of the World

© 2005 Rebo International b.v., Lisse, The Netherlands

Publisher and redaction: Dr. Manfred Leier

Autors: Hans-Joachim Neubert/ScienceCom (all text except pages 108-111 and 126-127), Winfried Maaß (pages 108-111 and 126-127)

Research: Dr. Onno Groß, Axel Grychta, Vera Stadie

Graphic Design: Bartos Kersten Printmediendesign, Hamburg, Germany

Photographs Redaction: Bildagentur Schapowalow/Stefanie Braun

Documentation: Dr. Onno Groß

Editorial technology: Bollmann & Rieprich, Hamburg

Production: HVK Hamburger Verlagskontor GmbH, Hamburg, Germany

Translation: First Edition Translation, Cambridge, Great Britain

Typesetting: A. R. Garamond s.r.o., Prague, The Czech Republic

Proofreading: Emily Sands, Sarah Dunham

ISBN 90 366 1578 X

100 Most Beautiful Museums of the World

A journey across five continents

REBO
PUBLISHERS

Foreword

Dear readers,

Before the 17th century, clerics and nobility of medieval Europe and sometimes the wealthy bourgeois citizens of major towns adorned their churches and palaces, municipal buildings, town halls and guild houses as well as their drawing rooms with works by the most important or the most popular artists and sculptors of the time. The 17th century showed a gravitation toward specialisation of separate collections of paintings and sculptures, which were subsequently exhibited in separate rooms. At first, these royal and municipal collections were accessible only to a selected audience of travellers, intellectuals, diplomats and nobility, but during the 18th century, a new attitude to art developed. The expertise of the great artists was enlisted to assist the wider public's intellectual and esthetic education. Establishment of the first public museum, the Capitolino Museum – which opened its doors in Rome in 1734, exhibiting a selection of exemplary antique sculptures – was a milestone. It became the standard throughout Europe, and the 19th century became age of museums.

The buildings themselves bear the signature of the great architects of the time. To this day, they house important noble and municipal collections of art that were given into their care in the 19th century. There is scarcely a European country that did not follow the museum trend – from Moscow to Florence, Stockholm to Lisbon, Prague to Athens, bourgeois society adorned itself with masterpieces by great artists, exhibiting them in museums that frequently assumed the roles of national treasure troves. The citizens thronged to these new temples of art and the tradition continues to this day. From Europe, the museum concept spread to North and South America, Asia and Africa.

Angels with dirty faces?
Two cherubs from
Raphael's panting
The Sistine Madonna?

Now almost every country has its national museum, in which native artists are represented by their most important works. At the same time, in the second half of the 20th century, a completely new form of architecture was established to house modern art. In many countries, new museum buildings have been erected which, because of present day structural possibilities and modern building materials, have become architectural works of art in their own right. The Guggenheim buildings in New York and Bilbao as well as the Pompidou Center in Paris, are striking examples. Not least because of these new architectural experiences, art museums have once again become much visited and admired meeting places for social circles interested in art. A form of art tourism has emerged as art lovers follow the paths of individual artists. At the same time, impressive exhibitions of global art travel the world, introducing people to new cultures and perspectives.

100 of the World's Most Magnificent Museums provides an overview of 100 museums whose collections place them among the most important cultural institutions of the age. The book is certainly dominated by big, well-known museums with massive collections, but certain museums that are particularly impressive, unique or interesting due to their particular location or concentration are also included. The Louisiana Museum of Modern Art near Copenhagen, with its surrounding parkland overlooking the Baltic Sea, the Dalí Museum in northern Spain and the Beyeler Foundation in Riehen near Basel are noteworthy examples. By offering the reader a panorama of art from all five continents, comprising hundreds of diverse cultures, we hope to provide further information for art lovers and experts and to fuel a passion for art in the occasional traveller.

The Editor

Contents

In honor of Rubens

The central room in the ANTWERP MUSEUM OF FINE ARTS is devoted to the master

ADDRESS:
Leopold de Wael Plaats, Antwerp

OPENING TIMES:
Tues.-Sat. 10 am to 5 pm, Sun. 10 am to 6 pm

INTERNET:
www.museum. antwerpen.be/kmska

PUBLIC TRANSPORT:
Tram, Lines 4, 8, 12, 24; Bus, Routes 1 and 23

OTHER ATTRACTIONS:
Rubens' House, Mayer van den Bergh Museum

This monumental Rubens' painting is entitled *Venus Frigida* and was painted in 1614 (above right).

Around 1450, Jean Fouquet painted *Madonna and Child*. Agnès Sorel, King Charles VII's lover, probably served as the model for this unusual representation of the Virgin Mary (below left).

He was a diplomat, a court painter and a great teacher of many artists. He held court in his richly furnished house in Antwerp and experimented with colors so lavishly that every vibrant shade in his joyous paintings was different. Peter Paul Rubens was the main proponent of – and embodies – Flemish Baroque and the most splendid room, regarded as the holy of holies, in the Museum of Fine Arts is devoted to him. The prince of painters' monumental paintings hang against dark gray velvet walls in the 66 foot high central gallery with its gold-decorated, coffered ceiling. Wine-red velvet benches invite visitors to ponder the paintings, a truly great way to present one of the princes of the art world.

After spells in Italy and at the Spanish court, Rubens, who came from Germany, settled in the city of Antwerp in 1608. Antwerp remains true to its reputation as an artistic city even today, not least because of the Royal Museum of Fine Arts. The building rises majestically, its grandiose, pillared front crowned by two whip-cracking charioteers.

Unlike many European museums based on a royal collection, Antwerp's collection is heavily influenced by the traditions of the artists themselves. From the end of the 14th century, resident artists had a place to gather decorated with works by members of the Guild of Saint Luke. The pieces later developed into a collection which merged with that of the Academy of Arts. While the Netherlands was under French rule, many works of art from churches and public buildings were carted off to Paris and only returned to the city in 1815.

Together with the collection of former mayor, Sir Florent van Etborn (1784–1840), which he willed to the city of Antwerp, and purchases of contemporary art, these masterpieces formed the basis of a collection that was soon so extensive, it needed a separate building. The architects, Jan Jacob Winters and Frans Van Dijk, designed a building in the Neo-Classical style, which opened in 1890.

From the 14th to the 20th century

A devotional atmosphere was fully intended and the facade was decorated with columns and loggias as well as the busts and medallions of great artists. The architects went for impact inside. A sweeping staircase housed the monumental painting by historical painter Nicaise de Keyser, tantalizing visitors with hints of the artistic delicacies to come. Today, the collection comprises exhibits from the 14th to the 20th centuries, including 3,300 paintings, 400 sculptures and 3,600 drawings – a treasure trove of Dutch–Flemish painting and more.

The oldest painting is a representation dated around 1333 by Simone Martini, showing scenes from the life of the Virgin Mary. Several paintings date from the era known as "Flemish Primitive," including Jan van Eyck's *Madonna and Child at the Fountain* and Rogier van der Weyden's *Portrait of Philippe de Croy*. An outstanding masterpiece is a painting by Jean Fouquet, showing the Virgin Mary with a snow-white, naked bosom. Its is probably a portrait of Agnès Sorel who, as King Charles VII's lover, had great influence at the French court.

Hans Memling is represented by the portrait, *Man with a Roman Coin*, and also by a singing host of angels. Joachim Beuckelaer shows bourgeois life in his painting, *The Vegetable Market*. The Museum owns 21 paintings by Peter Paul Rubens, including *the Adoration of the Magi* and *The Baptism of Christ*. Together with Jacob Jordaens and Anthony Van Dyck, Rubens forms the Antwerp Trinity. The works by the other two artists are also exhibited in the central room.

James Ensor and Rik Wouters

These 19th and 20th century painters have a place on the first floor and among them, James Ensor, who came from Ostend, is particularly outstanding. The Museum has the most important Ensor collection in the world. While paintings such as *The Oyster Eater*, *Afternoon in Ostend* and especially *Christ's Entrance into Jeru-*

salem radiate great domestic peace, Ensor's paintings depict the pious hypocrisy of masked bourgeois. The Flemish Surrealists, represented by the works of Paul Delvaux and René Magritte, transport visitors to faraway worlds.

The Museum is famous for the collection by Fauvist Rik Wouters, donated by friends of the Museum. Modern Belgian art is also represented, with works by Constant Permeke, Gustave De Smet and Frits Van den Berghe. The famous sculpture, *Job*, by Ossip Zadkine and Günther Uecker's nail picture are just two examples of international contemporary art.

In view of high art prices, the collection is growing only slowly, yet the Museum wants to be seen as a "living organism." The institution attracts a young public beneath its venerable, old roof with theater, music and other events.

EUROPE

James Ensor's *The Intrigue*, 1890, shows the masked world characteristic of the artist (below center).

The facade of the Antwerp Museum of Fine Art, with pillared portico (below right).

9

Poet among painters

The GROENINGE MUSEUM and ST. JOHN'S HOSPITAL combine forces in BRUGES

ADDRESS:
Groeninge Museum:
Dijver 12, Bruges;
St. John's Hospital:
Mariastraat 38, Bruges

OPENING TIMES:
Tues.-Sun. 9:30 am
to 5 pm

INTERNET:
www.brugge.be/musea

HOW TO GET THERE:
On foot from the city
center

OTHER ATTRACTIONS:
Gruuthuse Museum,
Beguine Convent

Gerard David's diptych,
*The Judgment
of Cambyses*, depicts
the judgment
(our image) and
subsequent gruesome
mutilation of a corrupt
judge (below left).

Bruges is a European city with an acclaimed artistic heritage. The city hums and buzzes with visitors. But just a short distance from the lively center, time seems to stand still. The canals shimmer with silvery light and the belfry chimes fall like a veil of sound over the medieval city. Past and present appear to blend seamlessly here.

A visit to Bruges' richest art gallery, the Groeninge Museum, is only half as impressive if you have not explored the town beforehand, because it is here that artists who spent the biggest part of their lives in Bruges – such as Jan Van Eyck, Petrus Christus, Hans Memling, and Gerard David – meet in a building erected between 1929 and 1930. Later extended. With an almost photographic precision, the artists captured scenes that bring to life again this former center of trade.

Bruges was the Promised Land for 15th century artists. Jan Van Eyck, who came from Maastricht in 1430, settled in the city that was home to the dukes of Burgundy. In 1436, he painted Madonna with Canon Van Der Paele, warts and all. Next to the Madonna appears a man past fifty years of age, whose strong-minded face bears poignant traces of ill health and extravagance. The portrait of Margareta Van Eyck, the artist's wife, is also extremely vivid. Her gaze pursues the visitor relentlessly.

Old museum mile

Above all, works of Hans Memling, together with paintings by Rogier Van Der Weyden and Hugo Van Der Goes, captivate visitors. The artist, who emigrated from Germany, is regarded as the "poet" of the Bruges artists. He acquired wealth and fame with his portraits of Bruges' bourgeoisie and painted his triptych for Mayor Willem Moreel was the first major family portrait in the Netherlands. Visitors who view the paintings of Gerard David, on the other hand, need strong nerves. In *The Flaying of Cambyses*, for example, a corrupt judge is skinned while fully conscious. Hieronymus Bosch's capacity for imagination seems almost inexhaustible; his *Last Judgment* is one of the Museum's highlights. Then let the Symbolists, such as William Degouve de Nuncques or Fernand Khnopff, spirit you away to a mystical dream world.

Bruges is proof that museum miles are not a modern invention. The Arenthuis is adjacent to the Groeninge Museum, followed by the Gruuthuse Museum, housing an unusual collection of high quality craftwork, as well as sculptures and paintings, in a former palace. The building is a superb example of the splendor in which the former metropolis' citizens once lived.

The Memling Museum, housed in the nearby St. John's Hospital, reveals a very different side of the mercantile city. It is one of the oldest hospitals in Europe and was first mentioned as early as 1188. Romanesque sections are preserved here from the time when ailing citizens and permanent invalid residents were cared for by nuns and monks. The building ceased to be used as a hospital in the 16th century, but remained devoted to the care of the sick until 1978. Today, St. John's Hospital is one of the most popular museum sites in Bruges, especially because of the masterpieces by Hans Memling, displayed in the hospital's biggest chapel and in the smaller Cornelius Chapel.

Magnets for disciples of art

Heavy vaulted ceilings and a wealth of pillars form the perfect background for an artist whose works, despite their religious themes, are so lifelike, vital and triumphant. There are "only" six Memlings exhibited along-

side individual works by other artists, but it is said that if you have not seen them, you have not been to Bruges.

The triptych, *The Adoration of the Magi*, the Reins triptych painting, *The Lamentation* of Christ (showing the removal of Christ's body from the cross), the *Portrait of a Woman*, and the two-section altarpiece *The Madonna and Maarten Van Nieuwenhove* are jewels in the city's crown.

First and foremost, however, disciples of art are drawn to the two masterpieces housed in the Cornelius Chapel. Here stands the winged altarpiece, *The Mystical Marriage of Saint Catherine*, intended as a commissioned work for the chapel of St. John's Hospital. The Madonna and Child can be seen in the center section and the side sections show the beheading of Saint John the Baptist and the visions of Saint John the Evangelist. Memling's complete mastery of olor is shown in the saints' clothing, whose luminous quality has never been surpassed.

Next is Memling's most famous work, the *Shrine of Saint Ursula*, which offers such a wealth of images that it is impossible to absorb them all. It shows the travels of Saint Ursu-la, which took her, via Cologne and Basle, to Rome and back. Legend has it that her travels ended in martyrdom in Cologne. The shrine is made of wood and painted by Memling. The figures are far ahead of their time because of their realistic and accurately detailed representation. The artist also proves that he knew the city on the Rhine well because of his accurate reproduction of the scenery in Cologne. He is supposed to have spent part of his apprenticeship there with Stefan Lochner, but he became famous, died and is buried in Bruges.

Brussels' royal inheritance

The **MUSEUM OF FINE ARTS** in **BRUSSELS** possesses one of the biggest collections of art, from medieval to contemporary, in the world

North Sea

English Channel

Brussels

BELGIUM

ADDRESS:
Old Palace: Régence 3,
Modern Collection:
Place Royale 1-2,
Brussels

OPENING TIMES:
Tues.-Sun. 10 am
to 5 pm

INTERNET:
www.fine-arts-museum.be

PUBLIC TRANSPORT:
Train or subway to
Central Station; Bus,
Routes 27, 38, 60, 71,
95, 96;
Tram, Lines 92, 93, 94

J.L. David's 1793 painting, *The Death of Jean Paul Marat*, reflects the French Revolution of 1789, which was also significant for the history of the Museum (below left).

Arcimboldo's *Allegory of Water*, 1566, is a masterpiece of Mannerism (below right).

The story of Belgium's biggest and most important art museum also begins, like so much in Europe, with the Emperor. Art could only be exhibited publicly when the Austrians had been driven forever from the southern Netherlands. In 1794, Napoleon's officials seized Belgium's collection of religious artifacts and sent the most important works to the Louvre in Paris. But because it was impossible for the Louvre to hold all the European art collected, in 1801, Napoleon ordered the establishment of 15 departmental museums, including Brussels, and 50 of the stolen art works were returned to the people of Brussels for the first exhibition. After Napoleon's downfall in 1815, most of the remaining exhibits then returned to Belgium. The Museum passed to municipal ownership under the patronage of the Dutch King William I. Sixteen years after the Revolution, and after the establishment of an independent Belgian kingdom in 1830, it was renamed the Royal Museum of Painting and Sculpture in Belgium.

Legendary gallery
The Museum continued to receive royal patronage and the collection expanded quickly as a result of donations and new acquisitions. A new building, constructed by Alphonse Balat and inaugurated in 1887, now had truly royal dimensions, especially what is known as the Forum, a 4,844 square foot foyer with a gallery running around the upper floor, which offered the necessary space for ladies in hooped skirts and men in ceremonial uniform. The room itself accommodated even the most massive Neo-Classical paintings and still provides an elegant setting for sculptures by Auguste Rodin and Jef Lambeaux today. Yet the hall is not the only building. The staircase leads to the upper floors where art treasures from the Dutch, Flemish, German, French, Spanish and Italian schools are housed.

The chronological – and color coded – arrangement in the Museum of Ancient Art is helpful because, with the wealth and quality of exhibits, it is easy to lose the big picture. The Royal Museum is still one of the richest collections in the world.

The blue tour is reserved for the 15th and 16th centuries, represented by the works of Rogier van der Weyden (*Pietà*) and the anonymous masters who painted various saints and legends. We can find Lucas Cranach the Elder's *Venus and Cupid and the Portrait of Dr. J. Scheyring*. Gerard David's *Madonna and Child with the Milk Soup* gives an insight into the daily life of the Holy Family. The 16th century is characterized by the works of Flemish painters such as Quintin Massys and Joachim Beuckelaer. Here we encounter Pieter Breughel the Elder's paintings, brimming with life, such as *The Census at Bethlehem* and *The Wedding Dance*.

The 17th century (brown tour) honors Peter Paul Rubens with, amongst others, the *Martyrdom of Saint Livinius*. We are guided to France and Italy, and into the 18th century, with works by Philippe de Champaigne, Tiepolo, Guardi and Tintoretto.

The 19th century (yellow tour) starts with a drum roll, because Jacques Louis David's *Death of Marat* is impressive in its strength of composition and expressive rendition. Here at the border with modernism, we also encounter the Symbolists, represented by works such as *The Caresses / The Sphinx* by Fernabnd Khnopff. In addition to Impressionist and Post-Impressionist paintings by Gauguin, Vuillard and Matisse, the exhibition's highlights including paintings by James Ensor.

Paul Delvaux, René Magritte

The 19th century works lead us into the Museum of Modern Art, whose dramatic architecture stuns visitors. The six floors of this new building, connected with the Museum of Ancient Art, are positioned so skillfully around an underground light that the individual exhibition levels appear to be flooded with sunlight. Visitors are drawn down almost dynamically, starting with the new acquisitions, then guided to the Fauvists, whose main representative in The Netherlands was Rik Wouters. Visitors also encounter the Belgian Expressionists, with the stark paintings of Constant Permeke and Jan Brusselsman. The Surrealists, mainly represented in Belgium by Paul Delvaux and René Magritte, also play an important role.

The collection with works by Brussels painter René Magritte is actually the biggest Magritte collection in the world. *The Empire of Light*, *The Treasure Island* and *The Art of Conversation* transport visitors to a fantastic world. Contemporary art is represented with works by Alexander Calder, Donald Judd and by Richard Long's stone *Utah Circle*, an invitation to meditate. The latest directions in art are also exhibited here on the lowest floor. The "sunken" rooms have a calming effect. Moving back into the daylight, the sculpture garden invites visitors to relax a while.

Fernand Khnopff's painting, *The Sphinx*, was created in 1896 and is one of the best-known Symbolist works (above).

Paul Delvaux's *Nocturne*, an example of Surrealism in modern Belgian art (right center).

View of the Forum with the encircling gallery (below right).

Flemish painter princes

The **MUSEUM OF FINE ART** in **GHENT** has collected the Belgium's art treasures since the end of the 18th century

ADRESS:
Citadel Park, Ghent

OPENING TIMES:
Expected to be closed until 2007. Temporary exhibitions will be shown in the Museum Pavilion, St Bavo's Cathedral and other city museums.

INTERNET:
www.mskgent.be

PUBLIC TRANSPORT:
Bus, tram and taxi

OTHER ATTRACTIONS:
S.M.A.K. Museum of Contemporary Art, Design Museum

A group of male intellectuals: *The Lecture of Emile Verhaeren* by Théo van Rysselberghe, 1903 (below left). The French writer, André Gide, can be picked out at the table, on the right.

Rysselberghe is the name of a highly regarded family in Ghent. Théo van Rysselberghe was one of the first painters to embrace Art Nouveau. The Art Nouveau style achieved noteworthy heights in Belgium, through men such as Henry van de Velde and Victor Horta.

For a little country that has been independent for only 170 years, Belgium's contribution to art is quite extraordinary. Noteworthy are James Ensor, who provided Rysselberghe with a great deal of assistance, Fernand Khnopff, Félicien Rops and – later – René Magritte and Paul Delvaux. Rysselberghe went to France, where he became part of the Pointillist circle surrounding Georges Seurat and Paul Signac. His most famous works date from that period.

His works hang in countless European collections and he is exhibited in the Museum of Fine Art in his home town of Ghent as well. This art gallery is one of the oldest of its kind in modern-day Belgium. Its origins date back to 1798, the age of the French Revolution. The Austrian Netherlands, as Belgian Flanders was

called at the time, rose up against the Hapsburg domination, finally becoming an integral part of the French republic, which implemented its domestic policy in the area, including secularization of the comprehensive monastery and church estates. Works of art from abandoned religious institutions were passed back and forth across the country. In Ghent, they provided the foundations of today's Museum.

The city itself has an honorable history, politically as well as artisitically. The late medieval port at the mouth of the Leie and Schelde rivers, the center of Flemish cloth manufacture, was governed by the counts of Flanders and had a rich and self-important mercantile class. The Austrian Emperor Maximilian I married Maria, the Burgundian heiress there. It was the start of the global Hapsburg Empire. The city's most famous work of art already existed at the time, in a

side chapel in the cathedral of St Bavo: the late Gothic altar polyptych by the brothers, Jan and Hubert Van Eyck, depicting the Adoration of the Lamb on a total of 12 altar panels.

Painter of the sinister

Numerous pictures that form part of the Museum of Fine Art's collection can be seen in this church. The main building is currently closed because extensive construction work is in progress. We can only speculate as to what the building will look like after work is completed in 2007.

The Museum opened in 1904. It is an important building in pale sandstone, with a Doric portico. Two rows of Gobelins tapestries, manufactured in Brussels, hung (and will hang in the future) right behind the entrance. One sequence of the tapestries, produced in the 17th century, depicts the old story of the Ancient Persian King Darius. The other, about one hundred years younger, shows the Glorification of the Gods. It was originally housed in Ghent's castle, the Gravensteen.

The various exhibition rooms, 30 in all, are interconnecting. Around 350 works are on display, mainly paintings and graphics. The collections from the time of the Great Revolution have been added to and expanded in subsequent decades by acquisitions and donations.

The aim was and is to provide a representative overview of the deve-

lopment of the fine arts, especially the fine art of Flanders, during the period between the 14th and the first half of the 20th century. In addition, there are works by artists from other countries such as Tintoretto, Gustav Courbet, Camille Corot and William Hogarth. The city has acquired another building for contemporary art which goes by the abbreviation S.M.A.K. It continues where the institution in Citadel Park leaves off and displays the not inconsiderable number of contemporary Belgian avant-gardes, such as the highly commercial Roger Raveel.

An even more recent star on the global art scene is the Flemish, Luc Tuymans. His paintings are nightmarish commentaries on our everyday reality. He thus continues his region's artistic legacy, which is collected in such an exemplary manner by the Museum of Fine Art in Ghent. Magritte and Ensor already depicted the sinister. The tradition dates back even further to the late Middle Ages, to Rogier Van der Weyden, the Eycks, Pieter Breughel the Elder and, above all, to Hieronymus Bosch. The Museum owns a *Christ Carrying the Cross* by the Bosch. The suffering Christ is jostled by many grotesque caricatures whose mocking laughter echoes through the ages.

There is a long tradition of still life in Flemish painting (above left).

The section from Hieronymus Bosch's *Christ Carrying the Cross* highlights with brutal mastery the devilish and grotesque participation of onlookers (above right).

Ghent's most famous work of art: *The Adoration of the Lamb* (section) by Jan and Hubert Van Eyck (right center).

The Museum's splendid entrance facade, founded in 1798 (below right).

Where art meets nature

LOUISIANA MUSEUM PARK in **HUMLEBAEK** near Copenhagen is one of the most atmospheric cultural centers in the world

DENMARK
Humlebaek
Copenhagen
Baltic Sea
North Sea

ADDRESS:
Gl. Strandvej 13, Humlebaek

OPENING HOURS:
Thurs.-Tues. 10 am to 5 pm, Wed. 10 am to 10 pm

INTERNET:
www.louisiana.dk

HOW TO GET THERE:
By car via the E47/E55 motorway. By rail from Copenhagen.

A backdrop of uninterrupted sky and a rippling lake with a mobile by Alexander Calder toying with the wind. Art amidst a natural setting. This is Louisiana in Humlebaek, a small village north of Copenhagen, which has become a legend among art lovers, thanks to its unusual museum – a unique symbiosis of architecture, nature and art created by its founder, Knud W. Jensen.

Jensen, who initially owned a food wholesale business and possessed a keen interest in art and literature, by chance came upon a 19th century estate situated on a rise above Øresund, the stretch of water separating Denmark and Sweden. It was named Louisiana because the owner had led a succession of three women to the altar, all named Louise. "Out of respect for such an achievement, we also named the museum 'Louisiana,' something we have never regretted," commented Knud W. Jensen later with regard to the name.

Shadow and light

In 1954, having sold off parts of his business, he bought the property with the intention of establishing a museum of modern art on the site. Two young architects, Juergen Bo and Vilhelm Wohlert, were commissioned to design the new building. They spent months carefully examining the terrain and finally produced plans for a pavilion-style complex in the unmistakable style of Scandinavian functionalism.

The old building was preserved and continues to serve as the main entrance area to the Museum, incorporating intimate exhibition rooms. Light and airy wings were added, extending out into the park or incorporated underground as severely purist structures. The contrast between shade and glaring light, between tunnel-like corridors and high ceilinged rooms, between inside and outside, is what makes the new building complex so captivating. People's gaze is almost inevitably drawn outward to the sculptures in the park, located in carefully chosen sites. There are more than 60 sculptures by artists such as Joan Miró, Max Ernst, Henry Moore and Alexander Calder, all competing with the natural backdrop. Henry Moore once said that he could not imagine any better place for his works.

Louisiana owes its fame to some outstanding masterpieces of modern art. Although the opening exhibition in 1958 was devoted exclusively to works by young Danish artists, it was not long before the focus shifted.

After visiting the 1959 *documenta* 2 exhibition in Kassel, Jensen realized that the future of the museum lay in international art. Despite having no immediate public funds available for the acquisition of new works, he nevertheless managed to accumulate some superior works – thanks to donations by Ny Carlsberg as well as by collectors and artists. The Museum is meanwhile renowned for its collection of international post-1945 modernist works.

Window onto the lake

His ambition did not, however, lie in documenting every single artistic direction. It was more important to exhibit individual artists and show how each one reflected his own period. The Louisiana Museum has a collection by Alberto Giacometti which is well worth a visit. His fragile figures in one of the rooms, the windows of which look out onto an enchanted lake, are so compelling that it is difficult to tear yourself away and explore the rest of the exhibits.

Works by Yves Klein, Lucio Fontana, Jan Tinguely and Martial Raysse serve to demonstrate the new realist movement. César's mighty sculpture of a thumb rears up like a warning. The world of Pop-Art is similarly represented with some world-famous masterpieces, including works by Robert Rauschenberg, Andy Warhol (including his portrait of Chairman Mao), Claes Oldenburg, Roy Lichtenstein and Jim Dine. Edward Kienholz provides the shock element with his revealing installations while the strong colors of Sam Francis's works are unmistakeable. Morris Louis, Frank Stella and Kenneth Noland are representative of a generation of artists who embraced "Colorfield Painting." Minimalist art is likewise well-represented with names like Ad

Dekkers, Robert Ryman, Sol LeWitt and Gerhard Richter. Mario Merz, along with Joseph Beuys and Richard Long, documents the 1970s and 1980s. There is a particularly impressive selection of works by Anselm Kiefer displayed in a subterranean room. They include a lead aeroplane entitled *Jason*. Another room is devoted to the monumental works of Danish artist Per Kirkeby. The same amount of space is devoted to his works as to the large-scale pieces by Georg Baselitz, Markus Lüpertz and A.R. Penck.

Anyone visiting Humlebaek on a summer day can see that the dream of art reaching the public has been fulfilled in Louisiana. Visitors congregate on the grass around the sculptures as if at a picnic, merging with the works of art like special forms of lawn decoration.

One of the park's famous new realism pieces is César's giant thumb (left).

The entrance to the Museum (above right) contrasts with the severely functionalist design of the new wings to the building.

A sculpture by Henry Moore, resembling a group of human figures, forms part of the park landscape above Øresund (below right).

Royal collections

The STATENS MUSEUM in COPENHAGEN houses the Danish royal art treasures as well as a collection of modern art

DENMARK
Copenhagen
North Sea
Baltic Sea

ADDRESS:
Sølvgade 48 - 50,
Copenhagen

OPENING HOURS:
Tues., Thurs.-Sun.
10 am to 5 pm,
Wed. 10 am to 8 pm

INTERNET:
www.smk.dk

VERKEHRSVERBINDUNG:
Suburban train to
Østerport or Nørreport,
Bus, Routes 6A, 14, 40,
42, 43, 184, 185, 150S

OTHER ATTRACTIONS:
Ny Carlsberg Glyptotek,
Thorvaldsen's Museum,
Royal Museum of Fine
Arts

A highlight of early German art: Lucas Cranach the Elder's painting, *The Judgement of Paris* 1527 (below left).

A contemporary-style new building was added to accommodate the modern collections (below center).

The Danes are regarded as the most relaxed people in Europe and they certainly boast the oldest monarchy. Denmark has been ruled by kings (or feisty queens) for over a thousand years, becoming not only an important nation, but also an important art center.

The royal art collections form the basis of the art housed in the Statens Museum, the country's largest and most important art museum. Boasting 9,000 paintings and sculptures, 300,000 sketches and examples of graphic art as well as 2,600 plaster casts of Greek, Roman and medieval statues, this is truly a collection fit for a king.

During the reign of Christian IV (1577–1648), the founder of Copenhagen, art collections were accumulated to furnish the newly built castles and palaces. His son, Frederik III, was more interested in curios and oddities, a trend during the period that influenced him when he set up a royal art chamber in 1650 which included, along with all kinds of trinkets, various examples of contemporary art. The royal collection of paintings and sculptures kept growing for decades and was displayed in an art gallery in Christiansborg Palace starting in the mid-18th century. During the period, the collection was substantially boosted by acquisitions made after 1765 on behalf of the monarchy by German art dealer and museum curator Gerhard Morell, who purchased the Italian, Spanish and Dutch paintings which now number among the Statens Museum's finest works. These collections were opened to the public in 1792.

In 1855, it was decided to construct a museum modeled on the kind of pretentious temples to art popular in Germany and Austria. The architects, Vilhelm Dahlerup and G.E.W. Müller, designed a positively palatial facade. Featuring pillars, allegorical statues, elaborate flights of stairs and bronze and sandstone reliefs, the Museum was a resplendent building. There was just one small problem: after opening in 1896, it was discovered to be too small to house the enormous collection of art and a large majority of the exhibits had to be placed in storage for a century. In 1986, it was decided to put an end to this sad state of affairs and plans were made for a new building.

"The Sculpture Street"

Italian-born architect Anna Maria Indrio and Danish Mads Müller designed an entirely separate museum. A glass complex was built running parallel to the old building in an extensive park landscape. The old and new museums were connected by an area known as "The Sculpture Street," in which sculptures dating from 1850 to the present are displayed, including works by Bertel Thorvaldsen. This seems to have solved the problem of space once and for all. Displayed over an area of 323,000 –134,000 square feet, the celebrated collections now have adequate space.

The exhibits have been organized to complement the different architectural styles. The old building, for example, concentrates almost exclusively on art until 1900. Starting with the 13th century, collections of Danish and international art are displayed in rooms with color schemes that enhance the different styles. Flemish paintings, for instance, are displayed in dark green rooms while Dutch paintings are hung in blue ones.

The collection of Dutch works ranges from early Flemish to the early

15th century, right up to the heyday of the Dutch School, featuring outstanding artists such as Rubens, Breughel the Elder, Hans Memling, Frans Hals, Rembrandt, Ruisdael and Jacob Jordaens. The Italians – including Tizian, Tintoretto, Tiepolo, Filippo Lippi and Barocci – are particularly well-represented, with Man-

tegna's painting, *Christ as the Suffering Redeemer*, as one of the main attractions.

Landscape as a subject

The German section is most famous for the largest collection of works by Lucas Cranach located outside his homeland. The most prominent 18th century Danish artists include Nicolai A. Abilgaard and Jens Juel while the 19th century is represented by artists such as C.W. Eckersberg and Constantin Hansen. The whitish gray interiors of Danish symbolist Vilhelm Hammershoi suggest loneliness. While in the old building, every effort has been made to intensify the impact of the paintings by careful choice of surrounding color, a different strategy has been followed in the new museum. Here the designers have taken into account that modern art – for instance, paintings by Asger Jorn and Per Kirkeby –

requires space and should not be hampered by colors. The entirely white walls, glass fronts and clear lines of the rooms encourage concentration on the exhibited work. The collection of 20th century French painters – a donation – has also found a home in the new building, where the works of Emil Nolde are likewise accommodated.

A separate children's museum, which provides opportunity for simple experimentation, was also integrated. A spacious cafeteria looks out over the park, reminding us that landscape has always constituted one of the main themes of Danish painting.

Michael Ancher is one of Denmark's best known painters. His dramatic work, *The Crew Rescued*, 1894, is a dramatic depiction of people being rescued from a shipwreck.

The modern section includes a drawing by Henri de Toulouse-Lautrec. The artist entitled his 1899 work, *At the Circus* (below right).

Declaration of love

The SKAGEN MUSEUM displays the works of Scandinavia's most famous painters

ADDRESS:
4 Brøndumsvej,
Skagen

OPENING HOURS:
May to September daily
10 am to 5 pm,
October to April 10 am
to 3 pm

INTERNET:
www.skagens-
museum.dk

HOW TO GET THERE:
By rail, bus, or car via
Frederikshavn

OTHER ATTRACTIONS:
Anna and Michael
Ancher's house,
Brøndums Hotel.

**The Skagen Museum
(in the foreground)
opened in 1928. Brøn-
dums Hotel, where the
painters met regularly
to dine and discuss,
can be seen in the
background (below
left). The hotel was
owned by Anna
Ancher's parents.**

*Returning from
the Meadow,* **above
left, shows artist Anna
Ancher. It was painted
by her husband,
Michael Ancher, in
1902.**

Two women are walking along the beach in the early evening light. In their long, light dresses, they become part of a landscape that seems to dissolve into the light. The picture is called *Summer Evening on the South Beach at Skagen.* It was painted by Peder Severin Krøyer in 1893 as a declaration of love to a place that was the center of Scandinavian art for almost twenty years.

Skagen was an isolated fishing village when painter Martinus Rorbye arrived there in 1833 and began painting people's everyday lives in the Danish classical style. Almost 40 years passed before Scandinavian artists such as Holger Drachmann, Carl Locher, Fritz Thaulow, Karl Madsen, Michael Ancher, Laurits Tuxen and Viggo Johansen visited Skagen again. They painted what they saw around them: scenes of fishing life, people and domestic interiors. But above all, they painted the landscape, whose uniqueness they recognized. Here, at the most northerly point of Denmark, where the North Sea joins the Baltic, there is a very special light that

becomes even more intense on midsummer nights.

At first, a rather academic style of painting prevailed. But under the influence of the Paris art scene, younger painters consciously distanced themselves from the forms of expression of the Copenhagen Academy. In 1882, the already celebrated, Norwegian-born Peder Severin Krøyer arrived in Skagen, making a considerable contribution to the town's reputation as the center of the new art.

Master of light

Krøyer worked tirelessly on the depiction of light and both his seaside scenes and his pictures of banquets are important elements in Skagen painting. Michael Ancher's pictures seem much more serious. By producing paintings like *Fishermen putting a Rowing Boat to Sea* and *The Drowned Man,* he made himself a part of the harsh everyday life of the fishermen. The third of the great Skagen painters, Anna Ancher (daughter of the hotel owner, painter and wife of Michael Ancher) went her own way, painting interiors and also the people in her immediate environment. One of her most famous pictures is *Sunshine in the Blue Room,* which depicts her daughter Helga.

Peder Severin Krøyer's paintings of his friends' gatherings have great charm. The group met regularly at Brøndums Hotel, the home of Anna Ancher's parents, to have dinner and stimulating discussions. The depiction of a champagne supper in the garden bears the descriptive title, *Hip, Hip, Hurrah.* This picture, apparently so delicate and spontaneous, actually took four years to finish.

There was, in any case, a yawning gap between the ideal and the reality. Though a cheerful, relaxed mood often prevailed in the pictures of the Skagen painters, it was not to last. Many of the artists were plagued by anxiety, depression and self doubt. Marriages like that of Marie and Peder Severin Krøyer broke up and friendships foundered. At the beginning of the 20th century, the artists' colony gradually dispersed. However, a few painters like the Anchers, Krøyer and Tuxen remained and, together with some of the townsfolk of Skagen, set up an independent foundation on 20 October 1908, with the aim of collecting as many works of art as possible in the place where they were created. With the help of donations, a collection was formed and it moved into a museum of its own, designed by architect

Ulrik Plesner, in 1928.

The dining room was preserved

The Skagen Museum was considerably extended by the bequest of the hotelier, Degn Brøndum, brother of Anna Ancher, who donated his entire art collection and his hotel to the Museum. In 1946, the magnificent dining room, the artists' former meeting-place – with all its paintings, paneling and furniture – was moved to the Museum and rebuilt there. Its gallery of portraits of the Skagen painters is legendary.

The fame of Skagen's Museum reaches far beyond Scandinavia. The building is generously proportioned, affording plenty of space for the large pictures. The central hall is surrounded by a gallery, which bathes the room in a perfect light. The garden is also part of the Museum. It formerly belonged to Brøndums Hotel and was used as a studio by some of the painters.

The hotel was sold in 1966, but it still stands close to the Museum and continues to be run in the traditional manner. The dining room and the hall with the great fireplace are hung with pictures from the time of the Skagen painters.

They show that many places in Skagen remain just as they were when

At the close of the 19th century, Peder Severin Krøyer painted his wife, Marie, and Anna Ancher with hats and long, white gowns. He named the painting, dated 1893, *Summer Evening on the South Beach at Skagen* (above).

Also by Krøyer is *At Lunch*, showing the Skagen painters in animated conversation round a table in Brøndums Hotel (below center).

The domestic idyll depicted: *Coffee is served* by Laurits Tuxen shows the artist's wife with their two daughters (below right).

the painters saw them: the yellow houses with gardens full of poppies, the bright light by the sea and the sky on windy days. Rarely is the viewer so aware of the connection between art and subject.

The Pergamon frieze

From the Hellenistic period: the preserved remains of the
PERGAMON ALTAR are exhibited on **BERLIN'S MUSEUM ISLAND**

North Sea
Berlin
GERMANY

ADDRESS:
Am Kupfergraben,
Berlin

OPENING TIMES:
Tues.-Sun. 10 am
to 6 pm,
Thurs. to 10 pm

INTERNET:
www.smb.spk-berlin.de

PUBLIC TRANSPORT:
Subway, U6; S-Bahn, S1,
S2, S25, S5, S7, S75, S9;
Tram, M1, M12, M2, M4,
M5, M6; Bus, Routes
100, 147, 200

OTHER ATTRACTIONS:
Museum
of East Asian Art

Pergamon was the capital of the Pergamon Empire, the part of Hellenistic Greece located in Asia Minor. Today, the city is part of the Turkish province of Izmir and is called Bergama. Pergamon was great during the last three centuries before Christ, when a dominant and wealthy kingdom developed under Eumenes I and his successors. It was as an expression of this earthly might that King Eumenes II ordered a shrine to be built, dedicated to the god, Zeus, and goddess Athena, between 180 and 160 B.C. An altar whose foundations measured approximately 118 by 111 feet, surmounted by a frieze of figures $7\frac{1}{2}$ foot high, with a total length of 394 feet, was raised on one of the upper town's steep terraces.

The shrine was one of Ancient Greece's last monumental religious art works. Asia Minor has long since become recognized as part of the Ottoman Empire and Pergamon was renamed Bergama by German archeologists. The undertaking benefited from Ottoman Turkey's lack of interest in non-Islamic culture, coupled with good political relations with the German Empire. Work star-

ted under scientists Humann and Conze in 1878. They showed that sections of the frieze had been used as building material. The sculptural decoration was damaged beyond repair.

Removal began in 1879, the frieze having being purchased for 20,000 imperial German marks. Imperial ambition and arrogance played a part as well as interest in history and art; the German Empire was trying to emulate Great Britain which had, three quarters of a century earlier, transported the Elgin Marbles from Turkish-occupied Greece to London, the high-

light of which was the frieze from the Parthenon in Athens. The Elgin Marbles are now in the British Museum.

A home befitting an altar

The Bergama artwork was re-erected on Berlin's Museum Island in the heart of the German metropolis, which lies in the middle of the River Spree that flows through the city, close to the palace square, forming the center of historic Berlin. The building housing the altar was the last of a complex of museum buildings to be built. After a temporary arrangement, the building

was erected between 1910 and 1930 according to a design by Alfred Messel, the highly regarded architect of many of Berlin's buildings. He created an impressive, three-winged building with a courtyard of honor, reached by a narrow bridge that crosses the Kupfergraben.

The museums on the island were all severely damaged during the Second World War. Parts of the altar were plundered by members of the Red Army and carried off to Leningrad and Moscow, only to be returned in 1958, whereupon the Museum building was rebuilt, although not very soundly. Restoration work has been necessary again and again, and the renovation plans stretch into the future.

Near Eastern collection

The Pergamon Museum includes several collections, including Islamic and Near Eastern art. The latter contains important evidence of Mesopotamian culture procured by German archeologists: the Processional Way with its blue glazed tiles from ancient Babylon, the golden mythical creatures before the Ishtar Gate and the facade of King Nebuchadnezzar's throne. The collection of antiquities combines the finds from excavation sites in Olympia, Samos and Miletus. The two-story market gate, a Roman piece erected under Emperor Hadrian and now one of the high-lights of the Museum's antiquities collection, originates from the last-named town, like Pergamon located in Asia Minor.

The star exhibit is still the altar and frieze from the palace at Pergamon. They have earned their own extended exhibition room with a glass ceiling. The layout of the original site has been imitated. Wide steps lead up to pillared gallery with roof sculptures which once surrounded the sacrificial altar. The frieze of figures runs beneath both projections to left and right and continues along the walls of the room. The material is marble. It is assumed that numerous sculptors from Pergamon and the Greek islands were involved in its creation.

The continuous picture represents the battle between gods and giants. It is known that Ancient Greek mythology referred to several recurring conflicts between a race of elder gods and primal beings. The last of these battles took place between Zeus and the Olympian gods, fighting the Giants, born on Earth and sent by their mother to defeat the rulers of Olympus. The conflict, called the Gigantomachy, was an important motif in Hellenic art. It is interpreted as the struggle of order over chaos, the victory of culture over barbarism. In Pergamon, it also served as a reminder of the victory of the nation's armies over the Galati-ans. With its dramatic battle scenes and extreme depictions of death, it is certainly the most vivid reproduction of the mythological theme.

The Pergamon Museum – which has only used this name in the post-war era, by the way – is also a location for theater performances. Extraordinarily popular gala dinners are held in front of the altar of Zeus. With around 800,000 visitors annually, it is the most frequented museum in Berlin.

The western section of the Pergamon altar, with the stairs (above left).

This scene from the frieze shows a section from the Gigantomachy, the Greek gods' battle against the Giants (above right).

The Ishtar Gate, originating from ancient Babylon, with its golden mythical creatures (below left).

Aerial view of Berlin's museum island with the Pergamon Museum (below right).

A museum temple

The OLD NATIONAL GALLERY in BERLIN shines with Romantic and Impressionist collections

ADDRESS:
Bodestrasse 1-3,
Berlin

OPENING TIMES:
Tues., Wed., Fri.-Sun.
10 am to 6 pm,
Thurs. 10 am to 10 pm

INTERNET:
www.smb.spk-berlin.de

PUBLIC TRANSPORT:
Subway, U6; S-Bahn S1,
S2, S25, S5, S7, S75, S9;
Tram, M1, M12, M2, M4,
M5, M6; Bus, Routes
100, 147, 200

OTHER ATTRACTIONS:
Hamburger Bahnhof,
New National Gallery

When big public museums sprang up all over Europe in the 19th century, people liked to talk – it was the Romantic era – of an "artistic church." Art was regarded as something glorious and it had to be housed appropriately. The National Gallery in Berlin thus took the form of a temple. Anyone entering the colonnaded courtyard was supposed to experience an intense spiritual sensation. The religious atmosphere is heightened by the subsequent climb up the palatial floors.

The building is modeled on classical Greek temples. The entire museum complex where the National Gallery stands is a frank imitation of the Acropolis. The form that the buildings later took, as well as their arrangement, is a deviation from the original idea. Only the National Gallery building is still reminiscent of Ancient Greece.

Initially a foundation

The first design came from King Frederick William IV of Prussia. As a politician, the man was a disaster, but he was commendable, on the other hand, as a patron of the arts. He was the force behind the completion of Cologne Cathedral as well as the conversion of the residential cities of Berlin and Potsdam into cultural centers with classical architecture. The architect, Karl Friedrich Schinkel, lent a helping hand and Schinkel's employee, Friedrich August Stüler, was entrusted with the final National Gallery design.

Prussia had been a major power since King Frederick II. After the wars, between 1864 and 1871, its capital, Berlin, became increasingly wealthy. Construction of the National Gallery swallowed up the massive sum, for those days, of three million German marks. Only sandstone from Nebra was used for the building. Stüler died during the project and its execution

The architecture of the National Museum was supposed to reflect the pride, power and culture of the German nation (below left).

passed to royal architect Johann Heinrich Strack. Construction dragged on from 1866 to 1876. In the meantime, Germany became a unified kingdom with Berlin at its center.

The National Gallery, as indicated by its name alone, was intended to celebrate Germany and to make the centralization of the country and its subsequent empowerment clear both in the external appearance of the museum and in the standard of art on display. An equestrian statue of Frederick William IV watches over the entrance.

In spite of all the ruling house's claims, the heart of the collection was donated by a citizen. Joachim Heinrich Wilhelm Wagener, banker and consul, donated 262 works by domestic and foreign artists. At the time, it was the most comprehensive collection of contemporary art in Germany, comprising works by Caspar David Friedrich and Eduard Gärtner as well as art from Belgium, France, Austria and Scandinavia. The Gallery's first director, Max Jordan, acquired two more important paintings by Adolph Menzel: the *Flute Concert at Sans Souci* and the *Iron Rolling Mill*. Both were already hung at the time of the opening. Jordan's successor was one of the great museum curators of the day, Hugo von Tschudi. He bought works by the French artists Manet, Cezanne, Renoir and Rodin in addition to paintings by the important German Impressionist, Max Liebermann.

Indignant Emperor

Tschudi was always controversial. His National Gallery was one of the first museums to take an interest in the Impressionists. The imperial family in particular, headed by William II, was highly indignant. The court preferred paintings with hackneyed, clichéd historical themes. The dispute escalated to such an extent that Tschudi resigned and returned to Munich, not without taking with him the paintings that he had just acquired by Van Gogh and Gauguin. Tschudi's successor was Ludwig Justi. To the furious amazement of the imperial family, he continued Tschudi's policy and expanded the collection with the latest, in this case avantgarde. The Anton von Werner battle paintings beloved by Emperor William were banished to the nearby Armory.

Consequently, the Berlin National Gallery possessed one of the most important collections of German Expressionism. Hitler's followers regarded it as degenerate. The pictures had to be removed; most went

abroad and are now treasured by other museums. When the Second World War broke out, the doors to the National Gallery were closed, the works of art were removed to storage and the building itself sustained considerable damage.

The government of the German Democratic Republic repaired the

building. Thereafter, it exhibited those pieces located in the Soviet Occupation Zone. The city was divided along political lines. The western section opened its own National Gallery in a highly praised, new building by architect Mies van der Rohe. After the city's reunification, the collections were reorganized. Classical modern art remained in the Mies van der Rohe building, now called the New National Gallery, while the 19th century works can be seen in the Old National Gallery on the museum island.

The building was again laboriously restored between 1998 and 2001. Since its reopening, the gallery has received an unrelenting flood of visitors. People flock around the Menzels and the Friedrichs. The most recent painting, chronologically, is by Max Beckmann, once considered degenerate by the Nazi government. His painting is now considered a jewel in the museum's crown.

Masterpieces in the Old National Gallery collection: Caspar David Friedrich's painting, *Moonrise by the Sea*, 1822 (above) and Adolph Menzel's *Flute Concert at Sans Souci*, 1852 (below center). Both are key works of German Realism.

The Gallery's Impressionist and Post-Impressionist collection includes Paul Gauguin's *Tahitian Fisherwomen*, 1891, (below right).

Saxony's cultural legacy

The **OLD MASTER'S GALLERY** in **DRESDEN** owns numerous important European art works

ADDRESS:
Semperbau am
Zwinger, Theaterplatz,
Dresden

OPENING TIMES:
Tues.-Sun. 10 am
to 6 pm

INTERNET:
www.skd.dresden.de

PUBLIC TRANSPORT:
Tram, Lines 1, 2, 4, 8, 11, 12

OTHER ATTRACTIONS:
Zwinger

The most famous portrait of the religious reformer, Martin Luther, was painted by Lucas Cranach the Elder in 1532 (below left).

The story of Dresden starts with the sumptuous Dresden Baroque époque including intrigues at the royal court and fantastic carnival celebrations; it continues with glittering appearances at the Opera House and an art scene that dominated the Expressionist era and ends with the inferno of February 1945, when the city lay in ash-covered ruins.

Recent reconstruction of the Frauenkirche supports Dresden's claim to be one of the great European cultural centers. The museums exert a magnetic influence, especially the Old Master Gallery of paintings, whose history is closely associated with that of the Saxon royal city.

As in many princely residences, this globally renowned collection started out as a collector's "cabinet," established in 1560, where Italian and Flemish paintings were collected alongside crafts, natural history specimens, instruments and curios. The Saxon Prince and Polish King Augustus the Strong recognized the paintings' value and removed the valuable pieces from the cabinet. An inventory was drawn up in 1722 and finally put on show for the court in the converted stable yard.

Yet, despite the efforts of Augustus the Strong, it was only through his son, Augustus III, who came to the throne in 1733, that the Dresden art scene achieved world fame. Augustus II purchased truly great works of art. In 1741, he acquired 268 paintings from the Wallenstein Collection, including Jan Vermeer's *The Procuress*, followed a little later by numerous works from the imperial gallery in Prague. Hundreds of the best paintings owned by Duke Francesco III were brought from Modena to Dresden and added to the collection, including works by Correggio, Velazquez and Titian. Finally, Augustus III crowned his collection with an altarpiece from San Sisto in Piacenza. Known as the *Sistine Madonna* and painted by Raphael, it is one of world's most famous masterpieces.

To designs by Gottfried Semper

The outbreak of the Seven Years' War (1756–63) and economic problems brought an end to the rise of "Florence on the Elbe." Just one hundred years later, the art world was reinvigorated and a prestigious museum was built.

Although initially a different location was preferred, the director of the Dresden State Architectural School, Gottfried Semper, designed a Neo-Renaissance style palace

Sistine Madonna in duplicate: the section from Raphael's painting shows an enlargement of the cherubs (above left), next to a complete reproduction of Raphael's painting (right).

The Dresden collection's pastels include Jean-Etienne Liotard's *Chocolate Girl* of 1744, a particularly impressive study (center right).

The Gallery building, designed by Gottfried Semper, seen from Theaterplatz (below right).

which was supposed to complete the square around Theaterplatz. Work commenced in 1847, but because Semper had been actively involved in battles for democratic freedom, he fled the city after the May uprising of 1849, pursued by the police. The Gallery building was still completed basically according to his designs, and opened in 1855. In 1931, the Gallery of New Masters and Gallery of Old Masters became separate entities.

The next few years were dark days for the Dresden art world. In 1937, numerous works, mainly Expressionist, were removed by the Nazis and destroyed for being degenerate. Although the majority of the remaining collection had been brought to safety in view of increasing air raids, almost 200 works of art were destroyed in the hail of bombs. The Semper Gallery was severely affected too.

In 1945, the Russians seized a considerable part of the collection and transported it to Moscow, Leningrad and Kiev. In a ceremonial document, the Soviet leadership returned 1,240 paintings to a government delegation from the German Democratic Republic in 1955. In 1956, it was possible to reopen part of the Semper Gallery. In 1960, the entire building was res-

tored and the city became once again a kind of outpost for Italian art, as more than two fifths of the works of art are by Italian painters.

Canaletto the superstar

In addition to Raphael's *Sistine Madonna*, the 16th century department also possesses a painting whose balance and vividness make it an outstanding example of the High Renaissance. Giorgione's *Sleeping Venus*, a work that inspired many artists, also belongs to the period. Canaletto is regarded as a kind of superstar in Dresden because the Venetian artist painted views of Dresden and its immediate surroundings that are almost photographic in their accuracy.

The Old Masters Gallery also has a real treasure trove of Flemish Baroque works, including 19 paintings by Peter Paul Rubens amongst others. Another highlight of the collection is the Dutch works, including paintings by Rembrandt. Because it was also possible to acquire the estate of the French citizen king, Louis Philippe, in 1853, visitors can experience an amazing variety of Spanish paintings by El Greco, Murillo and de Ribera, for example. There are shining examples of German art in works by Dürer, Holbein and Cranach.

The Dresden Gallery furthermore has a superb collection of pastels, including Jean-Etienne Liotard's *The Chocolate Girl*, which is particularly enchanting. Anyone would love to be served cocoa by the young lady with the serious expression. Luckily, the Gallery also has a cafe with a south-facing terrace. From here the view sweeps across Theaterplatz – also one of the city's notable works of art.

A collection with bourgeois origins

North Sea
Berlin●
GERMANY
Frankfurt

The **STÄDEL MUSEUM** in **FRANKFURT** owes its first-class exhibits to the city's patrons

ADDRESS:
Schaumainkai 63
Frankfurt

OPENING HOURS:
Tues., Fri.-Sun. 10 am
to 5 pm
Wed. and Thurs. 10 am
to 9 pm

INTERNET:
www.staedelmuseum.de

PUBLIC TRANSPORT:
Underground, Lines U1,
U2, U3; Trams, 15 and
16; Bus, Route 46

OTHER ATTRACTIONS:
Schirn Art Gallery,
Museum of Modern Art

Johann Wolfgang von Goethe, the poet prince, never saw the most famous portrait of himself, now hanging in Frankfurt's Städel Museum. It depicts the young Goethe, reclining in a leisurely pose, in the Roman Campagna, one stockinged leg turned toward the viewer. He is wearing a broad-brimmed hat, tilted back to reveal his face, and he is seated amidst temple ruins, apparently contemplating the transience of life.

In 1787, Goethe, a "refugee from the North," set up residence in Rome with painter Johann Heinrich Wilhelm Tischbein and a group of other artists, to explore art and the southern lifestyle. Tischbein drew sketches of his fellow housemates, one of which later became the painting, *Goethe in the Roman Campagna*.

The unfinished portrait ended up in 1840 in the possession of Karl Mayer von Rothschild, a Frankfurt banker, whose heirs bequeathed it to the Städel Art Institute. Goethe was, after all, a native of Frankfurt and once described the Städel collection as "priceless."

Nazi iconoclasm

The Städel Museum's roots are thoroughly bourgeois in origin, reflecting perfectly the enterprising spirit of this international merchant city. In 1816, a Frankfurt merchant, banker and collector, Johann Friedrich Städel (1728–1816), left his entire fortune of over one million guilders, his house and his art collection of 474 paintings and drawings to found an art institute in his name – with two provisos: the collection

should be accessible to all citizens and should be constantly augmented. Furthermore, young artists should be encouraged through teaching and financial assistance.

The collections, initially displayed in Städel's house on Rossmarkt, grew rapidly, an art school was soon founded and in 1833, the institute and art gallery moved into a larger building. Between 1874 and 1878, a splendid, new Neo-Renaissance-style building was constructed on Schaumainkai from a design by Oskar Sommer, a Semper student. In 1907, a municipal gallery was added to the building. When the Nazis seized 77 paintings, 339 drawings and prints and 3 sculptures in 1937, condemning them as "degenerate art," it seemed as if the Städel Museum's days might be numbered,

The painting, *Goethe in the Roman Campagna*, hangs in the Städel in Goethe's native city of Frankfurt am Main. It was painted in Italy after 1787 by Johann H.W. Tischbein (above left) and is arguably the most famous portrait of Goethe ever painted.

Panel by Hans Holbein the Elder, 1501, from the wooden altar of Frankfurt's Dominican church, depicting the Judas kiss (above center).

especially after the building was also badly damaged in a bombing raid in 1944. Thanks to the fact that many of the paintings had been removed to safety during the war, however, the Museum was able to reopen in 1966 following extensive reconstruction work. Today, the collection boasts 2,700 paintings, 600 of which are on permanent display and the Museum is one of the largest art galleries in Europe.

The Städel as sponsor

The Museum unites under one roof examples of every major European school of art, ranging from the 14th century to the present day.

The most significant example of early German painting is undoubtedly the *Little Garden of Paradise*, thought to have been painted around 1410 by a master painter from the Upper Rhineland. It depicts Mary, seated in a walled garden with the Christ Child at her feet. Grouped around her, like people at a picnic, are the figures of saints. The collection of old Dutch paintings is also one of the main attractions. Works such as Robert Campin's *Madonna and Child*, Jan van Eyck's *Lucca Madonna* and Rogier von der

Weyden's *Medici Madonna* are displayed alongside paintings by Hugo van der Goes, Hans Memling and Quentin Massys. There is also a fine selection of Italian works, including Sandro Botticelli's *Ideal Portrait of a Young Woman*, while the various eras of Italian painting are represented by Martino di Bartolomeo, Fra Angelico, Mantegna, Bellini and Tintoretto. The Baroque period is equally well documented, with superb works by Dutch masters such as Rembrandt and Peter Paul Rubens, while Adam Elsheimer is the main representative of German Baroque painting.

A great deal of space is also given over to 19th century art. It was not uncommon for the Museum itself to commission works, such as Overbeck's *The Triumph of Religion in the Arts*. Claude Monet's *Luncheon* and Edgar Degas' *Orchestra Musicians* are two of the outstanding works in the Museum's large collection of Impressionist paintings.

The collection of Expressionist art suffered badly at the hands of the Nazis. Thanks to new acquisitions and gifts, however, it has been possible to close many of the gaps. Contemporary art is represented by ar-

tists such as Gerhard Richter, Sigmar Polke, Piero Manzoni, Yves Klein and Anselm Kiefer.

The Städel Museum also played an important role in drawing other museums to the area: the Schaumainkai has now become a museum mile with a whole host of famous museums including the Museum of Architecture, the Film Museum and the Liebighaus with its sculpture collection, adjoining the Städel. Frankfurt's skyline with its gleaming financial buildings along the opposite bank forms a vibrant contrast to the world of art and museums.

The Städel Museum was designed in Neo-Renaissance style. This splendid building was opened in 1878 (below right).

Art on the Alster hill

The **HAMBURG ART GALLERY** possesses important works from the late Gothic era to the present

ADDRESS:
Glockengießerwall, Hamburg

OPENING TIMES:
Tues.- Sun. 10 am to 6 pm,
Thurs. to 9 pm

INTERNET:
www.hamburger-kunsthalle.de

PUBLIC TRANSPORT:
Subway, S-Bahn and buses to the main station

OTHER ATTRACTIONS:
Altona Museum

The port city of Hamburg is regarded as the "gateway to the world" and its citizens are proud that the Art Gallery is the biggest art museum in Germany. With a comprehensive collection of art from the late Gothic to the present – including 19th and 20th century sculptures and a collection of copperplate engravings that contains more than 100,000 sheets from seven centuries – the Gallery ranks amongst Europe's great museums.

Hamburg an artistic city? Hamburg, like so many cities, is plagued by contradiction and inconsistency. While some of Hamburg's citizens generously and courageously supported new ideas, others stuck so stubbornly to tradition that Expressionist painter Edvard Munch fled, horrified, from the city in 1907 and wrote, "I didn't dare attend my exhibition, the abuse rained down so." Munch's place among the ranks of exhibited stars, including Rembrandt, Lorrain, Tiepolo, Goya, Leibl, Menzel, Courbet, Böcklin, Feuerbach, Manet, Renoir, Monet, Corinth and Picasso, is only belated gratification for the patrons who once supported him against all odds.

"Respectably dressed" only

There was no art museum in the city when some of Hamburg's citizens founded the first art union in Germany in 1817. The first municipal art gallery opened in the Stock Exchange arcades in 1850 and 40 contemporary paintings were free for every "respectably dressed" person to view. But soon, as a result of donations, there was not enough room for the growing collection and the collection moved in 1869 to a splendid building erected on Alster hill on municipal land, a building that Berlin architects Georg Theodor Schirrmacher

and Hermann von der Hude designed as a brick shell decorated with sandstone and terracotta.

In 1924, an extension was added that was in keeping with the grandiose spirit of the age: a pale plaster facade and mighty domed rotunda. When the Contemporary Gallery opened in 1997, modern art found a home too, displayed in a new building. The addition of the Hubertus Wald Forum completed this generous complex and filled a major gap. The 10,770 square feet of exhibition space provide ideal premises for international temporary exhibitions.

It is precisely because of the various architectural styles that a tour of the Hamburg Art Gallery is like a theatrical production. Anyone entering the cupola building through the main entrance will soon access a high rotunda equipped with Doric columns, indicating an atmosphere of consecration to antiquity.

The second floor is reached via a wide staircase and the collection of Old Masters, as well as 19th century and classic modern art, is exhibited there. The two late Gothic altars, created by the Masters Bertram and Francke when the city flourished shortly before 1400, are invaluable treasures.

Lichtwark's contribution

Dutch painters of the 17th century, gathered by Alfred Lichtwark, are heavily represented, The collection's fame extended far beyond the borders of Germany. Lichtwark was the first director of the Hamburg Art Gallery. Between 1886 and 1914, he stockpiled such a rich treasury that Hamburg has today assumed a leading role in the field of Romantic painting.

Lichtwark collected practically every work by Philipp Otto Runge. He also acquired paintings by Caspar David Friedrich, out of fashion at the time. His paintings, such as *Wanderer above the Sea of Fog* and *Sea of Ice*, now exercise a magnetic attraction in the 19th century wing. The classical modern wing contains German Impressionist, Expressionist and Surrealist works.

One of the artists who worked in Hamburg at the invitation of Lichtwark was Max Liebermann, whose paintings *The Netmenders* and whose portrait, *The Surgeon Ferdinand Sauerbruch* are on display. The Museum's cafe is named after Liebermann. It is without doubt one of the nicest of its kind,

with splendid ceilings and paintings, perfect for a relaxing break between visiting the individual collections.

The problem of transition from the old buildings to the Contemporary Gallery, a stark cube designed by architect Oswald Mathias

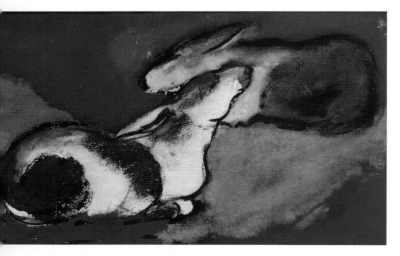

Franz Marc's colorful painting, *Two Sleeping Hares*, 1913, is one of the great works of German Expressionism (below left).

Ungers, has been solved in a genial manner in Hamburg. The installation, *Ceiling Snake*, created by Jenny Holzer, flickers like a red conveyor belt along the route and creates a magical suggestion. The temple of contemporary art contains four stories exhibiting works of Abstract Expressionism, Pop and Minimal art as well as Concept and Media art, including exhibits by Andy Warhol, Joseph Beuys, Bruce Nauman, Richard Serra, Mario Merz, Jannis Kounellis, Richard Long, Robert Morris and many others. Georg Baselitz, Gerhard Richter and Sigmar Polke are represented here as well, alongside Hamburg artist Horst Janssen.

The *Terrace at Restaurant Jacob in Nienstedten on the Elbe* was painted by Max Liebermann between 1902 and 1903. The terrace with its lime trees has survived the ravages of time and is now a protected monument. The Hotel Jacob, to which it belongs, still exists as well (above).

Caspar David Friedrich's painting, *Wanderer above the Sea of Fog*, dates from 1818. It is regarded as one of the masterpieces of German Romanticism (below right).

Hamburg Art Gallery buildings: the Contemporary Gallery's white cube designed by O.M. Ungers (below left) and the stairs to the second floor in the old main building (below center).

Treasure house of medieval panel painting

The **WALLRAF-RICHARTZ-MUSEUM** in **COLOGNE** houses the largest collection of works from the Cologne School

ADDRESS:
Martinstrasse 39
Cologne

OPENING HOURS:
Tues. 10 am to 8 pm
Wed. – Fri. 10 am
to 6 pm
Sat. and Sun. 11 am
to 6 pm

INTERNET:
www.museenkoeln.de/
wallraf-richartz-museum

PUBLIC TRANSPORT:
Bus to Town Hall
or Gürzenich, tram
to Heumarkt

OTHER ATTRACTIONS:
Roman-Germanic
Museum, Ludwig
Collection

Ferdinand Franz Wallraf, born in 1748, was a scholar and "a Renaissance man." From 1769 he taught as a professor at a Cologne high school and he was initiated into the priesthood in 1772. He was a scientist, medical doctor and mathematician, but his main interest was art – centered particularly on the art movement developing in his hometown of Cologne. He focused mainly on early Romanticism with its fascination for the German Middle Ages.

Wallraf was a collector. Napoleon's occupation of Cologne led to the secularization of the monasteries and churches after 1802, resulting in altarpieces and wood carvings becoming obtainable collector's items. Wallraf eventually accumulated an impressive collection of Cologne's medieval panel paintings. In 1824, he left his treasures to the city, a bequest that included 1800 paintings. In 1826, the Prussian government, which had jurisdiction over Cologne, provided the collection with a building which eventually grew into one of the first civic art museums in Germany. It opened its doors in 1827.

But the arrangement was only temporary. In 1854, a rich Cologne merchant, Johann Heinrich Richartz, donated the necessary funds to finance a more suitable building. It was built near to the Minoriten church, in the Classical style with Neo-Gothic additions. One of the architects involved in its design was Friedrich August Stüler, a pupil of Schinkel.

An art museum alongside a cathedral

The Museum continued to receive private donations. When he died in 1867, Jakob Ignaz Hittorf, a master builder, bequeathed his extensive private art collection to it. Other donors included Cajetan, Haubrich and Strecker. More recently, in 2001, the Swiss couple, Gérard and Marisol Corboud, presented the Museum with a permanent loan of 170 Impressionist and Post-Impressionist paintings.

The original building on the northern side of the Minoriten church was destroyed during the Second World War, along with the rest of Cologne's city center. A new building, designed by Rudolf Schwarz and Josef Bernard, was erected on the same spot and opened in 1957. It too soon proved too small. A bigger building was constructed, designed by Peter Busmann and Godfrid Haberer, bet-

ween the cathedral and the Rhine River. It opened in 1986 and the space, consisting predominantly of Pop Art from the United States, was shared with the Ludwig Collection.

In 2001, the Wallraf-Richartz-Museum finally moved into its present, extremely spacious quarters. This time, the architect was Oswald Mathias Ungers, a prominent exponent of German post-war modernism, pupil of Egon Eiermann and esthetically speaking, a follower of Josef Hoffmann, the Viennese architect, from whom he inherited his preference for the square as a constituent element. Having designed Frankfurt's Museum of Architecture and the extended section of the Hamburg Art Gallery, he was obviously experienced in museum architecture.

The city's greatest painter

The new Museum is located between the Town Hall and the Gürzenich, formerly a merchants' meeting place. Nowadays, it is used as a concert hall. The site of Ungers' building lies almost on the exact spot where the goldsmiths' and picture painters' street was situated in the Middle Ages. It was here that Stefan Lochner, an artist from the Lake Constance region and probably Cologne's greatest painter, once had his workshop. Ungers' building is extremely elegant in appearance. It boasts five stories, each covering an area of nearly 11,000 square feet. The space available allows virtually the Museum's entire collection to be displayed, a distinct advantage over other institutions, which are obliged to keep a large part of their holdings in storage.

The Wallraf-Richartz-Museum boasts a significant collection of Baroque works, notably paintings by Rubens and Rembrandt. It also has a selection of 19th century art and German Romantic painters, such as Caspar David Friedrich as well as Realist

painters, including Wilhelm Leibl, a native of Cologne. In addition, the Museum houses the Fondation Corboud, a collection of Impressionist works. The core of the collection, however, remains Wallraf's original collection of Cologne artists, spanning the period from the late Middle Ages to the early Renaissance.

Cologne was once the largest and richest town in Germany. Founded by the Germanic people and occupied and expanded by the Romans, it has managed to preserve its ancient heritage despite domination by Franks, Saxons and Salians. As a religious electorate with an archbishop at its head, it was dominated almost exclusively by clerics and burghers. Its history is reflected in its art. Church institutions were the painters' and woodcarvers' main sponsors, and their works – which stressed religious themes – grew into an individual school of panel painting. Only a few of these painters are known by name, notably Barthel Bruyn and Stefan Lochner. The latter created a particular type of Madonna, distinctive for her sweet, girlish grace. Approximately 700 works produced by the Cologne School have been documented and almost half are on display in the Wallraf-Richartz-Museum.

Stefan Lochner's Madonna figures are famous for their feminine grace. *Madonna in the Rose Arbor* was painted around 1450.

Two of the Museum's most famous paintings are August Macke's Expressionist painting *Lady in a Green Jacket*, 1913, right, and Rembrandt's *Self Portrait* (after 1665), center right.

The Museum building with its futuristic, elegant facade.

Old German splendor

The ALTE PINAKOTHEK in MUNICH houses a collection of works from the 15th to the 18th centuries

ADDRESS:
Barer Straße 27,
Munich

OPENING HOURS:
Wed-Sun 10 am
to 5 pm
Tues 10 am to 8 pm

INTERNET:
www.pinakothek.de

TRANSPORT:
Subway: Lines U2, U3,
U6, U8. Tram: Line 27.
Bus: Line 154

OTHER ATTRACTIONS:
Haus der Kunst

Two years before his death in 1526, Albrecht Dürer, perhaps the most famous of all German painters, created two upright panels, each of which contains larger than life figures of two apostles. On one panel are Saint John and Saint Peter, absorbed in reading an open book; on the other, deep in conversation over a closed book, are Saint Mark the Evangelist and Saint Paul, the first Christian missionary. Dürer donated the two pictures to the council of his home city of Nuremberg. There was to have been text at the bottom explaining the purpose of this gesture and warning the reader about the unwelcome consequences of the Reformation. Dürer himself was a staunch adherent of the Reformation, but he deplored the way it was denatured by sects such as the Anabaptists. The apostles were exhibit characteristics of the upright Christian: composure, steadfastness and energy.

Many experts consider that these paintings show Dürer's art at a peak he never again achieved. Familiar with contemporary foreign art through his travels, he now left all the late Gothic charms of stance, drapery and coloration far behind, attaining a Classicism that placed his works on a par with the most significant achievements of the Italian Renaissance, without sacrificing the brooding Old German faces and expressions which we recognize in his portraits.

Classical elegance

The panels hang in the Alte Pinakothek in Munich, which was founded by King Ludwig I of Bavaria. He was an art lover and he transformed Munich, previously a cramped and somewhat gloomy Baroque royal seat, into a spacious city. He paid a number of visits to Italy and accumulated art avidly while he was there. In his early years he was quite a liberal spirit and supported the Greek War of Independence. He

employed Leo von Klenze, one of the great architects of German Classicism, to design an art museum, the Pinakothek, for him, along with other buildings in Munich.

The Pinakothek opened in 1836, after ten years of construction. At the time, it was one of the biggest museum buildings in the world. The Classical elegance of the long building, the beautiful structuring of its facade and the exhibition rooms, which were the best possible at the time they were built, made it a masterpiece and a much admired example for museum buildings everywhere.

The collection it was built to house is one of the most valuable in

the world. It contains Old Master paintings from the 14th to the 18th centuries. It is the product, not only of King Ludwig's passion for collecting, but also of that of many of his ancestors, who were buying art treasures as early as the 16th century. Of course, what had until then been a possession for the purely private pleasure of the Wittelsbach family was now made accessible to the public, thanks to Ludwig. By doing so, he was pursuing his interest in national education, modelled on democratic experiments in France, where the French Revolution opened up aristocratic art collections to everyone.

Leo von Klenze, one of the great masters of German Classicism, designed the Alte Pinakothek building (below).

Lucas Cranach the Elder's *Adam and Eve* is one of the jewels of the Alte Pinakothek (above center).

Dürer's apostle panels, completed in 1526, show Saint John and Saint Peter (left panel) and Saint Mark and Saint Paul (right panel). The two large-format paintings are considered to be the principal works of an artist who is perhaps the most famous of Old German masters (above right).

One of the most famous Flemish works of art is *The Land of Cockaigne* by Pieter Brueghel the Elder. He acquired the nickname "Peasant Brueghel" at a very early stage (below right).

Focus on the Renaissance

The Alte Pinakothek collection contains Old German paintings from the beginning of the 15th century – the time of Stefan Lochner – to the time of Dürer, including artists such as Grünewald, Altdorfer and Holbein the Elder as well as Dürer himself. Old Dutch painting is represented by Van der Weyden, Bouts and Gossaert; the Italian Renaissance by Botticelli, Raphael, Leonardo and Titian; and 17th century Flemish painting by Brouwer, Van Dyck and Rubens. There are Dutch artists of the Baroque period such as Rembrandt and Hals. The time span is completed by Italians, Frenchmen and Spaniards such as Reni, Tiepolo, Poussin, Claude Lorrain, Boucher, Murillo and El Greco.

The museum has a stock of around 30,000 works. Many of them have been lent to other locations, churches and castles in the free state of Bavaria, and many gaps in the main collection have been filled by loans.

Immediately after the opening, the King decreed that access to the Pinakothek should be free on Sundays. The people of Munich arrived in droves – though not to visit the museum, but to sit and picnic on the grass in front of the building, since they preferred to enjoy beer and sandwiches to paintings by Holbein and Raphael.

During the Second World War, Munich was the target of Allied bombs and the Alte Pinakothek did not escape damage. The building has been restored and the collection appears in its former glory. The restorers took the opportunity to make careful changes to the arrangement of the collection, particularly in the Dürer Room, where there are now considerably more paintings on show than before. It brings together major works of the early German Renaissance by Grünewald and Altdorfer. Dürer's self portrait is given a place of honor. Dürer's relationship with Italy, which he visited twice, is well-documented and, of course, you can find the two panels with the pictures of Apostles Peter, John, Paul and Mark, which are so big you cannot miss them.

German temple of art

The NEW PINAKOTHEK in MUNICH and its 19th century collections

ADDRESS:
Barerstrasse 29,
Munich

OPENING TIMES:
Thurs.-Mon. 10 am
to 5 pm
Wed. 10 am to 8 pm

INTERNET:
www.pinakothek.de

PUBLIC TRANSPORT:
Subway, Lines U2, U3,
U6, U8; Tram, Line 27;
Bus, Line 154

OTHER ATTRACTIONS:
Pinakothek of Modern
Art, City Art Gallery in
the Lenbachhaus, Haus
der Kunst (House of the
Arts)

Carl Spitzweg's *The Poor Poet* (1839) is a caricature of a happy poet during the Biedermeier era (below left).

The poet wears a white nightcap on his head and a pair of spectacles on his nose. The way he is holding his right hand could mean that he is silently memorizing verses, yet a closer look will reveal that he is crushing a flea between thumb and index finger. Soon, however, he will write lines on the paper he is holding in his left hand. He has the quill clamped between his lips. He is half sitting, half reclining in his bed, which consists of a mattress on the floor. By his side he has quite a few tomes and over his head is an open umbrella, because the room he inhabits has a leaky roof. The room is gloomy and untidy, but it hardly seems to bother the poet.

Reminiscent of Italy

The painting is entitled *The Poor Poet* and dates from 1839. At 18 x 14 inches, it is unusually small. Its creator, the Munich artist, Carl Spitzweg, was a gifted genre painter, a pharmacist by trade and a self-taught artist. He captured the petit bourgeois worlds of the Biedermeier era and the German Industrial Revolution with unsurpassed precision, accurately identifying and capturing the inherent comedy of the subject, as his *Poor Poet* proves. The tiny scale, by the way, was his trademark. A considerable number of his paintings are owned by the New Pinakothek, in Munich.

The new Pinakothek was the third large museum building erected by the artistically inclined King Ludwig I of Bavaria, after the Glyptothek for antiquities and the Old Pinakothek for work up to the 18th century. Both these buildings were designed and constructed by Leo von Klenze, Munich's great classicist. The New

Pinakothek was the work of Friedrich von Gärtner. He endowed the city of Munich with such striking architecture as the Feldherrnhalle and the Siegertor, or Triumphal Gate. He was an experienced eclectic and used many different style features. His New Pinakothek was an extended building with a hint of Italian palazzo, faced in brick, with a colorful frieze of figures directly below the roof guttering. It stood on the other side of Theresienstrasse, opposite the Old Pinakothek.

Both buildings were severely damaged during the Second World War. Unlike Klenze's Old Pinakothek, no one took the trouble to reconstruct Gärtner's building; the architect had long been regarded as irrelevant and outdated. The new, purpose-built construction of 1981 was created by Alexander von Branca. The decision against Gärtner is bitterly regretted, but irreversible. The loss of the original building can not, however, detract

from the status of the newer collections the building contains.

It is an important collection of regional, national and international late 18th and 19th century art. Other genre artists in addition to Spitzweg are included in regional art. There is historical painting, in which Carl Theodor von Piloty was a famous specialist. There was an academy in the city that in its later years enjoyed a great reputation under Peter von Cornelius, appointed by King Ludwig, and which produced a number of important artists.

Loved by the bourgeoisie

Cornelius was a Nazarene. Like his Romantic friends, he wanted to repeat the art of the Italian High Renaissance. Other Nazarenes, such as Friedrich Overbeck, are represented in the New Pinakothek. At the same time, Munich became a leading artistic center, especially of landscape painting.

First, we must bear in mind that at the start of the 19th century, the genre was still regarded as a lesser category of art. It was only the influence of the English, the Danes and, above all, the French from the Barbizon School that elevated the status of landscape painting, with the result that it finally flourished, becoming the bourgeoisie's favorite art form. Munich, where a wealth of inspiration in the form of the Alps was on the doorstep, so to speak, contributed to the growing popularity of landscape painting with men such as Dillis, Achenbach, Schleich, Lier and Kobell. They are clearly represented in the New Pinakothek, together with landscape painters of other nationalities, such as the Austrian Waldmüller, the North German Friedrich and the Frenchmen Corot, Daubigny and Diaz de la Peña.

The Impressionists were also heirs to the rich inheritance of the Barbizon School. Apart from Germans Liebermann, Slevogt and Corinth, the New Pinakothek exhibits one of the famous water lily paintings by Claude Monet, for example. The museum largely has Hugo von Tschudi to thank for such acquisitions. Tschudi escaped to Munich, where he became director of the New Pinakothek, to avoid the Philistine Emperor Wilhelm II.

The first floor of this museum, opened in 1853, is occupied by a collection of more than three hundred works – predominantly by Nazarenes, Romantics and historical painters – belonging to King Ludwig I, who had abdicated by the time the museum opened. One of the former monarch's last purchases was a painting by Arnold Böcklin.

The collection has been enriched by private gifts. An early donation was received from Conrad Fiedler, the wealthy Munich art historian and patron; another from Hugo Tschudi. In 1919, Tschudi's widow donated the self-portrait of Vincent Van Gogh, dating from 1888, that was in her possession. In 1938, the Nazis labeled it "degenerate" and removed it from the collection, allowing it to be auctioned off in Switzerland. It now hangs in the United States.

The Hard Path is the name Fritz von Uhde gave his 1890 painting (above left). It is regarded as the most important work of German Impressionism.

Ferdinand Hodler's study, *Student at Jena*, 1908, (above right) betrays signs of the Art Nouveau style.

The new New Pinakothek building in the 1980s (below right).

The art of the Estonians

The Baltic state's **NATIONAL ART GALLERY** can be found in **TARTU**

ADDRESS:
National Museum
J. Kuperjanovi 9;
Tartu Art Museum:
Raekoja plats 18

OPENING TIMES:
Wed. 11 am to 6 pm

INTERNET:
www.erm.ee

HOW TO GET THERE:
On foot from the main
railway station

OTHER ATTRACTIONS:
Estonian Museum
of Literature,
Tartu Museum of Art

The National Art
Gallery houses
a collection of Central
African tribal art,
cultural-historical
jewels. View of the hall
(below left).

The painter Konstantin
Karlson painted
Portrait of Jüri Proben
in 1908 in the spirit of
19th century traditions
(below right).

Estonia is the northernmost, smallest and most successful of the three Baltic states. The economy is healthy, the political situation stable and the standard of living comparatively high. During the Soviet era, its proximity to Finland, whose language is mutually intelligible to Finns and Estonians, proved particularly advantageous. This linguistic closeness is the result of common Finno-Ugric origins. The emigration to the Baltic Sea region around the Gulf of Finland took place around the time of the birth of Christ.

Just two thirds of Estonia's not quite 1.5 million inhabitants are Estonians. They are hard working, inventive and artistic. They were not always so, because they were not allowed to be. Until the 19th century they were subject to external rule by the Germans, Swedes and Russians. Irrespective of tsarist Russia's political supremacy, the economic and cultural climate in the country was dominated by the Germano-Baltic aristocracy. The Estonians remained rural servants, in a state of bondage until the start of the 19th century. They were not permitted to purchase land until the mid-19th century.

Jacob Hurt as a pioneer

Awakening of the Estonian national identity occurred at the same time as similar movements in other ethnic states ruled by Russia, and by the same means and methods. The people concerned themselves with their own language and art, taking care to preserve their own history. A pioneer in this field was called Jakob Hurt.

He came from southeastern Estonia, from the comparatively archaic region of Põlva. He studied theology in Tartu and became involved in Estonian language and poetry at the same time. He started working as a supply teacher before he was given a parish, and he carried out linguistic research and collected cultural objects. He died in St. Petersburg in 1907.

Two years later, a national museum was established in Tartu, with the express intention of adopting and continuing his ideological legacy. Tartu, otherwise known as Dorpat, is the second biggest city in the country – after the administrative center of Tallinn – and is regarded as the launch pad for the Estonian nationalist movement, not least because of the impact of Jakob Hurt. The city's new museum was and is devoted to patriotic ideology. It not only offers an art collection in the usual sense – it is also a museum of folklore.

The collections are organized accordingly. They comprise 130,000 items, of which only around 2 percent can be displayed. Lack of space is a persistant problem. The institution has needed a suitably sized building since its inception.

A committee was formed to look for suitable premises. The Tartu City Council wanted nothing to do with the project initially and then it made a couple of rooms available free of charge in the center of Tartu. The museum moved in 1913.

It remained there until 1922. In the meantime, the state achieved independence and the prospects of a change of location seemed promising. In 1922, the museum found a new home at the Raadi House, a former manor house previously owned by a family called Liphart. Initially, the museum occupied four rooms and, by 1927, the whole building, but it still wanted a new, purpose-built museum building.

Delicate landscapes

The Raadi House was destroyed during the Second World War. The property

became a Soviet army base and the collection migrated to two abandoned churches, where it remained under lock and key. There were no exhibitions. In 1980, the idea of restoring the Raadi House surfaced, but it remained just an idea.

Estonia gained independence again with the collapse of the Soviet Union. The Estonian National Museum opened again in 1993, this time in a building on Kuperjanovi Street, previously the home of the Railwaymen's Club. A permanent exhibition has been on display since 1994, but the museum has not abandoned the idea of constructing a new building on the site of Raadi House. In the meantime, the Ministry of Culture has approved the scheme and there has been a design competition, won by two young Estonian architects. Collections have been held in churches for the cause, but no one can say when the work will begin.

Folk art, costumes, furniture, metalworking, household items, jewelry and agricultural equipment are on display, but above all there are pictures – etchings, drawings and watercolors. There are portraits by Konstantin Karlson, Friedrich Sigismund Stern and Karl Neff, and a vivid genre scene by Ernst Hermann Schlichting. There are extremely delicate landscapes, views and interiors. The fact that the names often sound German, Swedish or Russian is connected with the country's ethnic mix. Once the potential cause of conflict, such diversity has long since become an advantage and the National Museum in Tartu is proof of this.

Whilse, the National Museum's collections center on the culture and history of Estonia, the Art Museum, founded in 1940, focuses on 20th century fine art. It has collected modern Estonian art consistently, and even during the Soviet communist era, always engaged with modern, domestic art movements. Ulo Sooster is really the best known of 20th century Estonian painters, but Lepo Mikko has also made a name for himself in the art metropolises of Western Europe with his techno-futuristic pictures. The cultural and linguistic relationship with the Finns has contributed to the ability of Estonian artists to establish an interesting art scene in their country, even in difficult times. With its 3,500 paintings, more than 9,000 drawings and watercolors and 700 sculptures, the Art Museum in Tartu is now Estonia's biggest art gallery.

Estonian artists sought to access current movements even under communist rule. Ulo Sooster's *The White Egg* (above) is one example.

The museum building's facade (below right).

The heart of Karelianism

The ATENEUM ART MUSEUM in HELSINKI was inaugurated as the country's first national gallery in 1887

ADDRESS:
Kalvokatu 2,
Helsinki

OPENING HOURS:
Tues. and Fri. 9 am
to 6 pm
Wed. and Thurs. 9 am
to 8 pm
Sat. and Sun. 11 am to 5
pm

INTERNET:
www.ateneum.fi

PUBLIC TRANSPORT:
Metro, to Kaisaniemi;
Tram, 3B/3T, 7A, 6, or 2
to Kaivokatu: Bus, to
Rautatientori

OTHER ATTRACTIONS:
National Museum,
Museum of Culture,
Cygnäus Gallery,
Seurasaari Open-air
Museum

The first 18 works that formed the basis of the original art collection in Helsinki were donated by Tsar Alexander II of Russia. At that time, Finland was one of Russia's dependent territories and had been so since 1807, as part of the treaty of Tilsit signed between Napoleon of France and the reigning tsar. Until then, Finland had belonged to Sweden. Situated on the northeastern shore of the Baltic Sea with its population of Siberian immigrants, it had always long for, but never actually enjoyed territorial independence. Along with other ethnic groups under Russian rule, Finland was striving for autonomy, struggling to cultivate an individual language of its own, as well as encouraging and developing a national culture.

The Art Museum was intended to provide a home for all Finnish national culture. The idea was to establish a creative alliance of art galleries and educational establishments. An international competition was held. Carl Theodor Höijer, one of Helsinki's leading 19th century architects, won. He drew up a number of architectural plans for the building, largely in the Neo-Renaissance style so popular all over Europe at that time.

From 1860 to 1960

The aptly named Ateneum Art Museum celebrated its inauguration in 1887. The main facade of this three-story structure was divided into three sections. The middle portion was designed to reflect the Museum's main purpose and function. Four main arteries represent the disciplines of painting, sculpture, architecture and graphic art. Three busts, depicting Raphael, Phidias and Bramante, decorate the entrance.

The main entrance opens onto a hall with an imposing staircase leading up to the various floors of the gallery. The building was extended in 1900 and thereafter further expansion work has been constantly in progress, most notably during the 1990s. After the relocation of the Art Academy

and University of Industrial Design, which originally shared the Museum building before moving to a building of its own, the entire Höijer wing is now available for exhibition purposes.

The Museum boasts a collection of Finnish art, dating from the 18th century to around 1960, as well as some examples of 19th and 20th century foreign art. There is also a constantly changing series of temporary exhibitions as well as a related program of different events. The Ateneum is now regarded as part of the Finnish National Gallery.

Strong Swedish influence

The visual arts, like so many aspects of Finland's public life, were influenced by Sweden for a long time. Swedish continues to be the country's second official language. Swedish names crop up frequently among the exhibited artists. Many of the 18th century works on display could just as easily be hanging in Stockholm.

A noticeable change in style and theme occurred around 1850, when the Finnish people began to discover their cultural identity. Art was a way of expressing sensual perceptions, a direction in art better known as "national Romanticism," the main features of which were monumentality and recourse to traditional ornamentation. As far as Finnish fine art is concerned, the leading proponents were architects Herman Gesellius and Eliel Saarinen and painter Akseli Gallén-Kallela, who illustrated "Kalevala," Finland's national epic poem handed down by word of mouth until it was recorded and printed in the 19th century. It relates the deeds of mythical heroes. Gallén-Kallela illustrated the poem with evocative pictures in the French Romantic style, influenced by "Jugendstil," although the general effect was much more serious and gloomy, both in terms of color and expression.

France and the Barbizon School with its penchant for landscape also had an important influence on the new generation of Finnish art. It discovers its own topography as a theme, creating a unique new movement known as Karelianism. Albert Edelfelt and Eero Järnefelt are important representatives in this respect. The political undertones are obvious: Karelia, a region bordering directly on Russia, was and still is regarded as the heart of the national movement for autonomy, despite all Russian desires to the contrary.

Around 1880, Symbolism became popular in Europe. Odilon Redon and Gustave Moreau introduced "fin de siècle" *Weltschmerz* and decadence into their paintings. Hugo Simbert and Helene Schjerfbeck of Finland share a similar approach, but both retain a distinctly national basic tone. When they depicted death or mortality, it always took place in an alien, and consequently more unpleasant, environment.

Helene Schjerfbeck's self portrait, dated 1915, is a melancholy painting, bearing comparison with Paula Modersohn-Becker. Hugo Simberg's *The Garden of Death*, dated 1896, depicts three clothed skeletons watering plants and weeding. This macabre scene is vaguely reminiscent of the gloomy atmospheric paintings by Edvard Munch.

The Ateneum building, designed by Finnish architect Carl Theodor Höijer (below left).

Akseli Gallén-Kallela is arguably the most famous Finnish painter. His gloomy painting, *Lemminkäinen's Mother*, 1897, is a moving lament for the dead (above). It was originally an illustration for "Kalevala," Finland's national epic poem.

Hugo Simberg's painting, *Spring Evening*, was painted the same year. It too is dominated by gloomy colors (below right).

41

Home of art in the Bordelais

BORDEAUX'S MUSEUM OF ART
is one of the biggest institutions in the **FRENCH** provinces

ADDRESS:
20 Cours d'Albret, Bordeaux

OPENING TIMES:
Thurs.-Tues. 11 am to 6 pm

INTERNET:
www.bordeaux.fr

PUBLIC TRANSPORT:
Tram and bus to Palais de Justice

OTHER ATTRACTIONS:
Goupil Museum

The Bordeaux Museum possesses a large collection of Dutch paintings. Peter Paul Rubens' 1614 painting, *The Martyrdom of Saint George*, forms part of this collection (below left).

Albert Marquet, classed as a late Impressionist, painted *Rouen Harbor* in 1920 (below right).

Napoleon Bonaparte was more than just a brilliant field commander and an insatiable conqueror; he also achieved many things having little or no connection at all with war and the army, such as creating a civil code much admired and imitated outside France. He also occasionally distinguished himself as a friend and patron of the arts. Thus creation of art museums in the French provinces, inspired by the Louvre, can be ascribed to him.

In 1793, during the French Revolution, the royal art collection was made accessible to the public. Art treasures of which aristocracy and Church had been dispossessed were added to the collection. In the meantime, political developments continued to unfold. The Jacobins took over after the Directorate, which was overthrown in 1799 by France's most successful military man, Corsican artillery officer Napoleon Bonaparte. Napoleon became First Consul and assumed responsibility for domestic matters.

One of his activities consisted of dividing up the Revolution's art collection, still centralized at this time, and distributing it to several cities. An expert appraisal by the presiding Minister of the Interior, Jean-Antoine Claude Chaptal, also an important chemist and economic expert, formed the authoritative basis for the decision. Napoleon created a total of 15 provincial museums, one in Bordeaux, in southwest France, an old port city at the mouth of the River Garonne.

The founder and first director was Pierre Lacour, who established the Museum in 1801. Lacour is a painter virtually unknown outside France. Stylistically, he falls somewhere between Chardin and David. Lacour concerned himself with the collection, already comprising 45 pieces, including works by less known contemporary French artists as well as paintings by Rubens, Van Dyck, Titian, Perugino, Bassano and Veronese. Lacour was a skilled conservator. He cleaned and, if necessary, restored the paintings, which were housed in an old school building.

The Lacaze collection
Lacour died in 1814, the year of Napoleon's first exile. Lacour was followed by his son of the same name, also the Museum's director, a conservator and an industrious collector. He lived through the short-lived return and last exile of Napoleon, followed by the return of the Bourbon monarchy. The Bordelais was always a conservative region and it greeted the Restoration with a mixture of relief and triumph.

The younger Pierre Lacour's most important action was buying the Lacaze collection. He was able to persuade the city fathers that they should spend the money in question. The private collection contained 245 works by Flemish, Dutch, German and Italian artists. The fact that Bordeaux exhibits one of the most comprehensive collections of 17th century Dutch art in France today can mainly be ascribed to the younger Pierre Lacour's acquisition.

In 1851, weathy bourgeois individuals and families founded

a society for art lovers in Bordeaux. Their donations and support made it possible to acquire other works by Eugene Delacroix (whose family once lived in

Bordeaux), Camille Corot and Charles-Francois Daubigny.

Works by Redon to Lhote

The Museum was forced to abandon the old school building, which had become too small, and relocated to a building adjacent to the city's Town Hall. In 1861, a former mayor donated his private collection. A year later, a fire broke out, but thankfully the paintings were spared. They were first removed to storage and then returned to the Town Hall because during the Franco–Prussian war of 1870–1871, it was feared that if the city were be occupied by enemy troops, the collection would be seized and carried away.

Instead of Prussian art thieves, there was another fire. This time, valuable parts of the collection were destroyed, including a Delacroix of which the Museum had been very proud. Finally, it was decided that a new Museum buil-

ding should be constructed. A trusted municipal architect, Charles Burguet, was entrusted with its execution. He had been pushing for a new Museum building since 1862, which had given rise to much debate. The Museum was built between 1875 and 1881.

It was an imposing building with three wings, in the French Historical style. It forms a uniform architectural complex together with the Town Hall, a former abbey and the splendid late Gothic cathedral of Saint André in the Old Town, not far from the west bank of the Garonne.

Amongst others, the present collection includes works by two artists born in Bordeaux: Symbolist Odilon Redon and Cubist André Lhote. Other masters of classic modern art are represented as well: Rouault, Vlaminck and Kokoschka. A gallery connected directly to the Museum regularly holds exhibitions with international participants.

The existing exhibition space at the Museum has long since become too small. Of the 2,500 paintings and more than 500 sculptures in storage, no more than one tenth is on display at any time.

Odilon Redon painted *The Winged Man* around 1880 (above).

View of the present Museum building (below right).

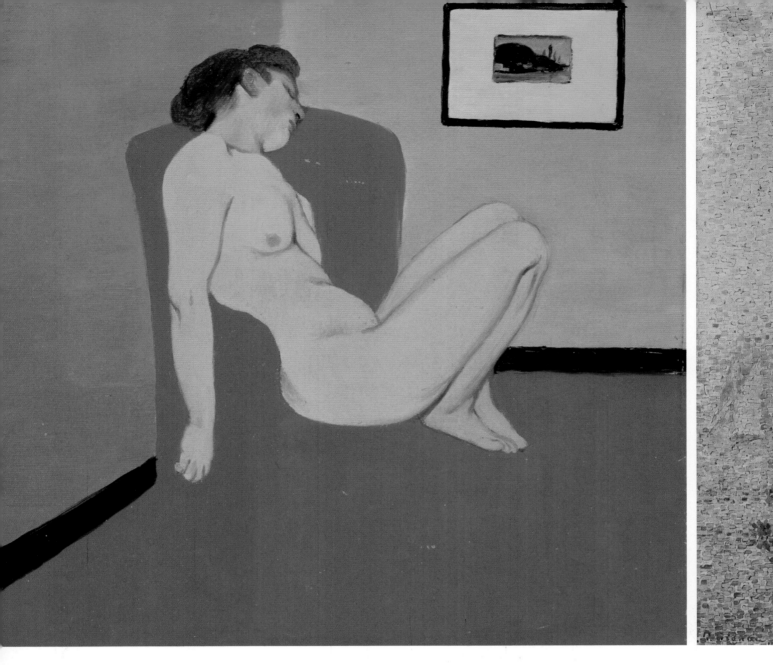

Art at the foot of the Alps

GRENOBLE MUSEUM has become something of a cultural institution in France – a *Who's Who* of modern art

ADDRESS:
5, Place de Lavalette, Grenoble

OPENING TIMES:
Wed.-Mon. 10:00 am to 6:30 pm

INTERNET:
www.museede-grenoble.fr

PUBLIC TRANSPORT:
Bus to Place Notre Dame

OTHER ATTRACTIONS:
Musée Bayard

Paris, that beautiful and celebrated city, is not one to share its exalted reputation lightly. Yet at least in the field of modern art, it is obliged to yield a certain amount of glory to a town that lies at the foot of the French Alps. Grenoble Museum possesses France's most significant collection of modern art outside Paris. Furthermore, the gallery boasts an outstanding collection of paintings, sculptures and sketches, dating from the Middle Ages to the end of the 20th century as well as a collection of Greek, Roman and Egyptian antiquities.

Grenoble has always been a town with an eye to the future. The Museum was established in 1796, during the Revolution, by Louis-Joseph Jay, and quickly gained a prestigious reputation for itself. The alpine town of Grenoble, boasting the first such institution of its kind outside Paris, became nationally famous for its collection of art treasures. In

the 19th century, its collections were augmented with works by Canaletto and Delacroix, along with various generous donations. General de Beylié, for example, presented the Museum with four paintings by Zurbarán, which now figure among its most popular attractions. The collections of old paintings were phased out at the beginning of the 20th century.

Rooms or environments?

Thanks to the efforts of Andry-Farcy, curator of the Grenoble Museum between 1919 and 1949, many works of modern art were introduced to the collection. He built up a selection of paintings covering all the main strands of artistic development during the first half of the 20th century, encompassing Fauve, abstract and Cubist works. Among these new acquisitions, special emphasis was placed on contemporary Belgian artists.

Towards the end of the last century, drastic measures became necessary to address the problems arising from an increasing shortage of space within the Museum, which was housed in a Neo-Classical villa situated in the Place de Verdun. A team of young architects known as Group 6 – comprising Antoine Félix-Faure, Olivier Félix-Faure and Philippe Macary – came up with a design for an impressive new building. It would no longer be located in the town center. Instead, the new rectangular structure, open to the sky, would occupy the site of a ruined fortress. The angular structure is divided into individual blocks and is clad in white stone.

The main entrance hall, lit by natural daylight, is entered from the atrium which also forms the central axis of the Museum. The right-hand side is devoted to temporary exhibitions of contemporary art. The circuit tours start on the left, beginning with 13th century works and pro-

The *Seated Female Nude* by Felix Edouard Vallotton, dated 1897 (top left), is one of the Museum's star attractions, as is Paul Signac's 1905 painting of St. Tropez (top right).

The two photographs below illustrate the artistically designed lighting in the Museum's rooms (above right) and the front entrance of the new Museum building (below right).

gressing through the Renaissance, Impressionist and Expressionist periods to end with kinetic and minimalist pieces. The area in between has been furnished with benches, providing an attractive rest area and high glass windows look onto an uninterrupted view of an artificial lake. This interaction between outside and inside is characteristic of the building; the exhibition rooms all enjoy views of the mountains towering in the background or the banks of the River Isère. Various sculptures have been installed in a park area around the Museum.

From Zurbarán to Sol LeWitt

Among the wealth of paintings, it is difficult to single out specific ones for special praise. One of the highlights, however, must inevitably be the collection of 17th century paintings, incorporating works by Philippe de Champaigne, Georges de La Tour, Laurent de La Hure and Francisco de Zurbarán. Similarly, the 19th century sculptures, displayed in a luminous hall, are worthy of note. The lists of artists in the new galleries read like a *Who's Who* of modern classical art, with works by painters such as Marquet, Derrain, Vlaminck, Van Dongen, Picasso, Matisse, Léger and Bonnard as well as Magritte, Tanguy, Miró,

Soulages and Max Ernst. All areas of contemporary art are represented with works by Sol LeWitt, Carl Andre, Christian Boltanski and Bertrand Lavier. Two stars of the collection are Picabias's Torso and Tom Wesselmann's *Bedroom Painting No. 31*.

This university town has always been blessed with an invigorating, intellectual atmosphere. Covering an expanse of nearly 200,000 square feet and divided into 65 rooms, the Museum has turned the relatively small town of Grenoble into a metropolis of art.

Where nuns once prayed

The **MUSEUM OF FINE ART** in **LYONS**, France's second biggest museum of art, is based in a former abbey

ADDRESS:
20 Place des Terreaux, Lyons

OPENING TIMES:
Tues.-Mon. 10 am
to 6 pm,
Fri. 10:30 am to 6 pm

INTERNET:
www.lyon.fr

PUBLIC TRANSPORT:
Metro, Lines A and C;
Bus, Lines 1, 3, 6, 13, 19,
40, 44

OTHER ATTRACTIONS:
Museum of
Contemporary Art

If you enter the portal of the grandiose Museum of Fine Art in Lyons today, you will find yourself in one of the loveliest museum inner courtyards in Europe. Its splendor can be ascribed to Abbesses Anne and Antoinette de Chaulnes, who ordered the complex of abbey buildings to be erected in the 17th century.

The daughters of a French marshal, they were nuns of the Benedictine Order of the Ladies of Saint Peter, which maintained a convent for daughters of the nobility at Place des Terreaux. Nuns had been living on this site since the 7th century.

In 1659, Anne de Chaulnes (1625–72) decided to rebuild and completely refurbish the abbey dating from the Middle Ages – a

massive undertaking – and entrusted the design to François Royers de la Valfrenière from Avignon. The main facade and two sides were built when Anne de Chaulnes died at the age of 47. The new abbess, her

sister, Antoinette, approached the work with the same dedication. She succeeded in securing the services of architect and painter Thomas Blanchet to decorate the convent's interior. Since his return from Italy,

Blanchet was treated like royalty in Lyons. He is also responsible for Lyons' ornate City Hall in the grandiose Place des Terreaux. To this day, Saint Peter's Abbey retains the staircase as well as the refectory designed by Blanchet. The nuns lived in Saint Peter's Abbey until the French Revolution. After the convent was closed, the building was initially used for administrative purposes, but very soon it was decided that it should be used as a museum.

"Lyons School"

The palace-like building was originally intended as a place to exhibit artistic examples from Lyons' silk industry, but this all changed in 1803. By decree of Napoleon Bonaparte, 15 museums were to be founded in France, including one at Lyons and, of course, what better location could there be for this temple of art than Saint Peter's Abbey? The School of Fine Art, which created floral designs for the silk-weaving industry, but which simultaneously established an independent style of painting, made a very sig-

nificant contribution to the Museum's rise. Parisian critics used the term "Lyons School" for the first time in 1819.

"Museum madness" at the end of the 19th century ensured that the abbey got a second splendid staircase, painted by Pierre Puvis de Chavannes, between 1884 and 1886. The Old Master and Modern galleries branch off here.

With 70 rooms, departments of antique art, *objets d'art* and medals, paintings, graphic art and sculpture, the Museum of Fine Art in Lyons is the biggest and most important French museum after the Louvre in Paris. Contemporary art, which was also on display in Saint Peter's Abbey until 1990, is now housed in a separate building. The collections in the Museum of Fine Art therefore cover the period from antiquity to the 1970s.

The collection of antique art displayed in 16 rooms offers an excellent overview of the civilizations of antiquity. Egypt, the Sumerians, Cyprus, Greece and the Roman Empire are all represented with valuable exhibits.

Large sculpture collection

The Museum's attention was drawn to sculpture at a very early date. It now has a considerable collection. Outstanding works stem from the French Romanesque, Italian Renaissance and the late 19th and early 20th centuries. The biggest sculptures are displayed to great effect in the convent's former chapel and include works by Rodin, Bourdelle, Maillol, Pradier and Pompon. The Albert Bartholomé frieze, *Monument to the Dead*, forms a focal point.

The department of painting and drawing on the third floor is regarded as particularly comprehensive and exhibits works from every age. Works by Spanish and Dutch masters, represented by, amongst others, Peter Paul Rubens' *Adoration of the Magi* and Francisco de Zurbarán's *Saint Francis of Assisi*, are displayed alongside works from the 17th to 19th century French schools.

But the collections of Impressionists, Expressionists and Abstract works too are present, with masterpieces such as Renoir's *The Guitar Player*, Jawlensky's *Head of Medusa* and Georges Braque's *Woman at the Mirror*.

Unlike many other museums, which soon gained donors and patrons, the Museum's collection was acquired predominantly by clever directors, yet there have also been major bequests.

One legacy stands head and shoulders above the rest: Jacqueline Delubac, an actress born in Lyons in 1907, bequeathed the collections which she and her husband had gathered, including works by Braque, Rouault, Léger, Picasso, Miró, Gauguin, Dubuffet and Bacon as well as Corot, Bonnard, Vuillard, Degas, Renoir and Monet.

In the face of so much female involvement, it comes as no surprise that even the bronze statue gracing the central fountain in the former convent garden is a woman. The charm of this little park, used by the public since the 19th century, does not merely lie in the statues erected beneath the trees. Its cloistered calm also invites visitors to take a stroll through the millennia.

Paul Gauguin's painting, *Delightful Day (Nave Nave Mahana)*, holds a special place (above left) in the Modern section.

A major collection with works by H. Fantin-Latour forms part of Lyons' treasures. The still life, *Roses and Glass Jug*, dates from 1889 (above right).

Pierre Puvis de Chavannes also has numerous works in the collection. The portrait of his wife (below right) was painted in 1883.

Of the Italians, Veronese's painting, *Bathsheba*, 1575, is an example of the Renaissance master's splendid use of light (below center).

The Museum is located at Place des Terreaux, the central square in Lyons' old town (below left).

Art in the triumphal arch

The MUSÉE D'ART MODERNE ET D'ART CONTEMPORAIN in NICE comprises an impressive collection of modern art

ADDRESS:
Promenade des Arts, Nice

OPENING HOURS:
Tues.-Sun. 10 am
to 6 pm

INTERNET:
www.mamac-nice.org

PUBLIC TRANSPORT:
City bus lines 1, 2, 3, 5, 6, 16, 17

OTHER ATTRACTIONS:
Musée International d'Art Naif, Palais Lascaris

Pastel-colored walls, flower markets like those in Rome and bubbling fountains… Nice, which did not finally become French until 1860, cannot deny its Italian origins. The southern city inspired many artists such as Matisse, Chagall and Dufy. Bonnard, who lived in nearby Le Cannet, described life in southern France: "Our god is light."

After Paris, Nice is the city with the largest number of museums in France. They include the Musée Matisse, the Musée des Beaux Arts, the Musée Raoul Dufy, the Musée Chagall, the Musée Massena and many others. But the whizz kid among these temples of art is the Musée d'Art Moderne et d'Art Contemporain, which took just three years to set up. European and American art from 1960 to the present day is displayed in a building that may itself be considered avant-garde.

Everything about the MAMAC – opened in 1990 – is unconventional, as the building was erected in the center of the city at the intersection of two axial roads, above the bed of the underground River Paillon. The museum was to form an architectural union with the octagonal, white marble theater of Nice, completed in 1989. The road on which the unusual architectural ensemble stands has been named the Promenade des Arts.

Niki de Saint Phalle's donation

The museum complex is laid out in a square with a total surface area of about 43,000 square feet. It has three floors and built in the shape of a kind of triumphal arch. The architects, Yves Bayard and Henri Vidal, linked four towers clad in grayish-white Carrara marble with transparent bridges that can be used as glass catwalks. Red walls

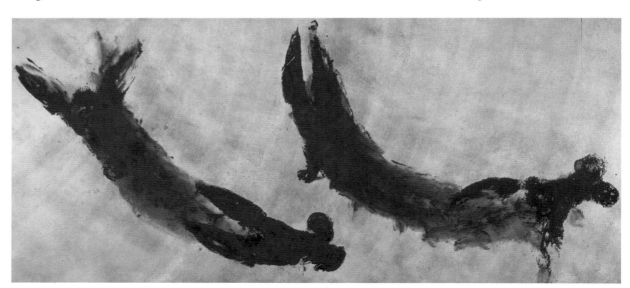

Yves Klein, who died young, was a co-founder of the "Nice School." *Anthropométrie sans titre*, **1960, is one of his best known works (below left).**

with olive trees growing on them contrast with the austere building and bring a Mediterranean flair to the city center. The sculptures of Niki de Saint Phalle, installed in the square in front of the entrance, are also astonishing. The artist donated 190 of her works to the museum in 2001, shortly before her death.

Like her husband, Jean Tinguely, Niki de Saint Phalle was a member of the Nouveaux Réalistes, the New Realist group founded in 1960, which originated in Nice – although it later shifted to Paris. Yves Klein, co-founder of the "Nice School," was the main driving force. His monochrome paintings in orange and blue aroused as much attention as his *Anthropométries* and visions of an airy architecture.

The son of artist parents, he was born in Nice on 28 April 1928. As an eighteen-year-old on the beach, he and his friends divided up the world. He chose the cloudless blue sky and remained faithful to that color throughout his life. The museum currently owns 20 of his works, as well as important pieces by other famous New Realists, such as Fernandez Arman, Raymond Hains, Jacques de la Villeglé, Mimmo Rotella, Jean Tinguely and Niki de Saint Phalle. Daniel Spoerri's *Hommage au Jardin d'hiver de la baronne de Salomon de Rothschild* is an environment every bit as impressive as César's *Dauphine*, a smashed red automobile. The New Realists came to a spectacular end when, ten years after their founding, they gave the group a ceremonial funeral in front of Milan Cathedral with a catafalque draped in lilac velvet bearing the initials NR.

Yves Klein's *Wall of Fire*

1960 marked the transition between modern art and the avant-garde, a period reflected in the museum program. Alongside the New Realists, you can see the heroes of Pop-Art, an American movement which paralleled New Realism. Works such as Andy Warhol's *One Dollar Sign*, Jim Dine's *The March Painting*, Tom Wesselmann's Still Life 56 and Roy Lichtenstein's Entablature figure among the exhibits. However, the museum also documents Minimal art, introducing it with works by Richard Serra and Sol LeWitt. Kenneth Noland, Morris Louis and Frank Stella represent American color field painting. The 1980s are exemplified by Ernest Pignon-Ernest's *David and Goliath*, Jean-Charles Blais' *El tiger del papel* and Ben's *Chambre à part*. The spectator is constantly struck by the amount of space allotted to each work of art.

However, because the interplay of nature and art, light and color reigns supreme in Nice, the museum has one additional surprise in store. *The Garden of Eden* laid out on the roof terrace was designed according to sketches by Yves Klein. His installation, *Wall of Fire*, is staged once a week. Art also reigns over the roofs of Nice.

The MAMAC is a temple of avant-garde art: view of the rooms with works by Robert and Christo Malaval (above left) and Niki de Saint Phalle (above right).

A Cerberus-like figure by Niki de Saint Phalle guards the entrance to the museum (below right).

France´s onliest museum

The **POMPIDOU CENTER** focuses on 20th century art

ADDRESS:
Place Georges
Pompidou, Paris

OPENING TIMES:
Wed.-Mon. 11 am
to 10 pm

INTERNET:
www.enac-gp.fr/
Pompidou

PUBLIC TRANSPORT:
Subway stations
Rambuteau, Hôtel de
Ville or Châtelet

OTHER ATTRACTIONS:
Picasso Museum

For centuries, the French capital's impressive buildings included the central indoor market, Les Halles, also known as the "belly of Paris." In 1972, it was demolished because it was too small and also unhygienic. A new, large-scale market opened on the southern edge of Paris. All who knew the iron architecture of Les Halles mourn its passing. A shopping center was erected in its place as well as a totally unique museum building.

The impetus came from the French head of state at that time, Georges Pompidou, the second president of the Fifth Republic after Charles de Gaulle. Like other potentates, he sought to immortalize himself through building projects and he promoted a building for modern art. "Paris should get a cultural center that is as much museum as it is workshop." With these words, in 1969, he invited architects from around the world to submit designs.

High-tech architecture

His words struck a resounding note. More than 650 tenders were received and carefully reviewed. The contract was awarded to two stars of the international architectural scene: Briton Richard Rogers and the Italian Renzo Piano, famous for their high-tech architecture, which esthetically highlights the technical aspects of the building, delighting in experimentation with new materials.

Their Paris museum building puts all the services, traffic routes and static elements on clear display, additionally emphasized by striking colors: blue for heating and ventilation, green for water and waste pipes, red for traffic routes and yellow for electrical installations. The ventilation pipe outlets, large curved metal funnels, rise up out of the square in front of the building, far from the foundations. They are reminiscent of pieces of abstract plastic art.

The forecourt that slopes down gently to the entrances is the scene of constant activity. Musicians, mime artists and magicians go through their routines. The visitors waiting in the long entrance queues, a permanent feature of the forecourt, watch the performers with interest and, whether the artistes realize it or not, they sometimes provide a little taste of some of the works housed by the museum.

The building was erected between 1971 and 1977 as a 545 foot long, 197 foot wide, 42 138 foot high prism. Parallels have been drawn with a steam ship. Each of the exhibition floors has a surface area of 80,730 square feet, optimum considering the building's layout; this is possible because services, elevators and escalators in big, diagonal glass tubes run outside in clear view of the forecourt. The internal walls can slide to one side or be removed, allowing the space to be used in different ways.

The museum contains many different things: a large library with reading rooms and computer screens,

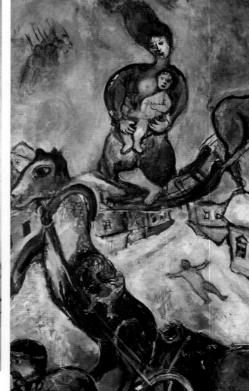

Marc Chagall's allegorical *The War*, from 1943, depicts the horrors of the Second World War (below right).

Picasso influenced the expressive world of modern art like no other painter. *The Acrobat (L'acrobate)*, from his Blue Period, was created in 1929 (below left).

a comprehensive movie collection with corresponding viewing facilities, an artisan crafts collection and drawing and craft activities for children. Experimental music is not forgotten here either – the famous avant-garde composer, Pierre Boulez, was curator at the museum for many years. Temporary exhibitions are introduced all the time. Some, like the major Surrealist exhibition of 2002, then go on tour.

World capital of avant-garde

The heart of the museum is the permanent exhibition of modern masterpieces. From the start of the 19th to the mid-20th century, Paris was the world capital of avant-garde. Many artists, including many foreigners, lived in France, and the scope and quality of the works on display are overwhelming.

The Centre National d'art et de culture Georges Pompidou building, to give it its official title, the Pompidou Center for short, or the Beaubourg (after its location), initially met with bitter opposition. Situated in the historic city center, many regarded it as an eyesore. But

the strife has long since ceased. Today the building is considered a masterpiece of modern architecture.

Frankly, it soon became clear that the building had not been constructed with the necessary care. The steel beams began to rust and other parts showed signs of wear. Thus, just two decades after completion, the building had to be closed so that it could be thoroughly overhauled. This took about three years. During this time, the district became rundown and resumed its role as the red-light district of Paris.

But since 2000, the fresh paintwork and fully functioning mechanics of the Pompidou Center glisten happily in the sun. The permanent exhibition has been reorganized and takes visitors on a successful tour of 20th century fine art, with works by around a hundred different artists, from Arp to Warhol. But the uncontested star is, and will always be, Picasso.

View of the beams, pipes and tubes embedded in the facade of the Pompidou Center (above) and of the entrance hall (below).

The museum of museums

With more than 300,000 works of art, the **LOUVRE** in **PARIS** is the biggest and richest museum in the world

ADDRESS:
Quai Louvre 34,
Paris

OPENING TIMES:
Tues.- Mon. 9 am
to 6 pm,
Mon. and Wed.
to 9:45 pm

INTERNET:
www.louvre.fr

PUBLIC TRANSPORT:
Subway, Louvre station

OTHER ATTRACTIONS:
Musée Carnevalet,
Musée Cluny

Leonardo's painting, *La Giaconda*, also known as *Mona Lisa*, 1506, (right), Delacroix's 1830 painting of the Revolution, *Liberty leading the People* (below center), and Canova's marble group, *Amor and Psyche*, 1787, (above left) have had a lasting influence on the development of art.

The immense scale of the Louvre (below).

It is absolutely impossible to get an idea of the Louvre in one day, even fleetingly, and even seven days will hardly suffice. The Louvre, with all its rooms and exhibitions, is a separate little city, with connections to several modes of public transport, malls, shops and restaurants. The Louvre station stands out from the other, often featureless, stations on the Paris subway system because of its beautiful decorations, notably copies of famous works of art found in the museum. There is direct access to the foyer of the Louvre from the platform.

The foyer proves to be an expansive space, flooded with light, from which various escalators lead upward. The airiness comes from the glass roof that covers it. It is shaped like a pyramid and is the work of the American architect I.M. Pei, who was commissioned by the former French President François Mitterrand to design this entrance. Like his predecessor, Georges Pompidou, Mitterrand had an ambition to make his mark on the world with particularly spectacular building projects. Pei's pyramid at the Louvre is just one of them.

Originally a palace

The pyramid has towered over the Louvre's square inner courtyard since 1989 and also provides the main entrance for visitors. While it was under construction, the pyramid was the subject of much heated debate, but it is now regarded as a masterpiece of modern architecture, not least because of the way it blends with the older architecture surrounding it. The Louvre was originally the palace of French kings, erected on the site of an even earlier fortress from the High Middle Ages. The builder was François I, the ruler from the house of Valois-Angoulême. Work began in 1546. The architect, who modeled his design on northern Italian palazzi, was Pierre Lescot. The buil-

ding work continued under François' successors until the 17th century. It ceased only in 1678, when the Sun King Louis IV moved his residence to Versailles.

Work resumed again under the Emperor Napoleon, halting temporarily under Napoleon III, by which time the palace had long since turned into a museum. Under Dominique Vivant-Denon, the French Revolution made the royal art collection, as well as precious works of art from the aristocracy and Church, accessible to the general public, thus creating one of the first public museums of art in recent history. The collections were constantly added to thereafter and Napoleon contributed the booty he brought back from Egypt. The Louvre was an inspiration to similar museum institutions elsewhere.

In 1940, when the Germans marched into the French capital, they discovered a palace that was, for the most part, empty. Practiced art thieves Hitler and Goering were amazed. The French had spirited their most precious art treasures away to safety in good time.

When the works of art returned to their old home, it soon became clear that all was not well with the fabric of the building. It was crumbling away on every side. Many people found the displays to be banal and visitor numbers fell. The renovation inspired by François Mitterrand did not come about primarily because of the need of every great statesman for self-engrandizement, but because the old building genuinely and desperately needed it. The Ministry of Finance, which had previously occupied a wing of the Louvre named after Cardinal Richelieu, now moved out and made room for an exhibition of sculptures and paintings. The collections that included the

Ancient Egyptian artifacts were completely reorganized. They are attractive because of their thoughtful arrangement, which not only permits an insight into life at the court of the pharaohs, but equally into the daily lives of ordinary people, with children's toys and information about meals and tools.

In the Grande Gallerie

The collection of paintings covers works up to the mid-19th century located in the Grande Gallerie, built during the reign of Henri IV, the first King from the house of Bourbon. Of all the paintings, the most famous is Leonardo da Vinci's portrait of the wife of a Florentine silk merchant, *La Giaconda*, also known as the *Mona Lisa*. The artist took the portrait on his travels in later life and because the last place in which he spent some timehe lived the invitation of François I – was Amboise on the Loire, the painting remained in France. The last private owner was Napoleon I. The *Mona Lisa* hung in his bedroom, over his bed. In 1804, he donated the painting of the woman with the mysterious smile to the Louvre.

Other famous exhibits worthy of note include the *Venus de Milo* and the *Winged Victory of Samothrace*. The collections contain more than 300,000 items and only a few of them can be exhibited at any time. The earlier decline in visitor numbers has slowly been reversed. Over five million visitors a year enter the famous museum beside the Seine.

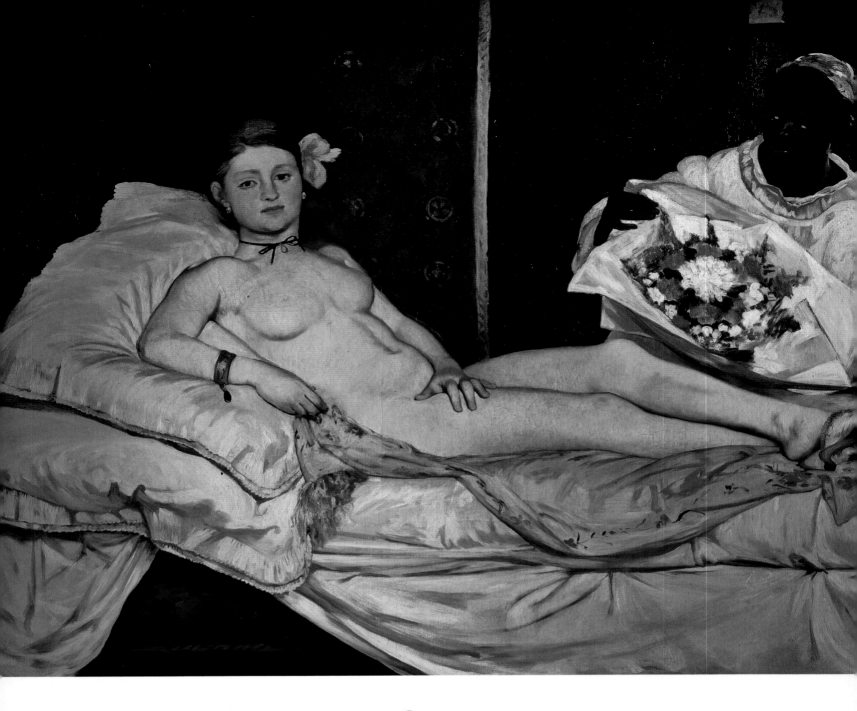

A station for art

Between Classicism and the Fauves, 1848-1914:
The **MUSÉE d'ORSAY** in **PARIS**

ADDRESS:
Square 1, rue de la
Légion d'Honneur
Paris

OPENING HOURS:
Tues, Wed, Fri and Sat
10 am to 6 pm
Thurs 10 am to 9:45 pm
Sun 9 am to 6 pm

INTERNET:
www.musee-orsay.fr

TRANSPORT:
Metro, Line 12,
Bus Lines 24, 63, 68,
69, 73, 83, 84, 94

OTHER ATTRACTIONS:
Musée des Beaux-
Sacré Coeur,
Notre Dame

Anyone traveling to Paris by train will arrive at one of Paris' famous stations, either the Gare du Nord or the Gare St.-Lazare, depending on which direction they are coming from. Passengers coming from the direction of Orléans will arrive in the French capital at the Gare d'Austerlitz. It was not always so. The terminus used to be the Gare d'Orsay, located on the left bank of the Seine, close to the French Foreign Ministry.

It is an absolutely splendid complex of buildings, the station itself and the Hôtel d'Orsay right next to it. Completed for the World Exhibition in 1900, its size and elegance are impressive. The architect was Victor Laloux. A contemporary admirer wrote: "The station is magnificent and reminiscent of a palace of fine arts and since the palace of fine arts also looks like a

station, I would advise Laloux to adapt it while there is still time!" It was a prophetic challenge.

When the Gare d'Orsay had served its purpose as a station, it remained unused for a time, started to crumble and was threatened with demolition several times, like the old Paris market halls, which finally gave way to a gigantic concrete shopping center. All those who knew them mourned the arrival of the modern steel architecture. Perhaps it was the resounding shock of the demolition of the market halls which saved the Gare d'Orsay from a similar fate.

When Paris was the capital of the world

The decision to turn the station into a museum was undertaken in 1977. Building work began three years later and was completed at the end of

1986. Four architects were responsible for the design. Most notably Gae Aulenti was responsible for the interior design. The Musée d'Orsay covers the period between Classicism and the Fauves, the years between 1848 and 1914. It was intended to cover the period between what is displayed in the Louvre and what is exhibited in the Pompidou Center, but the dividing lines tend to blur. Many of the artists represented in the Musée d'Orsay, such as Gustave Courbet, can also be found in the Louvre; others, like Henri Matisse, can be found in the Pompidou Center. In general, the Musée d'Orsay is home to art from the second half of the 19th century, the so-called Belle Époque, when Paris, according to the oft-quoted remark by Walter Benjamin, was the capital of the world.

Paris was certainly the capital of the artistic world. The bourgeois

landscape painting of the Realists and Impressionists was as much at home in Paris as the historical painting from the school of Delacroix and Géricault – just drawing to a close during the period in which the Musée d'Orsay specializes. The influence of French painting on neighboring counties and other art disciplines, such as sculpture, architecture and crafts during those years is also on show. Photography appeared for the first time during the Belle Epoque as well and the pioneers of the daguerreotype and the photograph are not forgotten.

The first impression on entering the museum is the majestic size of the main hall. A smooth path, bordered by paving stones and sculptures, lies where the tracks once ran. To the left and right are thematically arranged sections for painting and sculpture. Academic and salon art has not been suppressed; selected examples are on show, technically perfect and esthetically somewhat old-fashioned. Nevertheless, they are part of the cultural history of the 19th century, just like the pictures of Edouard Manet. A representative selection is on view here, including *Olympia*, the portrait of a naked courtesan, and *Déjeuner sur l'Herbe*, both of which once caused a scandal and have since exemplified Realist painting.

Rodin sculpted Balzac
The first floor of the station building contains art from 1848 to 1870, mainly covering the epoch of Napoleon III and his Second Empire. The modern age was ushered in by the Impressionists, including Claude Monet, Edgar Degas and Paul Cézanne; they were followed by the Post-Impressionists who comprised Georges Seurat, Vincent Van Gogh, and Paul Gauguin as well as Henri (le Douanier) Rousseau. Before the opening of the Musée d'Orsay, the movements were divided between various galleries like the Jeu de Paume; many items were in the Louvre and many more were in storage. Now it has its place in the Musée d'Orsay on the top floor of the building, where the magnificent restaurants and lounges were once located.

In one gallery, the visitor is received by Auguste Rodin's huge statue of the writer Balzac. The rooms where the paintings are hung have the slight disadvantage of being quite low, but they make up for it by letting in the light and by the delightful view they offer over the roofs and boulevards of the city which captivated so many of the Impressionists whose works are exhibited here.

The number of visitors to the museum was extraordinarily high from the day it opened. Long queues regularly form outside the entrances. The total number of visitors in the first ten years, including exhibitions in the Grand Palais, for which the Musée d'Orsay was responsible, was around 30 million.

Art in the open air

The Maeght Foundation in **ST. PAUL DE VENCE** has made room for 20th century artists

ADDRESS:
St.-Paul-de-Vence

OPENING TIMES:
Daily 10 am to 12:30 pm
and 2 pm to 6 pm,
10 am to 7 pm
in summer

INTERNET:
www.maeght.com

HOW TO GET THERE:
By car from Nice via
Cagnes-sur-Mer

Lovers under a Red Tree is the title Marc Chagall gave to his 1950 painting. It is one of splendors of the Maeght Foundation (below left).

Almost reverently, visitors climb the hill to the Marguerite and Aimé Maeght Foundation Museum. Set in a green frame, surrounded by tall pines, wild wisteria sways at the roadside and the chirping of the cicadas floats like an endless melody over the landscape. Both the white, concrete central buildings, overhung with semicircular roofs, are imbued with southern light and brightness. The dull red walls shimmer in the light and are reminiscent of the ochre rocks of Provence.

The estate is close to the artists' village of St.-Paul-de-Vence, approximately $12^1/_2$ miles north of Nice on the slopes of the Alpes Maritimes, which extend almost to the Mediterranean, in a landscape made to inspire artists.

The intention was that the museum buildings' architecture should respect nature as much as possible, should adapt to it and be part of it. But there was also a parallel agenda. This was not to be a place to honor painters and sculptors posthumously. In the Maeght Foundation, artists such as Chagall, Braque, Miró and Giacometti were challenged to help create the Museum for which Catalan architect Josep Lluis Sert created the setting. His design was based upon and inspired by the steeply sloping terrain, the perpe-

tual sunshine and the frequently turbulent wind. By creating internal courtyards, small gardens, patios and groups of walls, he created collusion between the environment and the sculpture installations. The Maeght Foundation opened in 1964 and has remained true to its beginnings as one of the most interesting private museums in Europe, assembled by a self-made man.

Various dedications

After his father fell in the First World War, Belgian-born Aimé Maeght (1906–81) spent his childhood and youth with his brothers and sisters in Gard, in the south of France. He attended school in Nîmes, became a brilliant lithographer and married Marguerite Devaye (1909–77) in 1927. Together they founded a printing company in Cannes in 1930 and a small gallery six years later. Thanks to a close friendship with Pierre Bonnard, the Maeghts got to know many of the painters and sculptors living in the south of France and, after opening a gal-

lery in Paris in 1945, became the art dealers for Matisse, Chagall, Braque, Miró, Bonnard, Giacometti and many others. They had a close friendship with all the artists, which can be deduced from the numerous works of art dedicated to the couple over the years.

The decision to make the works of art privately owned by the Maeghts accessible to the public was sealed by a tragic event. When the collectors' second son died of leukemia at 11 years old, his parents decided on a museum building as a permanent memorial. A small chapel near the entrance is dedicated to Saint Bernard, for whom the youth was named. The simple building is dominated by a 15th century altarpiece, as well as stained glass by Braque and Bazaine and a rosary by Ubac.

As in the chapel, visitors encounter sculpture installations by the artists everywhere. There is a Giacometti courtyard, where the figures look like they are sleepwalking; a Miró maze with birds, trees, statues and gargoyles; walls designed

by Chagall and a fountain by Pol
Bury. An abstract sculpture by Calder dominates a pine grove and a
pool mosaic by Georges Braque
causes sunlight to dance on the
water.

From Arp to Calder

The presentation of exhibits continues inside because the collection of 20th century art – with
paintings, sculptures, drawings
and graphic works – is regarded as
one of the richest in Europe.
Alongside works by Arp, Bonnard,
Braque, Chagall, Léger, Kandinsky,
Matisse, Germaine Richier, Adam,
Tal Coat and Calder, the Foundation owns 52 Giacometti sculptures and 150 works by Miró. The
library, one of the Maeghts' passions, consists of more than 30,000
volumes. With two to three temporary exhibitions a year and
numerous events, the Maeght
Foundation, in which members of
the Maeght family continue to
work, also provides new impetus
and guarantees the nearby village
of St.-Paul-de-Vence a veritable
stream of visitors.

The village, once a fortified hill-
top enclave, later an oasis for artists
and a society rendezvous, has its
own story to tell. Many artists have
lived and worked in St.-Paul-de-
Vence, but celebrities such as Greta
Garbo, Jean-Paul Sartre and Catherine Deneuve have also dropped by.
The fact that tourists today delight
in the scenic views and the artistic
ambience is due to the place's fame.

It's quieter in the little cemetery
outside St.-Paul-de-Vence. Here
lies the grave of Marc Chagall, who
lived in St.-Paul-de Vence from
1950 until his death in 1985.

Classical Greece

Antique sculptures and ceramics in the **NATIONAL ARCHEOLOGICAL MUSEUM, ATHENS**

ADDRESS:
Patission 44 St,
Athens

OPENING TIMES:
Mon 10:30 am to 5 pm
Tues-Sun 8:30 am
to 3 pm

INTERNET:
www.culture.gr.

PUBLIC TRANSPORT:
Bus, Lines 2, 3, 4,
5, 7, 8, 11, 12, 13

OTHER ATTRACTIONS:
Acropolis, Agora

Athenians curse the traffic and the hustle and bustle of their crowded, noisy metropolis, yet no sooner are they a couple of hundred miles away, than they long to be back in the Plaka, the Old Town, in Syntagma Square, or in the temple-dominated Upper Town. The Acropolis was constructed 2,500 years ago and is home to the longing pulsates of all those who, like poet Johann Wolfgang von Goethe "seek the land of the Greeks in their soul."

The passion for Classical Greece spread like an epidemic in the 19th century. Temples, sculptures and cult sites were excavated at every place known in antiquity, such as Olympia, Delphi and Mycenae – as well as in countless other sites that housed Classical Greece's unique culture and art.

Many of the excavated treasures went abroad, primarily to London (British Museum), Paris (Louvre) or Berlin (Pergamon Museum), yet a large proportion of the works of art that emerged into the daylight from official excavations were brought to Athens and stored at various places there. Thus, the establishment of a museum of antiquities became increasingly necessary and, finally, with the help of patrons, the construction of a monumental building was achieved.

Plenty of space for the exhibits
Between 1866 and 1889, a building arose, based on a design by German architect Ludwig Lange. The building was extended in the 1920s and 1930s, and again after the Second World War and it was reorganized to coincide with the Summer Olympic Games held in Athens in 2004. The National Archeological Museum houses the most valuable collection of Classical Greek sculptures and ceramics and is regarded as one of the most important museums in the world.

The external facade alone, built in a strict Neoclassical style, signals that it was to be built on a grand scale. Red walls glow behind mighty columns, as though a red carpet has been unrolled from above. The grandiose style continues inside; the rooms are furnished with valuables and leave plenty of space for the exhibits. Arrangement of the

The bronze figure of Poseidon, god of the sea, was found at Cape Artemision. The sculpture is therefore known as *Poseidon of Artemision*. The work was created around 460 B.C. (above).

The entrance facade of the National Archeological Museum, with both wings, reproduces the structure of a temple enclosure (below left).

exhibits, using extensive separation of the object categories, dates back to the 1950s and 1960s.

The dawn of Greek civilization is documented by clay vases from the Neolithic Age (6800–3300 B.C.), as well as by marble idols and statuettes from the Cyclades (3200–2300 B.C.). The treasure trove from Mycenae, deemed unique in the world, is displayed in the central hall opposite the museum entrance and in a smaller room. In addition to splendid daggers and sacrificial vessels, the treasure includes drinking beakers, diadems and gold masks, of which the so-called Agamemnon Mask is the most fascinating, showing as it does the face of a jaded old man.

The golden treasures date from the 16th century before Christ and the majority of them were recovered by the German businessman, Heinrich Schliemann, from the royal graves at Mycenae. The famous Minoan frescoes from Thera can be seen in the central area of the first floor. They tell of a ship's expedition and show women, children, fishermen, flowers and animals. A volcanic explosion preserved the colors and frescoes, so today it is still possible to get an idea of the original quality of the artworks.

Jockey of Artemision

The monumental tomb amphorae from archaic art, including geometric art, are impressive, as are the black-figured vases whose life-like detail is overwhelming. For most visitors, the main attraction is the collection of sculptures covering the period from the 7th century B.C. to the 4th century A.D. It shows works of art fascinating because of their harmony and powerful expressiveness, including the elegant archaic statues of youths, or *kouros*, of which the *kouros* of Sounion is the most famous, and the Kroisos *kouros*. In Room 14, you will see the marble relief of a young athlete crowning himself, the *Diadoumenos*, a masterpiece of Greek sculpture from the Classical period (around 460 B.C.).

The subsequent rooms exhibit Attic ceremonial reliefs, funerary steles and marble vases from the very end of the 5th century to the end of the 4th century B.C. In Room 21 stands the bronze statue, *Jockey of Artemision* – you can almost feel the passion with which the little jockey urges on the horse. Other famous works of art such as the colossal bronze statue of Poseidon and the marble group with Aphrodite, Pan and Eros, show the perfection of Greek art in its Golden Age.

Also worthy of note are sculptures from the Roman period, including the bust of Antinous, which shows a dreamy young man. The picture is completed by a comprehensive collection of bronzes and vases as well as a collection of Egyptian masterpieces.

The Gold Mask of Agamemnon dates back to Mycenaen times. It was worked in the second half of the 16th century B.C. (above right).

The relief, *Youths Wrestling*, was sculpted around 500 B.C. and impressively illustrates the Greeks' concept of beauty and their worship of the human body (below right).

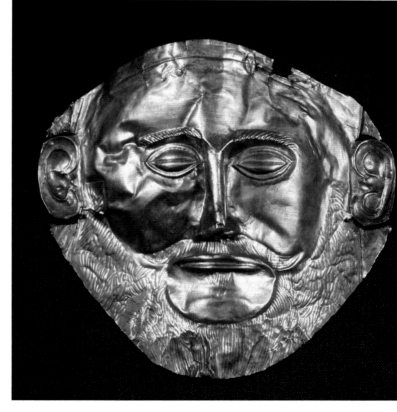

The theater of the Oracle

The finds from the sacred sanctuary at **DELPHI** can be seen in the on-site Museum

ADDRESS:
Delphi

OPENING TIMES:
Daily 8:30 am to 3 pm

INTERNET:
www.culture.gr

TRANSPORT:
Regional bus or hire car

OTHER ATTRACTIONS:
Shrine of Athena Pronaia

The countryside is like a prelude to a symphony as, arriving from the east past Mount Parnassus, visitors climb up through the gigantic mountain range of central Greece to Delphi. Set in a landscape of light and stone, pervaded by the scent of wild thyme, visitors finally reach the historic site regarded in ancient times as the dwelling of the most famous oracle in the world. The prophetess, chewing bay leaves and intoxicated by the scent of myrrh and incense, announced her prophecies, which the priests of Apollo interpreted, in a massive temple. Delphi was the spiritual and religious center of Ancient Greece and a place of pilgrimage, even today.

Countless myths

At the same time, it was also the center of the universe. According to legend, Zeus sent two golden eagles from Mount Olympus to either end of the earth to find the center of the world. They met in Delphi.

Since then, the site has been surrounded by countless myths. Ultimately it was Apollo, the god of light, youth and prophecy, who helped this sacred site achieve its reputation. He came upon this place, so favored by nature, killed a

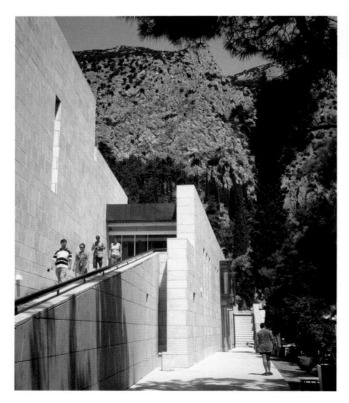

python and thereafter established, in the Oracle of Delphi, the most famous cult of antiquity. A temple was erected in honor of Apollo, in which simple citizens, alongside kings and generals, could ask the Oracle to prophesy for them, but not before they had cleansed themselves in a nearby spring. Delphi was in its heyday during the time between the 7th and 4th centuries B.C.

The offerings placed along the Sacred Way in honor of the gods were of great artistic value. Temple-like treasuries belonging to the great cities along the route up to the Temple of Apollo testified to their might and power.

After Christianity prevailed, Delphi was swallowed by a massive layer of earth and dust. Syste-

matic excavation began only in 1891, as part of a joint venture by France and Greece. The 1,000-house village of Kastri was moved and the ancient sacred site with temples, treasuries, amphitheater, gymnasium and stadium was revealed. It was possible to rescue valuable offerings intact. They were placed in the Museum on the edge of the excavations, opened in 1903, whose clear glass and stone facade blends harmoniously into the landscape. The Museum was built by French architect A. Tournaire, who also created the reconstructions of the holy sanctuary.

In subsequent times, the Museum has repeatedly been extended. The collection originates exclusively from ancient Delphi and gives a superb overview of the

development of art and the cult of this unique place.

In the Charioteer's Room

Entry to the cool, clear world of the purist Museum building present a stark contrast to scrambling over the ancient sites. Fourteen interconnecting rooms display statues and groups of statues, but also parts of the sculptural decorations, objects from daily life and cult objects. The rooms include the Omphalos Room, with an artistically shaped stone symbolizing the center of the world, and the Siphnian Treasury Room, which shows the building's eastern gable and the relief frieze that runs around it. In the Bull Room, a statue of a bull is on display, worked in beaten sheets of silver between 600 and 550 B.C.

The statue is almost life-size and is impressive for its naturalistic appearance, even if only preserved in fragments.

Numerous gold and ivory statues are testament to the donors' wealth and show the considerable skill of craftsmen of the time. In the Apollo Temple Room, a sculpture represents the god, Dionysius (beardless, for once), who was also worshiped at Delphi.

The greatest crowds congregate in the Charioteer's Room, where one of the most famous ancient works of art is to be seen. A young man in relaxed pose holds reins lightly in his hands and looks ahead, his head turned slightly to the left. The bronze statue once formed part of a yoke of four, with horses and chariots, and is a com-

plete work in the "severe" style from the early Classical period, between 475 and 450 B.C.

Delphi's particular attraction lies in the fact that the magic of the place can be felt all around the Museum. Walking down to the round temple in the shrine of Athena Pronaia in the bright midday light – accompanied by the chirping of cicadas and confronted by the unique natural backdrop of the broad slope with the temple buildings, every visitor can understand Lord Byron, who once wrote, "Sighed o'er Delphi's long deserted shrine, Where save that feeble fountain, All is still."

Reins in hand, the cast-bronze *Charioteer of Delphi* casually guides his horses. The statue dates from the period around 470 B.C. (above right).

Detailed view of the *Charioteer's* head (above left).

The finds from the shrine sanctuary are exhibited in a modern museum building. Entrance to the Museum building (below left).

Olympia's messengers

Treasures at the Archeological in **ATHENS**

ADDRESS:
Ancient Olympia,
Olympia

OPENING HOURS:
Mon 10:30 am to 5 pm,
Tues--Sun 8:30 am
to 3 pm

INTERNET:
www.culture.gr

TRANSPORT:
Bus connections from
Patras and Athens

OTHER ATTRACTIONS:
Ancient city of Elis,
Temple of Apollo
at Bassai

**A unique high point of
Greek art: the statue of
Hermes with Dionysos
on his arm, carved in
marble by Praxiteles
around 330 B.C.
(above).**

**The square in front
of the entrance to
the Museum is
decorated with
modern sculptures
(below left).**

It is considered the embodiment of perfection and one of the most famous of antique sculptures: the marble statue of Hermes in the Archeological Museum in Olympia, carved by Praxiteles in 330 B.C., enchants everyone that stands before it. The dreamy gaze and the soft features as well as the youthfully casual composure with which the messenger of the gods presents the beauty of his naked body inspire awe in every visitor. In his arms, he holds the boy, Dionysos, whom he is to deliver to the nymphs to be educated. The statue was found almost undamaged in the ruins of the Temple of Hera in Olympia in 1877, precisely where travel writer Pausanias saw it on his visit to Olympia between 160 and 180 A.D.

In an area of outstanding natural beauty, amidst the fertile plains of the western Peloponnese, lies the village of Olympia, which in ancient times was the most important center of worship in Greece after Delphi and Delos. The first Olympic Games took place here in 776 B.C. They were held without interruption every four years for almost 1,200 years, until the Roman Emperor Theodosius I banned them in 393 A.D. as a legacy of heathen times.

The area sank into oblivion, after being laid waste by the Romans, earthquakes and floods. Finally, a thick layer of soil covered the former shrine and Olympia was not rediscovered until the 18th century. Systematic excavations have been taking place since 1875. The archaeological work brought to

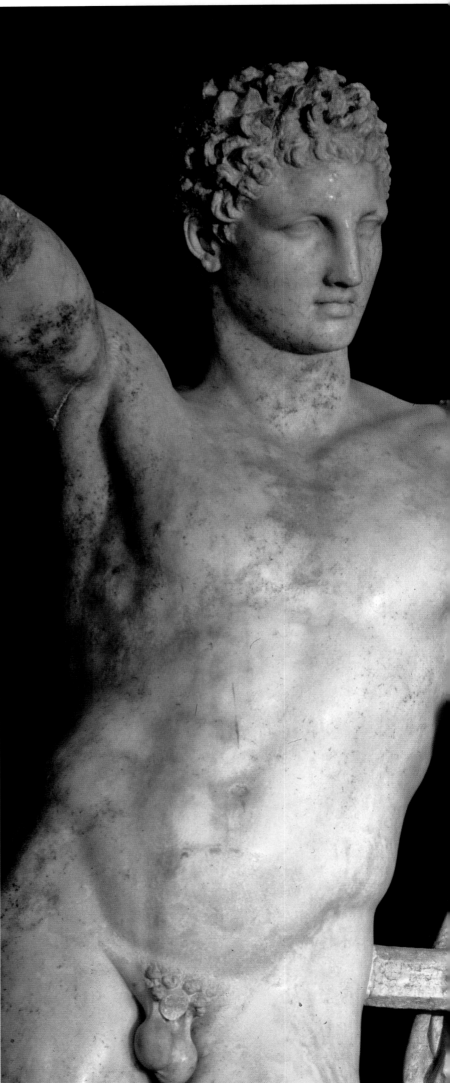

light more than just places of worship and competition. Olympia's high status in the Ancient World is confirmed by the rich treasures – sculptures, reliefs, bronzes and votive offerings – that can now be seen in the Museum.

A museum was built between 1883 and 1885 after the earliest finds were made, but it suffered serious damage in an earthquake in 1954. In 1982, a new building opened next to the archeological sites. Today, it has ten rooms housing the most important collection in the Peloponnese. Countless finds from the area are displayed in chronological order, divided into prehistoric, geometric, archaic, Classical and Roman periods. The ancient Olympic Games are also documented.

Founded by Heracles

The history of Olympia reaches far back, as the area was already settled as early as 2800 B.C. According to ancient legend, Rhea (Earth) and Cronos (Sky) were married here, even before Heracles, son of Zeus, organized the games in honor of his father. A regional festival developed into a grand pan-Hellenic event and envoys and competitors from the Greek motherland and the colonies traveled to the games. No fighting was allowed during the festival. The victors were honored with a wreath made of twigs from wild olive trees.

However, Olympia was more a place of worship than of sport, and a tour of the excavation site shows that the sacred grove with the Temple of Zeus and Hera, treasure houses, the Philippeion and other places of worship lay in the center. The sites of competition lay outside.

The Temple of Zeus, completed in 456, was considered a masterpiece. At 91 x 210 feet, it was one of the biggest and most impressive temples in Greece. Although the statue of Zeus, one of the Seven Wonders of the Ancient World,

sculpted by Phidias, fell victim to fire in Constantinople after being carried off by the Romans, it was possible to preserve the fragments of the sculptures on the pediment. They are now on display in the Museum, in a room that precisely matches the width of the front of the Temple of Zeus. The figures are very dynamic and show the tension that hung like a cloud before the start of a competition. The eastern pediment shows the preparations for the first Olympic chariot race between Pelops and Oenomaus. By contrast, the western pediment describes the battles between the Thessalonian tribe of the Lapiths and the drunken Centaurs.

Many of the exhibits are of high artistic merit, such as the statue of Nike, goddess of victory, by Paeonios (421 B.C.), the huge head of the goddess Hera (600 B.C.) and the clay head of Athena, made around 490 B.C. There is a terracotta statuette of Zeus and Ganymede dating from between 480 and 470 B.C. The god is running nimbly away with the boy, Ganymede, in his arms and a mischievous smile on his face. Two other exhibits remind us of the great deeds of the Greek golden age: the signed helmet that Miltiades wore in the battle against the Persians (490 B.C.) is kept in the Museum, as is the drinking vessel that sculptor Phidias used in his workshop in Olympia.

But it was not only ancient Olympia that awoke to a new life – the idea of the Olympics was also revived. The first modern Olympic Games took place in Athens in 1896 and 108 years later, competitors once again met in Olympia. On the occasion of the Olympic Games in Athens in 2004, the shot putt competition took place in the ancient stadium in Olympia – a memorable event. After 1,611 years, the head of an Olympic champion was once again crowned with a wreath of olive twigs on this historic site.

Olympic Games in Olympia: the small bronze (below right) from around 480 B.C. shows a runner at the starting line. He ran the competition course in the ancient stadium of Olympia, which has been preserved to this day. Our photo shows the 2,500-year-old starting line in the foreground (below right).

Scotland's National Gallery

Works by the great Scottish painters are gathered on Princes Street in EDINBURGH

ADDRESS:
The Mound, Edinburgh

OPENING TIMES:
Mon.–Sun. 10 am
to 5 pm,
Thurs. to 7 pm

INTERNET:
www.nationalgalleries.
org.

PUBLIC TRANSPORT:
Bus to Princes Street

OTHER ATTRACTIONS:
National Portrait
Gallery, Royal Museum
of Scotland, Royal
Scottish Academy

The man skates on a frozen lake. He's just pushed off with his right leg. He wears tight, dark trousers and a dark, knee-length coat. A tall hat sits atop his head and a lock of hair hangs down the back of his neck. He is in profile and seems to be about forty years old.

The man is Robert Walker and he was a clergyman by profession. The lake where he skates is Duddingston Loch in Scotland. Walker's image seems to be omnipresent in Scotland's capital, Edinburgh, as one of the images used by its tourist industry. The original painting hangs in the National Gallery of Scotland.

It was painted by Henry Raeburn, one of Scotland's first artists to achieve fame beyond his home country's borders. Born near Edinburgh in 1756, he was largely self-taught and specialized in portrait painting. His first painting, from 1776, still shows minor anatomical flaws, but he did not make such mistakes again and by the time his first exhibition in London had rolled around in 1793, he was very accomplished. He died in 1823. His paintings hang in numerous British museums.

George III's court artist

Another famous Scottish painter is Allan Ramsey. He lived earlier than Raeburn, between 1713 and 1784, and, in contrast to the latter, he underwent proper artistic training. Son of an Edinburgh man of letters schooled in London, he traveled to Italy, an almost obligatory trip for artists of the time and also visited France. Finally, he resided in London, where he was court artist to King George III. His style is Rococo and he is famous for his portraits of women, such as that of Margaret Lindsay, his second wife, painted in 1755, which also hangs in the National Gallery of Scotland. The Gallery stands on Edinburgh's Princes Street, on the border between the two historic quarters, the medieval Old Town and the Georgian New Town. The building was designed by William Henry Playfair, a renowned Classical architect, who lived from 1790 to 1857, and constructed other buildings in Edinburgh. He designed the Royal Scottish Academy building, later placing the National Gallery directly next to it.

The foundation stone was laid in 1850 by Prince Albert, Queen Victoria's Prince Consort, who was interested in both art and new buildings. It opened in 1859. Initially, the collection received only works previously owned by the Royal Academy. It was not until 1903 that it was able to undertake new acquisitions. Today, it is one of the most famous museums of art in the country.

A long tradition of national pride was behind the Gallery's creation. Ramsey still had to go to London to make a name for himself, but Raeburn succeeded in Edinburgh. The years between the two artists marked a historic change. In the mid-18th century Scotland's armed resistance to the English finally collapsed and at the same time, a series of important Scottish artistic figures emerged. National feeling and a desire for political autonomy was expressed through art and the English King made some efforts to satisfy the Scottish desire for prestige and recognition.

Pillared procession

The National Gallery of Scotland may collect important Scottish artists, but it places equal emphasis on the great Europeans, to place its own artists in an appropriate setting and to affim Edinburgh's Place among the great, metropolitain cities of the world. The Gallery owns Titians, Tintorettos, Holbeins, Rembrandts, Poussins and Chardins. The great British artists, such as Reynolds, Gainsborough and Turner, take their rightful places as well.

The Gallery itself is a beautiful, Classical structure of moderate size with a pillared facade. The first floor is a collection of paintings and sculptures from the 15th to 18th centuries. Works from the next century are on the second floor. The collection reaches Post-Impressionism, including exquisite South Sea paintings by Paul Gauguin.

In 1960, the modern collection was moved and exhibited as the Scottish National Gallery of Modern Art and is housed in a building erected in 1820, in Belford Road in the heart of Edinburgh's New Town. The landscaped garden contains sculptures by Barbara Hepworth and Henry Moore; the rooms contain paintings by French Cubists, German Expressionists and Russian Suprematists. British Art is also represented by Duane Hanson's resin figures and by the modern artists known as the Scottish Colorists.

*The **Reverend Robert Walker skating on Duddingston Loch** is the title Sir Henry Raeburn gave his legendary 1784 painting, familiar to every Scot today (left). The skater immediately became a national hero.*

*Philips de Koninck's 1666 landscape painting of is entitled, **An Extensive Landscape** (below center).*

Aerial view of the National Gallery (below right).

The home of British art

The **NATIONAL GALLERY** in **LONDON'S TRAFALGAR SQUARE** is one of the largest art galleries in the world

North Sea

GREAT BRITAIN

London

English Channel
ATLANTIC OCEAN

ADDRESS:
Trafalgar Square,
London

OPENING TIMES:
Mon.- Sun. 10 am
to 6 pm
Wed. until 9 pm

INTERNET:
www.nationalgallery.
org.uk

PUBLIC TRANSPORT:
Underground, Charing
Cross or Leicester
Square station

OTHER ATTRACTIONS:
Royal Academy of Arts,
National Portrait
Gallery

**The impressive
National Gallery
building, topped by a
large dome and fronted
by a row of Classical
pillars, dominates
Trafalgar Square
(below left).**

John Julius Angerstein was born in St. Petersburg in 1735. He was only 15 years old when he moved to England and found a job with Lloyds, the insurance underwriters. It did not take him long to make his fortune, partly through his connections with the coffee trade. He struck up a friendship with William Pitt the Younger, the long-serving conservative Prime Minister, eventually becoming his banker. At the same time, he discovered a growing interest in fine arts and began building up his own private collection of paintings by Italian, Flemish and German masters. By the time he died in 1823, he had amassed a total of 38 paintings. His art collection was then offered for sale to the government. In April 1824, the House of Commons approved its purchase for the sum of £57,000 and the paintings changed hands.

What was lacking, however, was a suitable building to display them. The paintings consequently remained in Angerstein's own London house, an exclusive residence on Pall Mall. Around the same time, George Beaumont, a renowned and extremely affluent British landscape artist, also offered to donate his own art collection to the state – on condition that it was properly housed and displayed. Beaumont's collection was handed over in 1826 and his paintings were likewise hung in the Pall Mall building.

Contemptuous comparisons

England was henceforth the proud possessor of its own national gallery. The collection of paintings was admittedly rather modest and housed in fairly makeshift conditions, a state of affairs that provoked a great deal of scornful criticism among the ranks of the London press, which derisively compared it to the Louvre, the main art gallery of England's old nemesis, France. Such public derision bore fruit. In 1831, Parliament voted in favor of constructing a centrally situated building in London's Trafalgar Square. The location was ideal: there was plenty of space for well-heeled visitors to drive up in their coaches, but the building was, at the same time, easily accessible by foot to less affluent visitors from the East End. The National Gallery was intended to

be a classless institution, belonging to the nation as a whole.

Trafalgar Square has remained home to the National Gallery. The building itself is an impressive example of Classical architecture, featuring a dome and an imposing portico. Its pillars came originally from Carlton House, which was demolished in 1826. They were rescued by architect William Wilkins and incorporated in the new building.

Expansion in 1876

After its completion, the National Gallery initially shared the building with the Royal Academy, which later moved into a building of its own in 1868. The number of exhibits in the National Gallery had meanwhile increased to such an extent, as a result of donations and various acquisitions, that Wilkins's construction proved too small. Once again, there followed a heated public debate in the newspapers. Edward Middleton Barry, the much admired architect of the Royal Opera House at Covent Garden, was approached to design a new building, yet the debate dragged on. Eventually, it was decided to retain, renovate and extend Wilkins's existing building. By 1876, seven new exhibition rooms had been inaugurated. The next enlargement scheme was carried out in 1907 and the last major rebuilding project,

the Sainsbury Wing, completed in 1991, now houses an exhibition of 13th to 15th century Italian paintings. Three male members of the wealthy Sainsbury family financed the project.

Masterpieces of art

The art gallery closed its doors at the start of the Second World War. Its treasures were removed to bombproof mine shafts for safety and the empty rooms became a venue for lunchtime music concerts, aimed at bolstering public spirits. The wisdom of removing the paintings to a safe location was demonstrated in earnest in the autumn of 1940, when several German bombs fell on the building.

London's National Gallery now counts as one of the world's largest art museums. It contains works by Raffael, Titian, Holbein the Younger,

Rubens and El Greco, and by great British artists such as Reynolds, Constable and Gainsborough. Its most important works include a self-portrait by Rembrandt, painted at the age of 34, and the ubiquitously copied *Sunflowers* by Van Gogh. Leonardo's sketch of Mary and the baby Jesus was damaged when a mentally ill visitor fired a gun at the picture, resulting in a nearly 1 inch bullet hole which necessitated an extensive restoration program. The sketch has only recently been returned to its former place.

The National Gallery frequently hosts special exhibitions, attracting much international acclaim, and organizes numerous educational events. Each month, a "painting of the month" is selected for special attention and discussed in detail.

The National Gallery's famous paintings include Thomas Gainsborough's *Mr. and Mrs. Andrews*, 1750 (above left). This work is typical of English society painting at that time. Piero della Francesca's *Birth of Christ*, 1470, is regarded as a major example of Renaissance painting (above right), while John Constable's *Salisbury Cathedral from the River*, 1820, is typical of the English Romantic period.

Colonial treasures

The **BRITISH MUSEUM** in **LONDON** boasts a wealth of art treasures from Ancient Egypt and European antiquity

North Sea

GREAT BRITAIN

London○

English Channel

ATLANTIC OCEAN

ADDRESS:
Great Russell Street,
London

OPENING TIMES:
Sat.-Wed. 10 am
to 5:30 pm
Thurs. and Fri. 10 am
to 8:30 pm

INTERNET:
www.thebritish-
museum.ac.uk

PUBLIC TRANSPORT:
Underground,
Tottenham Court Road
station; or bus

OTHER ATTRACTIONS:
Courtauld Institute
Galleries, Sir John
Soane's Museum

View of the glass-covered inner courtyard of the tradition-steeped British Museum (below left).

In 196 B.C., a priest in the Ancient Egyptian city of Memphis drew up a decree on behalf of the reigning King, Ptolomy V – one of the rulers who governed the land of the Nile in the wake of Alexander the Great. Ptolomy I was a close associate of the Macedonian conqueror and founded the following dynasty.

The Ptolomaic dynasty brought Greek–Hellenic influences which later became intermingled with Roman ones. One aspect of this culture was similar to that of the pharaohs: their kings, like the pharaohs before them, were venerated as deities. They were also obliged to take the multicultural structure of the country into account, which is why the priest in Memphis inscribed the text in two languages, Egyptian and Greek. The Egyptian text was produced in two types of script, the old-style hieroglyphics and the more modern demotic script. All this, as well as the Greek version, was inscribed on a single slab of basalt stone.

For 2,000 years this decree, carved in stone for King Ptolomy, lay buried under Egyptian soil. It remained undiscovered until 1799, when it was uncovered near Rosetta, a town situated on the Nile delta, near the Mediterranean coast. It was brought to Paris as a souvenir from Napoleon's Egyptian campaign and some years later – in 1821 – it came to the notice of a French scholar, Jean François Champollion.

Deciphering the hieroglyphics

Champollion taught history at the Royal College of Grenoble. He specialized in ancient languages and he realized that the Greek text might be used in conjunction with the hieroglyphics as the key to translating what had hitherto proved undecipherable characters. In 1822, he succeeded in unlocking the code. It has since been possible to read the vast number of scripts found among the temple remains between Abu Simbel and Cairo, all thanks to the Rosetta Stone.

The stone is now housed in the British Museum, an exhibit as unassuming as it is priceless, insured up to the hilt, yet displayed in such a way that it is unmistakeable. It also marks the entrance to the Ancient Egyptian section of the Museum, with its remarkable wealth of exhibits – ranging from human and animal mummies and sarcophagi to stone and clay statues. The Egyptian collection comprises just one part of the Museum. The Greek and Roman sections are equally outstanding and include artifacts from European prehistory, the

Middle Ages and the Renaissance period. There is also a collection of graphics as well as some parts of the British National Library.

The British Museum is still one of the world's largest libraries. Until 1973, the Museum and the National Library formed an integral unit. Thereafter, the British Library became an independent institution in its own right, with the exception of the reference library and the Old Reading Room, which have been retained as part of the British Museum. These resonate with nostalgic associations. Plaques near the entrance record the names of some of the famous readers who frequented these rooms, including a certain German immigrant by the name of Karl Marx, a regular visitor between 1857 and 1883, who spent his time reading and making notes. His efforts eventually resulted in his comprehensive treatise on political economy, *Das Kapital*.

Sculptures by Phidias

The Reading Room is self-contained and built in a round shape. It was integrated into the rest of the building as part of a major conversion project carried out over several years. The result is an intricate glass roof, designed by architect Norman Foster, covering the entire inner courtyard. The inner courtyard was thus turned into a weatherproof piazza complete with cafeteria, bookshop and souvenir shop. One of the Museum's biggest tourist draws, other than the Rosetta Stone and the Egyptian artifacts, is the Elgin Marbles. Thomas Bruce, Earl of Elgin and British diplomat, brought a large number of Greek art works back to London with him between 1803 and 1809. These included sections of the Parthenon in Athens, among which were some works by the sculptor, Phidias. They were handed over about ten years later to the British Museum, where they now occupy two rooms.

The Museum itself was more than 50 years old by then. It was founded in 1753 as a result of the amalgamation of three private collections. The British royal family donated books, coins and medals. The oldest of the surviving buildings was constructed in the Classical style between 1823 and 1852 by architect Robert Smirke; the Reading Room was built between 1855 and 1857. The British Museum attracts around 5.7 million visitors each year.

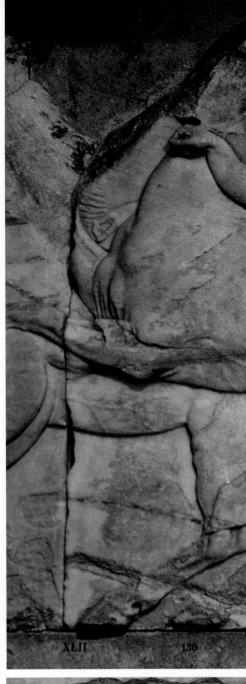

131   132   North Frieze XLII, 130 - 134. The north frieze begins with a preparation scene reminiscent of those on the west. A boy helps a rider to adjust the length of his tunic, while another horseman waits in readiness. As he restrains his horse, he   133   134   The North Frieze ran along one of the long sides of the building. The cavalcade that had begun on the west side continued here for twenty-one of a total of forty-seven slabs. Chariots preceded the horsemen and ahead of them came different

One of the British Museum's main showpieces is the marble frieze from the Parthenon, one of the temples on the Acropolis in Athens. It depicts a scene from the Pan-Athenian procession (above) and was created around 440 B.C. by Phidias, arguably the most famous Greek sculptor.

This Egyptian wall painting dating from around 1350 B.C. depicts an official, Nebamun, hunting (below center).

The basalt Rosetta Stone (below right) is inscribed in hieroglyphics, demotic and Greek script, with a decree promulgated by King Ptolemy. The Greek text helped to decipher the hieroglyphics.

Masters of landscape

The **TATE BRITAIN GALLERY** houses the largest collection of British art, right up to the threshold of modernism

ADDRESS:
Millbank,
London

OPENING HOURS:
Daily 10 am to 5:50 pm

INTERNET:
www.tate.org.uk/britain

PUBLIC TRANSPORT:
Underground,
Westminster, Pimlico or
Vauxhall station

OTHER ATTRACTIONS:
Victoria and Albert
Museum

The Tate Britain Gallery was ceremonially opened in 1897. The photo (bottom left) shows the columns, typical of the period, adorning the main entrance.

As far as visual arts are concerned, the 19th century was the century of landscape painting. Initially dismissed as a discipline of secondary importance, it rose to become the most popular of all visual arts for two reasons. The increasingly rich and powerful middle classes discovered an interest in aestheticism. They lived in an environment, however, characterized by burgeoning and multiplying towns, in which nature, and particularly landscape, had lost its significance. It was for this reason that paintings portraying nature began to find their way into people's households all over Europe. However, Great Britain, as one of the first countries to witness the growing influence of the middle classes, led the way. The tradition of landscape painting consequently has a longer history in Britain, beginning with 18th and early 19th century artists such as Thomas Gainsborough and John Constable. Both are regarded as the first painters to produce landscapes no longer based on fantasy and memory, but reflecting an actual scene painted in an open-air location.

A true genius of landscape portrayal was Joseph Mallord William Turner. Born in London in 1775, he was widely traveled and painted in both Italy and Germany. His overriding theme was nature, although the figurative increasingly gave way to atmosphere, mood and light during the course of his life. Many of his later works appear virtually non-representational and anticipate the advent of abstract art.

His work was not widely appreciated by the British public at first, but thanks to the timely intervention of John Ruskin, an influential critic, Turner was greatly admired by the time he died. A large part of his considerable works is now owned by the Tate Britain Gallery, one of London's 250 most important museums.

In contrast to the National Gallery, the Tate Britain Gallery is devoted solely to British artists – Blake and Hogarth, for example – as well as to some of the great open-air painters of the 19th century. Its founder, Henry Tate, after whom the Gallery is named, the Lancashire-born son of a preacher and merchant, amassed a vast fortune as a sugar manufacturer. Following the example of Angerstein the banker, whose art collection formed the basis of the National Gallery, in 1892, Tate placed his substantial art collection at the disposal of a new museum which opened in 1897.

The Tate Britain stands on Millbank on northern bank of the River Thames. There was previously a large prison on this spot. The architect, Sidney R.J. Smith, initially built a rotunda along with seven rooms. In 1899, a further nine rooms were added, likewise financed by the sugar magnate, Tate. Like the National Gallery in Trafalgar Square, it was expanded and extended to mark the hundredth anniversary of the building and, most recently, the beginning of the new millennium between 2000 and 2001. A whole new complex was created with a new entrance. In 1987, the extended Clore Gallery, designed by one of England's most eminent postmodernist architects, James Stirling, opened its doors and provided a home to the many Turners which hang here.

Center of the Pre-Raphaelites

During the 19th century, landscape painting was one of Great Britain's greatest artistic strengths. Another was the Pre-Raphaelite movement. The Pre-Raphaelite Brotherhood was founded in London in 1848, comprising artists and literary figures. It represented a reaction against oppressive historical paintings and embraced the influence of early Italian Renaissance art instead, thus becoming a successor to the Nazarenes, a group founded in 1809 in Vienna and rooted in Romanticism. The most significant exponent of the Pre-Raphaelite movement was Dante Gabriel Rosetti, a poet and son of a writer, who immigrated to Britain from Italy.

He created a series of mystical and religious paintings and later turned his attention to illustrating ancient poems such as Dante's *Divine Comedy* and the myths surrounding the legend of King Arthur. He and his contemporaries, John Everett Millais, William Holman Hunt and Edward Coley Burne-Jones, developed a mystical, decadent style, which evoked both religious as well as faintly erotic overtones. Rosetti also created arts

and crafts and the Pre-Raphaelites were the forerunners and instigators of the Jugendstil movement, which grew to prominence in Great Britain thanks to exponents such as Mackintosh and Beardsley.

All are represented in the Tate Britain Gallery, next to artists from the Bloomsbury Circle, including avant-

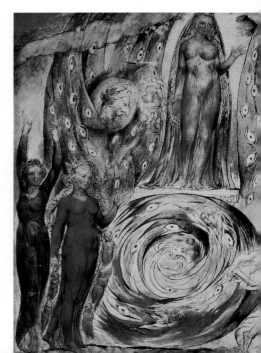

gardists such as Vanessa Bell, painter and sister of the writer Virginia Woolf. The significance of her artistic work has achieved full recognition only in recent years.

During the past two decades, the Tate Gallery has been divided into various sections. Its collection of international modern art has been transferred to the Tate Modern across the river. The Tate Liverpool was founded as well as the Tate St. Ives in Cornwall, where an influential and flourishing artists' colony exists, revolving around artists Ben Nicholson and Barbara Hepworth.

The Tate Gallery on Millbank organizes the Turner Prize, an extremely prestigious annual art award recognized not only in Britain, but throughout the whole world.

Highlights of English painting:
William Turner's *Morning – Going to the Ball in Venice* **(above), painted in 1845, is an almost abstract work, William Blake's 1824 depiction of purgatory is based on Dante's** *Divine Comedy* **(below center) and John Everett Millais painted** *The Death of Ophelia* **in 1851-2 (below right).**

Art on the Thames

The **TATE MODERN GALLERY** in **LONDON** boasts the largest collection of contemporary British art

ADDRESS:
Bankside,
London

OPENING HOURS:
Sun.-Thurs. 10 am
to 6 pm
Fri., Sat. until 10 pm

INTERNET:
www.tate.org.uk

PUBLIC TRANSPORT:
Underground or bus to
Southwark or
Blackfriars, Tate boat on
the Thames

OTHER ATTRACTIONS:
South Bank Cultural
Centre, Saatchi Gallery

The South Bank of the Thames was dismissed for many years as one of London's least attractive and significant areas. The industries that once thrived in this area had been abandoned, the buildings left to fall into disrepair. All changed at the end of the 20th century following the reconstruction of Shakespeare's Globe Theatre, which has since become an extremely successful venue for the staging of Elizabethan dramas. It has become London's main center of modern art: the Charles Saatchi Gallery produces exhibitions of British art, including Damien Hirst's sliced-up cows and pigs while the Tate Modern presents an exquisite collection of avant-garde work. The Tate Modern Gallery opened its doors on 11 May 2000 after a decision was made to transfer a collection of international contemporary art, on which the Tate Gallery in Millbank was based since 1917. The two Tate galleries founded in Liverpool (1988) and St. Ives (1993) were already devoted exclusively to modern art. It was decided to base the London collection in a disused power station on Bankside. A competition to find the best design attracted 148 entries; the

winners were two Swiss architects: Jacques Herzog and Pierre de Meuron. Once the plans for the renovation and rebuilding work were decided upon, the critics had a veritable field day disparaging the design.

No attempt has ever been made to gloss over the building's origins. The architects were, on the contrary, anxious to respect the aesthetic charm of old industrial buildings, Herzog and De Meuron retained the interior with its turbine hall, revamping its rundown appearance and creating what is now an impressive environment for modern art.

The environment

The exhibits include collections of preserved photographs and film. The actual exhibition rooms extend over three of the total of seven floors. The permanent displays are supplemented by a series of constantly changing exhibitions. The former are organized according to a revolutionary principle different from that adopted by all other major art galleries. The exhibits are arranged neither chronologically, nor even by the different schools of art or country of origin. The traditional separation of con-

temporary art works into paintings, graphics, sculpture and design has been largely abandoned. The setting is just as important here as ordinary objects or their arrangement, a factor which lends additional charm to the thematic grouping of the exhibits.

The curators decided to opt for four main blocks or suites, arranged thematically. Each of these is divided, in turn, into three linked sub themes. One is entitled "Still Life / Object / Real Life," another "History/Memory/Society." The "Nude/Action/Body" suite is the closest you can get to the traditional concept of visual art, although even here it is clear just how much the notion of art and the techniques of artistic production and appreciation have broadened over the past hundred years. Finally, the theme of the fourth section is "Landscape/Matter/Entertainment," where you will find a nude painting by German painter Christian Schad, executed with cool attention to detail and daring objectivity, alongside an installation by Louise Bourgeois, representing a cynical commentary on sex.

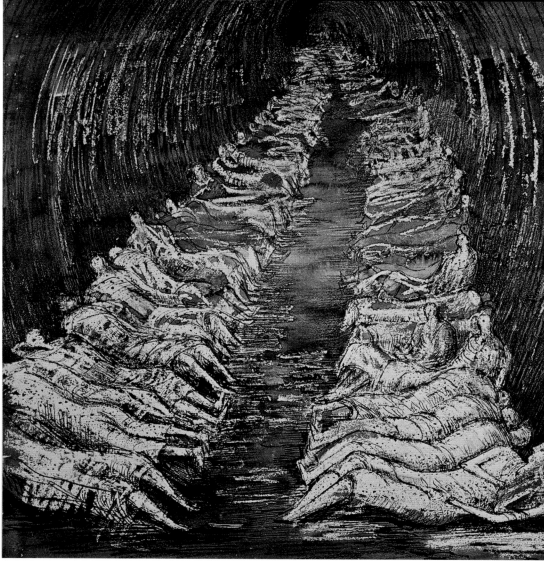

A multitude of contemporary modern artists

Nudes by Henri Matisse and Pablo Picasso, featuring the formal distorted representations characteristic of these artists, are on display alongside a bronze statue by Alberto Giacometti – the tall, elongated vertical lines of which echo all the attributes of the naked female figure. Austrian artist Arnulf Rainer prefers to disguise them with his technique of overpainting. Only Lucien Freud, the grandson of the founder of psychoanalysis, endows his large female nude with an almost Rubenesque voluptuousness.

All the classic painters of modern art are represented by at least one outstanding example of their work: Jackson Pollock with a wide-format sample of his action painting, Andy Warhol with his silkscreen images of Marilyn Monroe, Marcel Duchamp with his ironically named Fountain urinal. There is also a fabric object by Claes Oldenburg, an example of George Braque's Cubist abstractionism – involving a coat pocket, a musical instrument and a bottle of rum – and Salvador Dali's black telephone with its red lobster earpiece.

Particular attention is given to prominent British artists, such as sculptor Barbara Hepworth and Ri-

chard Long, a proponent of Earth or Land art. Damien Hirst is likewise represented, not by the corpse of an animal, but with an installation of a pharmacy. Alongside all this is a running video showing a plate full of fruit, gradually losing its colors. It shrinks, disintegrates and rots to the point that it is full of worms and flies – a potent and prvocative symbol of the transience of life. At the same time, it illustrates the ephemeral nature of beauty.

The Tate Modern boasts many classic works by the younger generation of modern artists: Andy Warhol's 1962 diptychon, *Marilyn* (top left), Richard Hamilton's silkscreen painting, *Swinging London*, 1970, (above center) and Henry Moore's wartime picture, *Tube*, dated 1941, depicting Londoners sheltering in the subway stations from German bombing raids (above right)

The photo (bottom right) shows the main hall of the former industrial building, now converted into the museum space.

73

Ireland's first art house

The NATIONAL GALLERY in DUBLIN documents the art of the Emerald Isle

ADDRESS:
Merrion Square West,
Dublin

OPENING TIMES:
Mon.-Sat 9:30 am
to 5:30 pm,
Thurs to 8:30 pm,
Sun 12 noon to 5:30 pm

INTERNET:
www.nationalgallery.ie

PUBLIC TRANSPORT:
Bus, Lines 5, 7, 7A, 10,
13A, 44C, 48A

OTHER ATTRACTIONS:
National Library
and National Museum,
Municipal Gallery
of Modern Art

Sackville Street in Dublin, now O'Connell Street, is regarded as one of the city's most splendid streets. Irish uprisings against the British often began here. This painting by Michael Angelo Hayes shows Sackville Street in the mid-19th century (below left).

The Yeats family was full of high achievers. The best-known was William Butler Yeats, the poet, awarded the Nobel Prize for Literature in 1923. His father, John Butler, was a highly regarded painter, as was William, who studied art before being lured away by literature. His brother, Jack, six years younger, became an important artist.

Jack Yeats was born in 1871 and spent his childhood in Sligo, on the west coast of Ireland, whose topography he loved and to which he returned time and again in his paintings. His early works were illustrations to accompany texts by John Millington Synge, who founded the Abbey Theater, Ireland's national theater, jointly with his brother, William. Together with Synge, Jack traveled through the west coast county of Connemara. Initially his style is that of a Realist, as became customary throughout Europe in the wake of Impressionism.

Celtic Renaissance

Like William, Jack Yeats was among the followers of the Celtic Renaissance, a movement at the end of the 19th century which embraced Irish spiritual life as part of the battle for Irish political independence through a return to Ireland's history and mythology. Jack B. Yeats's brushstrokes became ever more edgy and expressive until they bordered on the Abstract; the viewer is reminded of Kokoschka or Nolde. Increasingly, the move-

ment paid homage to scenery in the west of Ireland, with its fishermen, rocks and waves, meadows and horses. After residing in London for many years, Jack finally returned to Sligo, where he died in 1957.

Dublin granted his paintings a place of honor in the National Gallery. Its museum building stands on lovely Merrion Square, the quarter of Dublin, the Irish capital where the beautiful Georgian houses can be found; the family of John Butler Yeats once lived here as well.

The National Gallery of Ireland has existed since 1864. The initiative for its creation came ten years earlier, backed by all kinds of influential people, including Irish railway king William Dargan and later supporters included dramatist George Bernard Shaw, also a recipient of the Nobel Prize for Literature.

One of the building's four wings has since been named for William Dargan. It contains the paintings of Jack B. Yeats and the family's other celebrities. The father, John, painted portraits of his two famous sons that now hang here. William's portrait shows a narrow-headed young man. A lock of dark hair hangs low on his pale brow; he has a penetrating gaze and his lips are pursed somewhat mockingly. The painting is impressive. John Butler Yeats, so little known, was an accomplished painter.

There are big collections of international art. The Italian Old Masters are comprehensively represented, with Titian, Mantegna, Fra Angelico and Caravaggio; there is a lovely Dutch Baroque collection, including Ruisdael and Hobbema; there are the Spaniards, including El Greco, Velázquez, Murillo and Picasso as well as four nice Goyas. As for the British, Hogarth, Reynolds and Gainsborough are represented. It is possible to see sculptures and all kinds of works of

Romantisizing poverty

Acquiring, conserving and exhibiting Irish art is the greatest priority of the Gallery. The works shown date back to the dawn of Irish art in the 17th century. However, in the 19th century, national sentiment took a political turn and the harsh social conflicts also excited the artists' sympathy. Initially, as elsewhere in Europe, a certain tendency to romanticize poverty displayed itself, as in Joseph Patrick Haverty's *Blind Piper*, for example, and *The Houseless Wanderer* by John Henry Foley. *An Ejected Family* by Erskine Nichol is testimony to the brutal practice of the expropriation of peasants' land under English sovereignty.

Jean-François Millet first emphatically took up the theme of life on the land on behalf of European

art. The graphic collection spans folios from the 15th to the mid-20th century.

painting in the 19th century. Millet lived in Barbizon. Together with Théodore Rousseau, he established the first colony of artists who became significant, above all, for landscape painting. In addition to countless French artists, it also attracted foreign painters. The Irishman Nathaniel Hone Jr. (1831–1917) also lived in Barbizon for a time. He studied in Paris and spent almost two decades in France before returning to his homeland of Ireland, where he lived in Malahide, on the coast northeast of Dublin. He married the wealthy daughter of a whiskey distiller, a stroke of luck which allowed him to freely pursue his art. The National Gallery possesses his entire estate and, in the opinion of many art historians, he is one of Ireland's most important painters. His paintings show melancholy Irish landscapes, dairy meadows and stormy seas.

The latest structural expansion of the Gallery occurred in honor of the Millennium and accordingly bears the name the Millennium Wing. The museum contains study areas and offers all kinds of multimedia information. Visitor numbers are considerable, not just because of the quality of the collection, but also because of Fitzer's. Fitzer's has more to do with the culinary arts than the fine arts; this restaurant is considered one of the best in the city.

This painting by Philip Reinagle, *Mrs. Congreve and her daughters*, shows a Georgian English family idyll. It was painted around 1800, when 10,000 Irish men, women and children starved to death under British rule. The painting (above) exhibited in the National Gallery, in Dublin (photo below), is a far cry from such hardship.

The Bolognese school

The **NATIONAL PICTURE GALLERY** in **BOLOGNA**, Italy, began with the Accademia degli Incamminati

ADDRESS:
Via Belle Arti 56,
Bologna

OPENING TIMES:
Tues-Sun 9 am to 7 pm

INTERNET:
www.pinacoteca-bologna.it

PUBLIC TRANSPORT:
Bus, Lines 36, 37

OTHER ATTRACTIONS:
Morandi Museum,
Museum of Archeology

Ludovico Carracci was one of the founders of the Accademia. His painting, *Virgin with Child*, completed in 1588, is displayed in the collection (right).

Raphael's *Saint Cecilia* depicts the patroness of religious music. She is represented with organ pipes in her hand in this work, painted in 1514 (below right).

Guido Reni's view of Bologna from 1616 shows the patrician towers erected by wealthy families to demonstrate their power (below center).

The Museum building (below left) is located on the University campus and was opened to the public in 1875 (below left).

For many years, the most important school of painting in Italy was located in the northern city of Bologna. It was founded in 1582 by the artist brothers, Agostino and Annibale Carracci, and their cousin Ludovico. Initially, it was nothing more than a big studio, although it was known, rather ambitiously, as the Accademia degli Incamminati, 'the Academy for those who are on the right path,' an artistic direction rigidly defined as Classicism, based on the classicism of the Italian High Renaissance and classical antiquity.

Systematic lessons were taught. Figures were painted from life, nude, for the sake of anatomical accuracy; the Accademia degli Incamminati was instrumental in the development of nude painting. Contrary to Caravaggio, whose bloody, sensual verismo style of painting was inordinately popular at the time, the school promoted the moderate art of Titian, Michelangelo and Raphael.

A series of painters who later became extremely famous graduated from the school, including Domenichino, Guercino, Francesco Albani and Guido Reni. The young Cardinal Odoardo Farnese, a scion of the aristocratic clan that had also produced a pope, summoned the Carracci brothers and all their pupils to Rome in 1595 so that they could decorate his palace there, an enormous undertaking.

Center of art close to Florence

After Reni left Bologna to work in Rome, Carlo Cignani and Marcantonio Franceschini continued the Accademia's tradition. Both were extremely influential painters and draughtsmen who were supported by the writer, Carlo Cesare Malvasia. Together, they turned Bologna into an artistic center on par with Florence.

Today, works from this school of painters make up a significant portion of the collection in the city's National Picture Gallery, the Pinacoteca Nazionale di Bologna. Its existence can be ascribed directly to the Accademia. For many years, the city made efforts to provide itself with a picture gallery and gradually this came about. Above all, Bologna is important as a place of academic education, possessing the oldest university in the world. However, it must share the claim with the Sorbonne in Paris.

At any rate, the original institution, founded as a school of law, has been in existence since at least the late 12th century. It lent an important secular aspect to the city which, until it joined the kingdom of Italy in 1860, belonged to the Papal States since 1278 with only brief interruptions. The National Picture Gallery, in turn, is so closely linked to the University that it is located on the University campus.

The Museum does not content itself with presenting works by the Bolognese School of painters alone. It also possesses art by the great Renaissance artists on whom the Carracci brothers, who were not the first important Bolognese painters, modeled their works. This status should rather be accorded to Vitale d'Aimo de' Cavalli, known as Vitale da Bologna, a painter born around 1390 whose work is in the tradition of Giotto. He worked in Udine and Pomposa, as well as in Bologna, and his paintings are characterized by strong color and powerful movement. Some art historians believe that the Bolognese School really started with him. Amongst other items, the National Picture Gallery owns four altarpieces by Vitale da Bologna which recount the story of Saint Anthony. They hang near works by Giotto, Vitale's predecessor and

inspiration. The exhibited works date from the 14th to 18th centuries and are organized in three sections – the Late Middle Ages, the Renaissance, including the Mannerists, and the Baroque.

Patroness of church music

Raphael's portrait of Saint Cecilia is generally regarded as the highlight of the second section. The considerable popularity of this early 3rd century Roman martyr during the Reformation and Renaissance can be explained by her elevation to patroness of church music at the very time when great innovations were taking place in religious music, led by the outstanding composer, Giovanni Pierluigi da Palestrina.

Raphael's painting originally hung in a church dedicated to Saint John. Cecilia is shown surrounded by Saints John, Paul, Augustine and Mary Magdalene. She herself is holding something in her arms that on closer inspection proves to be organ pipes – legend has it that she invented this instrument. She gazes upward at cherubim on a cloud, delighting in pious music. The earthly figures display the harmony of expression and stance typical of the artist, and the light is gentle. The National Picture Gallery has been open to the public since 1875.

The Medici treasures

The **UFFIZI** in **FLORENCE** possesses the most important collection of late Gothic, Italian Renaissance and Baroque art

ADDRESS:
Piazzale degli Uffizi,
Florence

OPENING TIMES:
Tues- Sun. 8:15 am
to 6:50 pm, open
longer in summer

INTERNET:
www.polomuseale.
firenze.it/uffizi

PUBLIC TRANSPORT:
Bus, Line 23 from the
Santa Maria Novella
railway station

OTHER ATTRACTIONS:
Pitti Palace, Opera del
Duomo Museum,
Palazzo Vecchio

Giorgio Vasari (1511–74) is known today primarily as a writer. His *Vite de' più eccellenti pittori, scultori et architettor*, or *Lives of the Painters, Sculptors and Architects* (1550), is a reliable description of the important Italian Renaissance painters and architects. Vasari was multitalented, no different from Michelangelo Buonarotti, his inspiration. Vasari was also active as a painter and architect. He designed the Uffizi Gallery in Florence and decorated the immediately adjacent Palazzo Vecchio with frescoes. He was commissioned by the Medicis, a family descended from burghers. During the various interstate conflicts, the Medicis acquired power and wealth. They produced popes and two queens of France. The family was ennobled and governed the whole of Tuscany from the city-state of Florence. The head of

the family bore the rank of grand duke. Their rule lasted until 1737, when the dynasty died out. Parts of northern Italy were occupied and ruled by the Austrian Habsburg family.

Patrons and collectors

The city of Florence was the cradle of the Renaissance. The poet, Dante Alighieri, whose *Divine Comedies* became the linguistic basis for modern Italian, lived and worked here; it was here that interest in the art and philosophy of the ancients began. The Medicis were heavily involved in everything, as financiers, patrons and collectors. The art treasures they stockpiled over the centuries were donated to the city of Florence by their last heiress, Anna Maria Ludovica, Electoress of the Palatinate, and form the basis of the present-day Uffizi Museum.

The Italian word *uffizio* means office. The commission which Count Cosimo de Medici I awarded his court painter, Vasari, actually only comprised construction of a government building. The architect decided to use a technique revolutionary in its day, namely the use of cement strengthened with iron, which made it possible to execute unusually large windows. The Gallery's upper floor was designed for the family art collection.

The building was constructed between 1560 and 1580. It consists of two linked wings, adorned with arcades.

The Uffizi contains a total of 45 exhibition rooms, not including the so-called Vasari corridor, which was originally a kind of secret passage for the Medicis. It leads over the old bridge, the Ponte Vecchio, across the River Arno to the Pitti

Palace. The Corridoio Vasariano now serves as a gallery for a collection of self portraits by famous artists, from Vasari to Delacroix.

Italy's greats

The art work collection in the Uffizi runs to around 4,000 items. The artists are Dutch and German, like Lucas Cranach the Elder, but the majority are Italian, spanning from the first late Gothic painter, Giotto – via Cimabue, Masaccio and Fra Angelico – to Piero della Francesca. There are works by Leonardo da Vinci, Raphael and Michelangelo as well as examples of Italian Mannerists and Italian Baroque. The collection ends in the late 18th century, with works by Canaletto, Goya and Chardin.

One of the main attractions is located in Rooms 10 to 14 of the eastern gallery. Paintings by artist Sandro Botticelli hang there, including two of the most spectacular – *Spring*, 1478, and the *Birth of Venus,* around 1485. Indeed, the second painting owes more to pagan antiquity than the first. Its elegance and almost naked eroticism, in fundamental defiance of Catholic moral precepts, represents a high point in the creativity of the artist, commonly known as Alessandro di Mariano Filipepi, who got his nickname ('little barrel' in Italian) by association with his brother, who was known for his corpulence.

The Uffizi's collection also includes sculptures, carpets, drawings, jewellery, weapons, scientific instruments and archeological items. The Pitti Palace, on the other side of the river, also formerly owned by and the home of the Medicis, is the second exhibition site for the extraordinary collection of art compiled by the Medici family.

The Uffizi has long been one of the most important museums in the world. The historic building is no longer able to cope with the hordes of visitors created by modern tourism. The consequence is massive lines. So tourists stand in line and have time to admire the elegant structure and beautiful evenness of the building's pale yellow walls, and to realize that Giorgio Vasari was much more than a writer.

Art and theology

The **PINACOTECA DI BRERA** in **MILAN** contains major works by Piero della Francesca and Raphael

ADDRESS:
Via Brera 28,
Milan

OPENING HOURS:
Tues–Sun 8:30 am
to 7:15 pm

INTERNET:
www.brera.
beniculturali.it

TRANSPORT:
Subway lines MM2,
MM3
Tram Lines 1, 4, 8, 12,
14, 27.
Bus Lines 61, 97

OTHER ATTRACTIONS:
Civica Galleria d'Arte
Moderna,
Museo del Duomo,
S. Maria delle Grazie

Those who travel to Milan to experience the fine arts start off with three addresses in mind. The first is the cathedral of Santa Maria Nascente, the second biggest ecclesiastical building in the country and the most spacious cathedral of the Gothic era. The second is the Teatro alla Scala, perhaps the most famous opera house in the world, where many of Giuseppe Verdi's operas premiered. The third is the Dominican monastery of Santa Maria delle Grazie, whose refectory, the Cenacolo, houses Leonardo da Vinci's fresco, *The Last Supper*, which has been reproduced thousands of times and restored seven times to allow us once again admire it in its original form.

Unfortunately, for many people, the Pinacoteca di Brera is less familiar. "If you haven't seen the Brera, you haven't been to Milan," was a long-time slogan of the local tourist office and, apart from being perfectly true, it shows how urgent it is to promulgate this truth. The Pinacoteca is one of the country's great museums and many people mention it in the same breath as the Uffizi in Florence.

Baroque brick building

The museum is situated to the north and behind La Scala. It takes its name from the district, the bohemian artists' and restaurant quarter. The beautiful brick building was originally a Jesuit college, whose builders included the Ricchini, father and son Baroque architects. The Jesuit order came into being during the Counter-Reformation. When it was dissolved by the Pope in the 18th century, the Palazzo di Brera was considered to have outlived its purpose.

However, an art collection was then set up, together with a training center for artists and the Biblioteca Nazionale Braidense, a library founded by the Empress Maria Theresa in 1770. It was opened to the public in 1786 and now contains more than a million volumes.

The Pinacoteca experienced the greatest growth in the number of its exhibits, which had risen to 600, when it underwent the secularization spead by Maria Theresa's son, Josef II, across northern Italy. Monasteries were shut, church goods were expropriated, and the altar paintings were taken to the Brera gallery, where they were subsequently to serve aesthetic rather than pious purposes.

The museum is predominantly concerned with art created between the 13th and 18th centuries. There are a few works by non-Italians; Rembrandt, Rubens, Breughel the Elder, Jordaens and Van Dyck. Most of the artists are Italian, however, from Lombardy and the Veneto.

Bramante and Lorenzo Lotto

You will encounter well-known names as well as the lesser known. Right at the start of your tour are rather stiff male figures by Donato Bramante and Bernardino Luini as well as a wonderful depiction of *Saint Bernardino of Siena* by Andrea Mantegna and an emotionally charged *Pietà* by Lorenzo Lotto. You can find Veronese and Tintoretto, but the exhibition room that most visitors want to see is number 24, the room in which the two most popular pictures in the collection hang.

One is the *Virgin and Child with Saints* by Piero della Francesca. Piero della Francesca was perhaps the most influential painter of the early Italian Renaissance, remarkable for his modern use of central perspective, flat representation of the figures and pale, almost pastel coloration. The Milan painting shows Mary, accompanied by saints, in an almost statuesque pose; the naked child is already quite big and lies in his mother's lap.

Raphael's masterpiece

One of the artists whose influence on Piero della Francesca can be most clearly seen was Raphael. His *Marriage of the Virgin*, which hangs in the Palazzo di Brera, is considered one of his early masterpieces. In front of a flight of steps leading to a circular temple, Mary exchanges rings with Joseph, under the supervision of a clergyman who is half Rabbi and half Christian priest. Witnesses stand by, some taking part in the event or looking on indifferently. All are dressed in robes of Raphael's time. There is an ancient temple in the background and the sky above is a soft blue.

The gallery's collection continues on to Caravaggio, Tiepolo and

Bellotto. The last of the 38 rooms supplements the great Italian paintings of the Renaissance and Baroque with portraits, still-lifes and 19th century genre paintings. None of it is radically different from what

was going on elsewhere in Europe at the same time. One of the late works is a picture of spring by Giovanni Segantini. A dun cow grazes peacefully in a meadow with mountains rising in the background.

Segantini, born in 1858, received excellent artistic training at the Brera Academy. His main subjects were landscapes and rural life. His style is not boringly realistic, but resembles whimsical symbolism. His technique, known as Divisionism, consisted in the use of minute brush strokes of pure color to create contour and coloration. It subtly presaged the Pointillism developed later by French artists Seurat and Signac.

Giovanni Bellini's *Pietà* **stands out among the religious works in the collection (above left, detail).**

Piero della Francesca's *Virgin and Child with Saints* **is one of the seminal works of the early Renaissance (above right).**

View of the museum buildings of the Pinacoteca di Brera (below).

Greco-Roman splendor

The **NATIONAL ARCHEOLOGICAL MUSEUM** in **NAPLES** has an important collection of antiquities

ITALY

Rome
Naples

Tyrrhenian Sea

Mediterranean Sea

ADRESSE:
Piazza Museo,
Naples

OPENING TIMES
Tues.-Mon. 9 am
to 8 pm,
until 5 pm in winter.

INTERNET:
www.marketplace.it/
museo.nazionale/
museo_home.htm

PUBLIC TRANSPORT:
Subway, Museo station
and Piazza Cavour

OTHER ATTRACTIONS:
Naples Old Town
(Unesco World Heritage
Site), Castello d'Ovo
on rocks in the Bay
of Naples, excavations
in Pompeii and
Herculaneum.

The royal house of Farnese originated in Umbria, central Italy. It became famous because of Alessandro Farnese, who took charge of rejuvenating the spiritual and secular life of the Catholic Church when he reigned in Rome from 1534 to 1549 as Pope Paul III. He became the leader of the Counter-Reformation and permitted Saint Ignatius Loyola to form the Jesuit Order. His piety did not prevent him from fathering a son, however. Furthermore, he had a splendid palace built on the banks of the River Tiber, where he housed many Greco-Roman antiquities which were, of course, purely heathen in nature.

The male line of the Farnese dynasty died out in 1731. In 1735 the family's collection of antiquities passed to King Charles III of Naples. In 1787, he housed them in a building that was originally called the Real Museo Borbonico (Royal Bourbon Museum), because the Neapolitan kings were Bourbons. Now it is called the National Museum.

Hercules the demigod

A couple of exquisite pieces are on display, such as the *Farnese Hercules*, named after its penultimate owner. The statue was found in Rome, in the Caracalla Baths, and is a 10 foot representation of the popular demigod of antiquity, Hercules. The naked, fully bearded man is standing contraposto, with his right hand behind his back, looking obliquely down at the floor. The statue is a copy; the original from the 4th century B.C. has been lost.

Another splendid piece is the *Farnese Bull* group. Amphion and

The National Archeological Museum building dates from 1586, but has been renovated several times (right).

Zethos, the twin sons of Zeus and Antiope, avenged their mother by chaining the Theban Queen Dirke, Antiope's oppressor, to the horns of a bull, which then gored her to death. The Neapolitan reproduction of this mythical theme is regarded as the biggest preserved ancient marble group. It too is a copy found in the Caracalla Baths. The original stood on the island of Rhodes and was the work of the sculptors Apollonius and Tauriskos.

The Farnese collection also comprises the group of two tyrannicides, *Harmodius and Aristogeiton*. The original once stood in the market square in Athens. There is a relief depicting *Orpheus and Eurydice*, and a figure of the spear-bearing Homeric hero *Achilles*. They are all replicas. To these are added numerous Greek and Roman portraits.

The Farnese collection takes up the first floor of the Naples National Archeological Museum, renowned as the biggest and most important museum of antiquities in Europe. The building dates from 1586 and was initially used as a cavalry barracks. In 1612, it was converted for use by the University of Naples. Following further rebuilding work post-1777, the Farnese collection made its home in the building from 1787.

The Museum's main exhibits are made up of finds from Pompeii and Herculaneum. Both ancient cities, located close to the volcano of Mount Vesuvius were destroyed and

buried in Roman times, first by an earthquake in 63 A.D., then as the result of a volcanic eruption 16 years later. Excavations started in 1748 and the German architect, Johann Joachim Winckelmann, was involved. In Pompeii, archeologists were able to uncover the outline of roads and houses that had been covered and preserved by ashes, mud and lava. The Naples National Archeological Museum collections now contain many finds from these sites.

From the school of Praxiteles

These finds are located on the second floor, for example. They include bronzes whose patination gives a clear indication of where they were found – green oxidation indicates Pompeii, dark means Herculaneum. One of the masterpieces exhibited here, formerly known as the *Statue of Narcissus*, is actually a representation of the god of wine, Dionysius. The work originates from the school of Greece's most famous ancient sculptor, Praxiteles.

Many ancient mosaics are displayed on the mezzanine floor. Combining colored stones of glass or clay to form pictorial representations is an old Mediterranean art form. The Ancient Romans used them for floors, internal walls and frescoes. The art of mosaics was then passed down to Christian art, above all Byzantine, and to the art of Islam. Countless mosaics have been removed from excavated houses in

The battle of Issus in the year 333 B.C., during which Alexander the Great overcame the Persians, was depicted on a Pompeian mosaic. Alexander is on the far left of the picture, the fleeing King Darius in the center (above).

The fresco from Pompeii shows the three Graces: Aglaia, Euphrosyne and Thalia. It is regarded as a particularly beautiful work of ancient Roman erotica (below center).

A bronze copy of a statue of the Greek god Apollo, *Apollo Citarista*, was also found in Pompeii. The original is presumed to have been created by the legendary Greek sculptor Phidias in the 5th century B.C.

Pompeii and brought to the Naples Museum. The best known is the depiction of the battle of Issus, in 333 B.C., where Alexander the Great conquered the Persians under King Darius III. The Greek leader appears on the left edge of the picture, the fleeing Persian King dominates the center. It is presumed that the mosaic was modeled on a Greek original. The basement contains the Egyptian collection, donated by the noble Borgia family. It is only since 2000 that the collection of erotica found in the excavated towns of Pompeii and Herculaneum has been freely accessible.

The collection of the popes

From the Sistine Chapel to the Museo Pio-Clementino – Rome's **VATICAN MUSEUM**

ADDRESS:
Viale Vaticano,
Vatican City, Rome

OPENING HOURS:
Mon-Sat 8:45 am
to 4:45 pm; only until
1:45 pm in winter

INTERNET:
mv.vatican.va

TRANSPORT:
Metro, Line A,
Bus: Lines 32, 49, 81,
98, 492, 990. Tram:
Line 19

OTHER ATTRACTIONS:
Pantheon

In the western part of Rome, the capital of Italy, lies the Vatican, an independent state with its own station, its own post office and its own press. It is the smallest state in the world, with a surface area of just 0.16 square miles and only 850 inhabitants. Its current constitution goes back to the Lateran Treaties of 1929, concluded between Italy and the then Pope. The agreement was necessary after the Papal States – which until 1870 had been an extensive central Italian territory – were absorbed into the kingdom of the Risorgimento, whose seat of government eventually moved from Florence to Rome.

The Vatican consists of the cathedral of Saint Peter, Saint Peter's Square (which lies in front of it), and the Vatican palaces, a large proportion of which are used as museums. The Vatican, so the saying goes, is a state that is a museum and a museum that is a state. The range of its collections is extraordinary. Only the Louvre in Paris can compare. Since 2000, it has had a new visitors' entrance, with spacious halls offering, among other things, three guided tours of varying lengths, the most extensive of which is over 4 miles long.

Patron of Michelangelo

Julius II, one of the major Renaissance popes from 1503 to 1513, came from the mendicant Franciscan order. However, he was a man who loved life and fathered three daughters. As the patron of Michelangelo and Raphael – the latter also painted him – he loved the fine arts, which did not in any way restrict his aesthetic interest in contemporary Christianity. In 1503, he began to collect antique sculpture. One of the first pieces was a statue of Apollo, which he set up in the inner courtyard of his Palazzo Belvedere. It is still there and is known as the Apollo Belvedere.

Another gem acquired by Julius II was the figure of Hermes from Olympia, a work of the famous sculptor, Praxiteles, as well as the Laocoon group in 1506, one of the most spectacular sculptures of Ancient Greece which depicts the Trojan Laocoon and his sons

View of the painted ceiling of the Sistine Chapel (below left).

Michelangelo's legendary *Pietà*, which stands in Saint Peter's, is also part of the Vatican Museum's collection (below center).

The Creation of Adam, **painted by Michelangelo in the Sistine Chapel between 1510 and 1512. Detail from the ceiling (left).**

being strangled by snakes sent by the sea god, Poseidon. One of the boys is in the throes of death. The father in the middle struggles in vain against the threat awaiting the other son: an allegory of past, present and future.

Raphael painted the rooms

A later pope, Clement XIV (1769–1774) reorganized the Renaissance collection. He is considered the true founder of the Vatican Museums. In 1771, he set up the Museo Profano, later called the Museo Clementino. Starting in 1776, his successor, Pius VI (1775–99) had the huge building of the Museo Pio-Clementino erected, with its magnificent staircase and imposing domed hall.

From this time on, the collections were supplemented and expanded with Etruscan antiquities, manuscripts, icons, gold and ivory work, Egyptian and Babylonian antiquities, contemporary art and ethnological items. The total number of items in the collections is around 50,000. The headquarters of the greatest and most powerful branch of Christianity now owns a treasure house of antiquities, only a very small part

of which has anything to do with its theological mission. The existence and maintenance of the museum demonstrates an appreciation of the sacred history of the Vatican as well as for cultural diversity.

Visitors to the museum may view the former papal apartments, the "stanze" decorated by Raphael, his teacher, Perugino, and some of Raphael's pupils. The pictures are among the most perfect in the history of European art. Some are allegorical, some biblical in content; others illustrate events from the history of the church. But Raphael's *School of Athens*, in which the most famous philosophers of the Ancient World are gathered around Aristotle, Plato and Socrates, is also to be found here. The Scholastics were convinced that Classical philosophy was a forerunner of Christian thought.

The Sistine Chapel also exhibits such gifts from the ancients. The Sibyls depicted in the frescoes belong to Greco-Roman mythology, companions of the god Apollo. This chapel is where the conclave of cardinals meets and the site of the fireplace in which the voting papers are burned, sending out

dark or white smoke, indicating the result. Here too, images with Christian and biblical content predominate – from the creation of Adam through the Last Judgement of the Revelation of Saint John, both depicted in the incomparable frescoes of Michelangelo. Fifteen years were spent restoring the Sistine Chapel. In 1994, it could be seen in all its original beauty once again.

The aerial photograph shows Vatican City with its huge complex of palaces and museums (below).

Canova and the rich patrons

The VILLA BORGHESE in ROME and its sculpture collection

ITALY
Rome
Tyrrhenian Sea
Mediterranean Sea

ADDRESS:
Piazzale del Museo
Borghese 5,
Rome

OPENING HOURS:
Tues-Sun 8:30 am
to 7 pm

INTERNET:
www.galleriaborghese.it

TRANSPORT:
Metro, Line A to Piazza
di Spagna. Various bus
lines

OTHER ATTRACTIONS:
Galleria Nazionale
d'Arte Moderna, Museo
Nazionale Etrusco di
Villa Giulia, Galleria
Doria Pamphili

**Napoleon's sister
Paulina was the model
for the reclining female
figure, the *Reclining
Venus*. Canova created
the sculpture between
1805 and 1808
(below left).**

In her left hand, she holds the apple that, according to Homer, Paris awarded to one of the Olympian goddesses for her matchless beauty. He gave it to Aphrodite – or Venus in Latin – the goddess of love, and now she reclines there, leaning her head on her right hand. Her upper body is naked; only her loins are swathed in fabric. The couch on which she rests is antique in its effect, rather than a true relic of the ancient world, inasmuch as it is decorated with motifs typical of European Classicism. It is a wooden divan which once contained a mechanism that could set the whole figure in motion. The spectator remained in his place while Venus rotated on her axis before him. Whenever possible, this took place by candlelight, causing the smooth marble surface of the stone, which had been treated with wax, to gleam softly.

From Classical times

The turning mechanism was the specialty of its creator, Antonio Canova, the leading sculptor in Italy in the age of Classicism. His *Reclining Venus* dates from between 1805 and 1808, when the Apennine peninsula was ruled by Napoleon. The figure was commissioned by the Emperor's family and Canova's model was Napoleon's sister, Paulina. She married Camillo Filippo Ludovico Borghese in 1803 and thus became a member of one of Italy's most powerful aristocratic families.

The Borghese originally came from Siena in Tuscany, but a branch of the family had lived in Rome

since the 16th century. Their ranks produced distinguished churchmen, including one pope, Paul V. Another, Cardinal Scipione Borghese, the nephew of Paul V, had a country seat with gardens built for himself on the Pincio in Rome by architects Flaminio Ponzio and Giovanni Vasanzio.

As was customary among rich Roman families, the Borgheses owned a palazzo in the city and a country seat, known as a villa. (The word, 'villa' denotes a house surrounded by extensive parkland.) The Villa Borghese was built on a former vineyard that was once the gardens of Lucullus in ancient Roman times. The 200 acre site comprises avenues and plantations, summerhouses, statues, fountains and an artificial lake with an island. Taken as a whole, it is the second biggest area of parkland in the Italian capital.

One of Scipione Borghese's favorite artists was Gianlorenzo Bernini. The great Baroque artist was responsible for the sculpture, *Apollo and Daphne,* and for the statue of the biblical David, whose facial features are those of Bernini himself. A good hundred years after

Scipione's death, Marcantonio IV Borghese took over the villa, restored and extended it, and supplemented the collections. He died three years before Paulina Bonaparte married into the family.

Titian's wedding portrait

Antonio Canova survived the fall of Napoleon, but Paulina Bonaparte was forced to separate from her Borghese husband in 1815. By then Canova had become the superintendent of the Vatican art collections, charged with the task of bringing back the many works of art that Napoleon had stolen from Rome and carried off to Paris, including many objects from the Villa Borghese. Camillo, Paulina's husband, had been compelled to sell them to his tyrannical brother-in-law in 1807.

The villa has been publicly owned since the beginning of the 20th century. The previous owner, Paolo Borghese, sold the collections, this time voluntarily, to the Italian state. The casino built at the villa by the architect, Vasanzio, now serves as a museum. Famous for its sculptures, which include works by Bernini and Canova as well as

many pieces from antiquity, it houses one of the most valuable art collections in Rome.

Many of the works in the museum were collected by Cardinal Scipione Borghese, including the paintings. Today, it includes art by Raphael and Caravaggio, Bassano, Rubens, Cranach and Lorenzo Lotto. One famous painting depicting heavenly and earthly love was painted by Titian in 1514, when he was still only 25 years old. It shows two female figures, one nude, grouped around a marble sarcophagus with a winged boy. The boy is Cupid and the naked figure is Venus. The clothed woman represents Laura Bagarotto, bride of the Venetian, Nicolò Aurelio. The sarcophagus is decorated with his coat of arms. The picture was painted for their wedding.

In 1899, one of the Rothschilds was desperate to buy it and offered a price higher than the total value of the villa. The deal did not go through and today, the Titian is one of the jewels of the Villa Borghese art collection.

One of the showpieces of the collection is Gianlorenzo Bernini's *Rape of Proserpina*, 1622 (above left).

The opulently decorated Galleria degli Imperatori shows off all the splendor of the interior design of the Villa Borghese (above right).

Leda surrounded by Zeus in the Form of a Swan and the Twins Castor and Pollux dates from 1513-16, but is thought to be only a studio copy. The original by Leonardo was lost (below right).

87

Venetian style

The GALLERIA DELL' ACCADEMIA in VENICE houses masterpieces by Titian, Veronese and Tiepolo

ADDRESS:
Campo della Caritá
Dorsoduro n. 1050,
Venice

OPENING HOURS:
Tues-Sun 8:15 am
to 7:15 pm,
Mon. 8:15 am to 2 pm

INTERNET:
www.gallerie-
accademia.org

TRANSPORT:
Vaporetto,
Lines 1 and 82

OTHER ATTRACTIONS:
Ca' d'Oro, Palazzo
Grassi, Basilica di San
Marco

Leonardo's drawing of a nude, influenced by Vitruvius, utilizes a scheme for the proportions of the human body. The drawing dates from 1490 (below left).

Many people believe that Venice, or at least the part which stands on 118 islands where the rivers Po and Piave flow into the sea, is the most beautiful city in the world. Visitors to Venice crave the ecstatic experience of a city which is a work of art in itself – composed of palaces, bridges, squares, canals and churches. It seems almost absurd to maintain special museums in Venice since the city is a museum in and of itself. However, two museums deserve special attention: the Archaeologische Museum and the Galleria dell' Accademia.

The wealth that poured into the city from the medieval maritime trade with the Levant benefited cultural activities as well as the construction of palaces, both secular and ecclesiastical, churches and public monuments. The churches are overflowing with important paintings and should be the first stop for anyone interested in Venetian painting.

The Renaissance gains acceptance

The powerful artistic desires of the established strata of Venetian society, as well as the ample supply of money available to indulge them, created a lasting tradition and a special style known as the Venetian Renaissance. Venice had its own school of painting which cannot be linked to a particular institution, but arose through common ideas and similar tastes shared by the Venetian patrons, artists and individual workshops. What is most striking is that it lasted several centuries – almost five hundred years, in fact – and came to an end only with the decline of the old trading republic and its annexation by the Austria of the Habsburgs.

Venice was exceptional because it embraced the Renaissance well into the 14th century, considerably later than in other cities in northern Italy where the Renaissance had long been accepted. Because of its ties to Byzantium, Venice remained committed to the Byzantine tradition of art known as the Maniera Greca. The first Venetian to diverge from this esthetic canon was Paolo Veneziano, who was active between 1320 and 1358 and was briefly influenced by Giotto. In his late works, however, he returned to the all-powerful Maniera Greca.

After Veneziano, there followed a short period of Gothic style with Jacobello del Fiore and Gentile da Fabriano before the Renaissance finally won acceptance in Venice. Painting during the period was dominated by brothers Bartolomeo and Antonio Vivarini and by the Bellinis – Jacopo and his sons, Giovanni and Gentile. The last two were also the brothers-in-law of Andrea Mantegna. Jacopo Bellini is known for his small landscapes and his experiments with central perspective. Giovanni was the first painter in Venice to use oils. Gentile Bellini portrayed the life of the city in pictures of monumental proportions, in keeping with Venetian tradition until the time of Canaletto.

Museum on the Grand Canal

The most important characteristics of the Venetian style include warm, finely graded tones and colors, an emphasis on mood and light that almost effaces outlines. Such characteristics evoke the moisture-laden atmosphere of the city and its surrounding lagoon. The great masters of the Venetian style were Titian, Tintoretto and Veronese, the Tiepolos – father and son – and the veduta painters, Belotto and Guardi, when the end of political autonomy also heralded the end of artistic creation in the city.

Many works of the Venetian School can be seen in the Galleria dell' Accademia, which is one of Italy's most important museums. It stands on the bank of the Grand Canal, just before the point where it joins the Canale di San Marco. The banks are linked by the Ponte dell' Accademia.

Established in a former *scuola*, buildings housing the Venetian Christian brotherhoods and eccle-

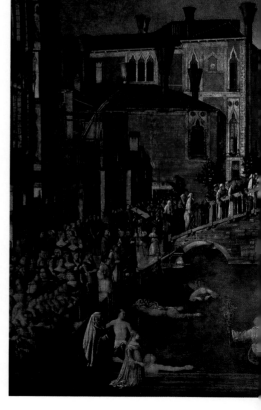

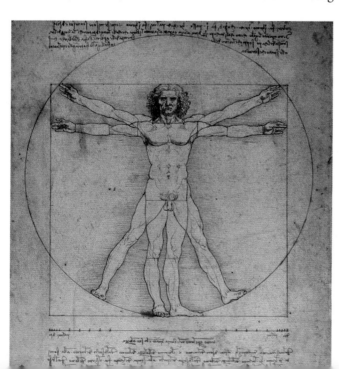

siastical communities, the building today known as the Galleria dell' Accademia once bore the name, Scuola Grande di Santa Maria della Carità. The collection is mainly the result of secularization under Napoleon, who conquered the city in 1797 and swore that he would become the Attila the Hun of Venice. It is estimated that 25,000 works of religious art were scattered all over the world at that time.

The Galleria dell' Accademia today owns about eight hundred paintings, mainly Venetian, but also *Portrait of a Young Man* by Flemish artist Hans Memling. Among the highlights of the collection are Giovanni Bellini's Sacra Conversazione, Mantegna's *Saint George,* Giorgione's *Tempest*, Veronese's gigantic *Feast in the House of Levi* and Tintoretto's *Miracle of Saint Mark freeing the Slave.*

Detail of Cupids from Tiepolo's *The Rape of Europa*,1730 (above).

Gentile Bellini's *Recovery of the Relic of the True Cross* was painted in 1500 and shows a Venetian canal (below center).

The Galleria dell' Accademia is the most famous art museum in Venice (below right).

A capital of art

ZAGREB has important collections in the MIMARA MUSEUM and the MUSEUM OF MODERN ART

ADDRESS:
Rooseveltov (Roosevelt Square), Zagreb

OPENING HOURS:
Tues., Wed., Fri., Sat.
10 am to 5 pm,
Thurs. 10 am to 7 pm,
Sun. 10 am to 2 pm

INTERNET:
www.mimara.hr

HOW TO GET THERE:
Tram or walk from Ban Jelacic Square

OTHER ATTRACTIONS:
Croatian Museum of Naive Art

A kind of national gallery: the Mimara Museum (below, upper picture).

The artist's impression of the new Museum of Modern Art, to be opened in 2007 (below, lower left).

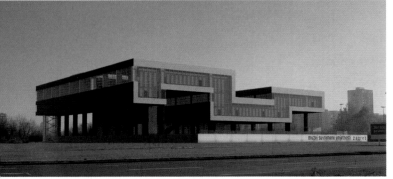

Zagreb is a magnificent old city with a very youthful flair. In summer, the street cafes are filled to overflowing and the art scene flourishes between the lower and upper towns. You continually come across galleries showing interesting contemporary art.

Visitors to the city are confronted with a dilemma because there are more than thirty museums and galleries to choose from. For the fine arts alone, there are four museums with famous names. Besides the Strossmayer Gallery with its Old Masters and the Museum of Modern Art which stands opposite it, there is the Museum of Contemporary Art located in the intimate setting of Catherine's Square in the upper town. The Museum of Modern Art is temporarily closed. It will be reopened in a spacious new building in 2007. This Museum documents the most important artistic movements of the 20th century.

The flagship museum is the Musej Mimara, which stands on Roosevelt Square, behind Baroque gardens. It houses the collection of the painter, restorer and art collector, Ante TopićMimara (1898 –1987). The Museum was opened in 1987 in a former secondary school, six months after his death. He only recently returned to Croatia after a lifetime spent abroad. However, art critics are divided about the importance of the collection, as there are doubts as to whether several of the paintings are genuine.

The Museum, erected in 1895 –1896 in the style of a Neo-Renaissance palace, does not really look like a school building. But then, the complex was intended from the start to be a place of artistic education and an integrated museum was planned in order to inspire the students. Even though this plan came to nothing, the palace, with splendid atrium, its imposing staircases and suites of rooms, still affects the spectator in a special way.

Remarkable glass

The current collection, which consists of a total of 3,750 items in various materials and from various artistic movements and cultural areas, benefits from the generous amount of space. Around 450 paintings representing a wide variety of schools are displayed, including works by Raphael, Velásquez, Rubens, Rembrandt and Goya. There are 200 sculptures covering the period from antiquity to the 20th century. Then there are archeological finds from Ancient Egypt, Mesopotamia, Persia, Crete, Greece and Rome. The Far and Near East are also represented, with three hundred items from ancient China alone. A textile collection of 80 carpets dating from the 16th to the 19th centuries bears witness to the collector's passion for wall hangings.

The glass collection is particularly noteworthy, consisting as it does of more than 550 items. It shows the development of glass from Ancient Egypt to the second half of the 19th century. There is a bottle in the form of a Janus head, dating from the 2nd century B.C., and a bottle in glowing blue made in the Roman Empire in the 3rd or 4th century A.D. Valuable pieces also await the visitor in the European glass section, where Bohemian craftsmanship has a special place.

It began with icons

You might treat yourself to a rest in the Museum cafeteria, which bears the name "Gymnasium" as a reminder of this grandiose building's past, before going up to the third floor. The collection of paintings that occupies eleven rooms is largely responsible for prompting people to refer somewhat flatteringly to the Mimara as the "Louvre of the East."

The collection starts with icons from the 6th to the 12th centuries, followed by panels from the 14th to 17th centuries from Cyprus, Russia and the Venice-Byzantium areas. The collection of paintings that follows is in chronological order. Thus works from the Late Gothic and Early Renaissance periods are followed by the paintings of the Italian High Renaissance and the Baroque for which the Museum is famous: the schools of Bugiardini, Veronese and Titian are represented in addition to Caravaggio and Luca Giordano. The highlights of the Flemish Baroque are Peter Paul Rubens and Anthony Van Dyck. Dutch art is represented by Rembrandt, van

Ruisdael and Cuyp, among others. Spanish painters also play an important part, with pictures by Murillo, Goya and Velázquez. Mimara had a special liking for English painting, as can be seen from pictures by Constable, Bonington and Morland. Impressionism is also represented. Besides Camille Pissaro, Edgar Degas and Edouard Manet, Auguste Renoir's *Bathers* attracts everyone's gaze. In the painter's early work, the viewer is captivated by the perfect harmony between nature and the female body. The picture is arranged so that viewers feel the pleasure of summer sunbathing.

Camille Corot's *Figure of a Girl* dates from 1868 to 1870. The picture is one of the showpieces of the Mimara Museum (above left).

The altar wing, *The Holy Family*, painted by Barna da Siena, dates from the middle of the 14th century (above right).

An iron sculpture by Croatian artist Dusan Dzamonja, who has become world famous for this kind of sculpture (left).

Pictures from many worlds

The collections in the **STATE MUSEUM OF ART** in **RIGA** also represent the history of Latvia

ADRESSE:
10 A K. Valdemara Street, Riga

OPENING TIMES:
Tues.-Mon. 11 am
to 5 pm, April-Sept.
Thurs. to 7 pm

INTERNET:
www.vmm.lv

PUBLIC TRANSPORT:
Trolley bus, Lines 3, 5, 21 Bus, Line 11

OTHER ATTRACTIONS:
Cathedral, Castle Museums, Museum of History and Seafaring Museum

Inga Bruvere was born in Riga in 1963. She attended a school specializing in art, named for artist Janis Rozentāls, and studied for six years at the Latvian Academy of Art in Riga. In 2003, she attained her master's degree in art. She took part in numerous exhibitions, including ones outside Latvia, had one-person shows, participated in international workshops and won awards.

Bruvere paints in the abstract style on a large scale. Her paintings are colorful compositions in the style of Op Art and works with letter-like symbols, vaguely reminiscent of Cy Twombly, but more regular and differently colored. Her paintings have been acquired by many museums, among which is the State Museum of Art in Riga.

The Museum is right next door to the Academy of Art, where Inga Bruvere studied, and is housed in a building constructed between 1903 and 1905. The architect was Wilhelm Neumann, who designed the building in the historic style of the late 19th century. Drafted by Neumann on Elisabeth Street, his design shows absolutely no sign of the Art Nouveau from which it is not far removed historically. Subsequently, Neumann became the institution's first director.

Vilhelms Purvitis was one of his successors, in the 1920s. A highly regarded landscape painter and also teacher at the Academy, he put a lot of energy into assembling a collection of Latvian art. At the time, the country was a republic, having become an independent state after centuries of domination by the Russian tsars. The Russians returned in 1940 after the start of the Second World War. The Soviet Russians subsequently renamed the country as the Latvian Soviet Socialist Republic and made it a Soviet satellite state for the next 50 years.

Artistic examples

Today, one third of Latvia's population, of which more than half are Russian, lives in Riga. Russian influence in Latvia dates back to the time of the tsars. During the republic from 1918 to 1940, the Baltic Germans living in the country played a dominant role, especially in Riga, the former Hanseatic town founded by Canon Albert of Bremen and populated predominantly by German mer-

chants, with not a single Latvian among them. The city's nobility was made up of Germans and a wealth of prominent German literary figures came from Riga.

Until 1918, Latvians with artistic talent customarily studied at the academies in St. Petersburg, Moscow, Odessa and Kasan. Russian taste was dominant and widespread, especially in modernism. *Negro Art*, a book instrumental in the development of the avant-garde movement, was published in St. Petersburg in 1919 and dealt with the artistic example set by African art. It was written in Russian. The name of the publisher was shown as Markov, but his real name was Matvejs and he was a native of Latvia.

In the Expressionist style

Other inspiration came from Scandinavia, France, The Netherlands, Italy and Germany. The Latvian Artists' Group, founded in 1919, was influenced by German Expressionism. There were exhibitions of Latvian art in Berlin and Paris.

The State Museum of Art in Riga provides material information and its collection runs to almost 32,000 items: paintings, graphics and sculptures. The main building on Valdemara Street has two floors of exhibits. The first floor contains works dating from 1750 to 1850; the second floor shows mainly Latvian art from the mid-19th century to 1945. There is a comprehensive collection of Russian art, with works by Ivan Aivasovsky, a renowned 19th century marine artist, as well as by Nicholas Roerich, born 1874 in St. Petersburg. This Symbolist, a member of the influential *Mir Isskustva* association of artists, later traveled extensively in Asia, and died in India.

He became famous as a set designer for Sergei Diaghilev's ballet troupe.

The Museum of Art has another exhibition space, the *Arsenals* in Tornaiela, opened in 1989 to display post-1945 Latvian art. Numerous immigrants, from Sweden, Australia and the United States, are represented here. Inge Bruvere's works also hang here, amongst many contemporary Latvian works.

Jékabs Kazaks painted the colorful *On the Beach* (above left) when influenced by the style of German Expressionists. The painting, completed in 1920, is one of the Latvian artist's last works.

Vilhelms Purvitis ranks as one of the great patrons of a national Latvian collection of art. His painting, *Winter*, 1910, is one of the most impressive works in Riga's Museum (above right).

The main facade of the Museum, officially opened in 1905 (below right).

Lithuania's cultural heritage

The **LITHUANIAN ART MUSEUM** in **VILNIUS** exhibits the biggest and most important collection of Lithuanian art

ADDRESS:
22 Konstitucijos
Avenue, Vilnius

OPENING TIMES:
Tues.-Sat. 11 am
to 6 pm,
Sun. 12 noon to 5 pm

INTERNET:
www.ldm.lt

HOW TO GET THERE:
The Museum is best
reached by traversing
the pedestrianized city
center on foot.

OTHER ATTRACTIONS:
Cathedral

Jonusas Radvila lived from 1612 to 1655. He was Governor of the city of Vilnius, Vilna in Polish. In the 14th century, the Grand Principality of Lithuania entered into a union with Poland, which is why Vilnius, like the whole of Lithuania, had – and has – a considerable Polish population.

Radvila built a palace for himself in Vilnius, which was made over to the Vilnius Philanthropic Society by one of the Governor's descendents in 1807. Until 1940, the society owned and ran the building. It now belongs to the Lithuanian Art Museum, which organizes exhibitions and concerts there.

The Museum has a history of its own. It started out as an art society, founded in 1907 during the period of tsarist Russian domination, but Russian pressure on the Lithuanians had relaxed slightly. There was a national press in the by that time Lithuanian language, a Lithuanian spiritual life and in 1907, an exhibition of Lithuanian fine art was held in Vilnius for the first time. The society retained possession of some of the exhibits and these were added to, mainly with acquisitions from later exhibitions.

It started with the art society

The First World War ended with the formal independence of the three Baltic states. All three suffered communist revolts and civil wars. In the case of Lithuania, Poland intervened again. A few committed people ensured that the existing art collection was protected and preserved. The republic that was finally formed soon turned in a para-fascist dictatorship. Furthermore, the country was destitute. These were not ideal conditions for a lively artistic life, but, be that as it may, its artists painted, built and modeled, and they took note of artistic happenings over the borders.

In 1933, the Vilnius municipal authorities created a city museum which took over the existing art collections stored at various locations. The first exhibition opened in the Town Hall in 1941. The country was overrun by the Russians again; in accordance with the German – Soviet non-aggression pact, the Soviet Union annexed the Baltic states at the start of the Second World War.

Stalin was people's commissar of nationalities affairs under Lenin. Part of Soviet domestic policy consisted of granting a certain amount of autonomy to the various ethnic peoples under their rule. This was restricted to use of the ethnic language and preserving folklore, but during the years of the Lithuanian Soviet Socialist Republic, the country managed to retain something approaching its own cultural identity.

Since 1941, the collection has had the official title of Lithuanian Art Museum. It has been constantly added to and expanded by works of art from deconsecrated churches, and by determined collecting on the part of Museum staff. Contemporary works have been included too, in response to the aesthetic diktat of so-called socialist realism that prevailed throughout the USSR, but this diktat was not applied quite so harshly in the Baltic region as elsewhere.

Lithuanian emigration

There has always been a Lithuanian tradition of national art. From 1797 to 1832, an academy of art in Vilnius exhibited its output. Around the turn of the 20th century, M.K. Ciurlonis, born 1875, composer and Art Nouveau artist, became extremely influential. His paintings, especially the later ones, verged on the abstract. After 1945, the graphic arts in Lithuania followed him and Western European- inspired avantgarde artists of the inter-war period, thus maintaining a standard that stands up to international comparison.

Lithuanian emigration should not be forgotten either. There were frequent waves of emigration from 1900, and these always included artists. Australia became one of the important focal points for Lithuanian exiles. After 1990, many emigrants returned, temporarily or permanently, and donated items they had brought home to the Museum, which is how the Radvila Palace comes to exhibit Australian aboriginal works.

Today, the palace is just one of nine institutions owned by the Museum of Art: eight in the capital and one on the Curonian Spit. They include a clock museum, a restoration center, the amber museum and exhibition rooms for the prehistory collection, coins, graphics, folklore exhibits, applied art, and paintings. There are more than 200,000 objects, paintings and drawings from all over Europe, mostly sreated by Lithuanian artists.

Vienas is the title of this painting by Leonardas Tuleikis painted in 1997 (left).

Ferdynand Ruszczyc's painting (below right) is one of the Museum's most important exhibits. It was painted in 1902 and is entitled, *Refugees*.

Two buildings that form part of the Art Museum - the Radvila Palace and the main building (above right).

Holland's Golden Age

The RIJKSMUSEUM in AMSTERDAM has the largest and most valuable collection of Dutch paintings

ADDRESS:
Jan Luijkenstraat 1,
Amsterdam

OPENING TIMES:
Mon-Sun 9 am to 6 pm

INTERNET:
www.rijksmuseum.nl

PUBLIC TRANSPORT:
Tram, Museumsplein
stop

OTHER ATTRACTIONS:
Historical Museum,
Jewish Historical
Museum,
Rembrandthuis

In the Netherlands, marksmen guilds were formed by the militia to protect a town or city. The title "guild" indicates that they were organized along the same lines as the guilds in cities during the Middle Ages. The original military purpose became lost in the mists of time and, like many similar organizations today, the marksmen guilds simply became traditional clubs whose main aim was camaraderie. That they had once been armed seemed just an old wives' tale.

Dining and carousing were the principal activities of the guilds and the only prerequisite for membership was material wealth. They had their own companies, *doelen*, housed in buildings where pictures of the officers and their subordinates hung. The guild members were important patrons of the Dutch artists. Guild members portrayed themselves as a close-knit group, similar to a sports team today.

Master of light and shade

When Captain Frans Banning Cocq and Lieutenant Willem van Ruytenburch of the Amsterdam Company of Marksmen acquired a new banqueting hall in the Kloverniersdoelen guild house around 1642, they wanted to decorate it with six group portraits. One of the commissions went to the 36-year-old artist, Rembrandt Harmenszoon van Rijn, a well-to-do citizen famed throughout the city as a portrait painter and creator of religious pictures. His artistic specialty was chiaroscuro, the experimentation with light and dark already used by Leonardo da Vinci.

He put the Kloverniersdoelen company into the picture and, in so doing, completely departed from usual practice, namely by painting them not in static poses, but as they are about to depart. The Captain, dressed in dark clothes, gives the

The present Rijksmuseum building was completed in 1885 (below left).

command. His arm is outstretched. The Lieutenant beside him, wearing light-colored clothing, listens attentively. The members of the guild arm themselves with weapons; the drummer beats his drum. A little girl stands amongst them, half curious, half baffled. The shaft of light streaming down adds to the drama.

The scale is vast – almost 15 by 11$^1/_2$ feet. Rembrandt's painting, usually known as *The Night Watch*, now hangs in the Rijksmuseum in Amsterdam and is the main attraction. A barrier protects it from over-eager visitors. Years ago, a mentally disturbed person attempted to destroy the canvas, but it has been completely repaired.

The Rijksmuseum's collection is dominated by Rembrandt and other Dutch Baroque painters. The Museum has Louis Bonaparte, brother to the Emperor of France, to thank for composing the collection. He ruled Holland for a brief period at the start of the 19th century and placed the paintings collected by the Dutch royal house of Orange under state ownership at Huis ten Bosch in The Hague, making them accessible to the public in the manner of revolutionary France. The move to the Paleis op dem Dam in Amsterdam, took place in 1808.

The present building opened in 1885. It is a massive structure by master architect Peter Cuypers, with the appearance of a water fortress. At that time, the collections from the Dutch Museum of History and Art were housed there. The building was extended between 1909 and 1919, and again between 1962 and 1969.

The Golden Age

Today, the collections cover Dutch painting from the 15th to 19th centuries; designs and drawings from the period are testimony to the history of a nation. Sculptures and paintings also have their place. In addition, there is a Department of Oriental Art, because the Netherlands was a colonial power in Asia for a long time, but attention is focused primarily on the Netherlands. The Rijksmuseum is the kingdom's national museum and the biggest museum establishment in the country.

The Golden Age, the 17th century, was a long, peaceful period of economic prosperity, international communication and flourishing culture. While the Thirty Years' War

raged until 1648 in other parts of Europe, the country at the mouth of the River Rhine bought art because it was beautiful and valuable. It was the age of the great Dutch Baroque painters: Rembrandt, Franz Hals, Vermeer, Fabritius, de Hooch, Hobbema, ter Borch and Ruysdael.

The Rijksmuseum displays a famous late work by Rembrandt, *The Jewish Bride*, in which the man's lascivious hand rests on the woman's breast – probably based on the biblical figures of Isaac and Rebecca. There is also Rembrandt's *Self Portrait as the Apostle Paul* and the

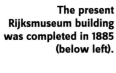

famous *Landscape with a Stone Bridge*, which insired the great Dutch landscape artists, Salomon van Ruysdael and Jacob van Ruisdael.

There are the captivatingly beautiful genre paintings by Johannes Vermeer from Delft, *Woman in Blue Reading a Letter* and *The Milkmaid*, a girl pouring milk from a jug into a bowl. There is Jan Steen's *The Morning Toilet*, with the woman sitting on a bed, putting on her stockings. The Museum documents the gradual progression of Baroque Dutch iconography until it reached a new peak with Van Gogh.

Two legendary works by Dutch painters: Rembrandt's *Night Watch*, 1642 (above), and Jacob van Ruisdael's *Mill at Wijk-bij-Duurstede*, 1670 (below right).

The hallowed halls of Vincent Willem Van Gogh

AMSTERDAM honors its Master of Expressionism

ADDRESS:
Paulus Potter Straat 7,
Amsterdam

OPENING TIMES:
Mon-Sun 10 am
to 6 pm
Fri until 10 pm

INTERNET:
www.vangogh-
museum.nl

PUBLIC TRANSPORT:
Tram, Lines 2, 3, 5, 12 to
Museumsplein

OTHER ATTRACTIONS:
National Museum of
Modern Art (Stedelijk
Museum)

Van Gogh painted this self-portrait (left) in 1888.

The artist painted several versions of *Sunflowers* (below left).

The Sower is just one of the many paintings in which Van Gogh depicted life on the land. It was painted in 1888 (below right).

The Museum building, completed in 1973, is reminiscent of Bauhaus architecture (center right).

Vincent Willem Van Gogh was prolific. In his short life, he was active as a painter, he produced 2,200 works, equating to roughly 220 works per year. He had an obsessive personality, which manifested itself in both his work and his personal life, right from the outset.

Born the son of a minister in 1853, Van Gogh left school at 15 and then worked for an international art house that also employed his younger brother, Theo. He embarked on a theology course before finally abandoning his studies. He went to the Belgian coal-mining district of Borinage and worked as a teacher, preacher and nurse. In 1881, he studied for a short time at the Academy of Art in Brussels and then traveled to The Hague to visit a cousin, a landscape painter, who taught him the basics of water-color technique and oil painting. Nevertheless, Van Gogh remained largely self-taught.

He lived in Paris with his brother Theo, now an art dealer. Theo supported him financially and fostered his innate creativity. His early works, painted in dark, earthy tones, illustrate Dutch landscapes or depict the life of miners and farmers. The style and manner is reminiscent of Jean-François Millet.

Meeting with Gauguin

During a stay in Paris, Van Gogh was introduced to the Impressionists and Pointillists and, under their influence, lightened his color palette. He also made the acquaintance of Paul Gauguin, who followed him to southern France. Here in Arles, Provence, Van Gogh finally discovered the style that was to make him famous.

Life with Gauguin became complicated. After an argument, Van Gogh mutilated himself by cutting off part of an ear with a cutthroat razor. He underwent psychiatric treatment, was discharged as cured, continued painting, suffered a relapse and once again returned to Auvers-sur-Oise, near Paris, to receive treatment from the psychiatrist, Paul Gachet. His bouts of depression communicated themselves in his art. In 1890, he committed suicide.

Largely ignored during his lifetime, he was soon to become a great source of esthetic inspiration, both for the Fauvists and German Expressionists. His paintings sold for high prices: many big art museums bought them, and nowadays, at auctions, his works are among the most expensive. His homeland, the Netherlands, discovered in him someone whose global fame was as mighty as that of any of the great masters from the Golden Age. It made sense therefore to devote a museum solely to Van Gogh.

A great inspiration

It opened in Amsterdam in 1973. The main building was based on a design by Gerrit Rietveld, an architect and designer associated with De Stijl, the group of Dutch artists whose aesthetic was that of strict Constructivism, also embraced by Piet Mondrian.

In 1999, the Rietveld building was extended by a new exhibition wing, designed by Kisho Kurokawa, one of Japan's most internationally renowned architects, equally acclaimed in Asia, Europe and the United States. His architecture attempts to combine elements of traditional Japanese art with the style of Western Avant-garde.

The Vincent Van Gogh Museum is one of the most visited attractions in Amsterdam. The collection is considerable, comprising 200 paintings, 500 drawings and 700 letters covering all of Van Gogh's creative periods, in addition to numerous self-portraits. Van Gogh's personal collection of Japanese woodcuts can also be found here. Previously, much was owned by the family of Theo Van Gogh, but at the instigation of the Dutch state, his descendants set up a foundation to protect the paintings, which are on permanent loan to the Museum.

In the meantime, there are countless institutional sponsors and donors who not only finance the purchase of new works by Van Gogh, but also works by the artist's friends and contemporaries: Jean-François Millet, Paul Gauguin, Léon Lhermitte, Kees van Dongen and Claude Monet, among others.

Loan exhibitions are organized, but the Museum's main purpose remains the conservation and display of Vincent Van Gogh's works. At present, they are once again housed in the main building. The large entrance hall exhibits an installation on the life, work and significance of this exceptional artist; the display itself is organized chronologically, making it easy to follow the general development from the realistic, sociocritical style – of which the *Potato Eaters* of 1885 was a particularly famous example – to the final, feverishly expressive paintings he made when mentally ill.

Iris, from the fruitful years in Arles, is on display; the *Yellow House*, where Van Gogh lived with Gauguin, hangs here, as does what was probably his last painting, *Wheatfield with Crows*, without which it would be difficult to imagine artists such as Emil Nolde and Oskar Kokoschka.

The Royal Cabinet

The **MAURITSHUIS** in **THE HAGUE**, Holland, houses the second biggest collection of artists from the Golden Age

North Sea

The Hague • Amsterdam

THE NETHERLANDS

ADDRESS:
Korte Vijverberg 8,
The Hague

OPENING TIMES:
Tues.-Sat. 10 a.m.
to 5 p.m.
Sun. 11 a.m. to 5 p.m.

INTERNET:
www.mauritshuis.nl

PUBLIC TRANSPORT:
Tram, Binnenhof stop

OTHER ATTRACTIONS:
Gemeentemuseum,
The Hague

The story of the Netherlands' rulers is somewhat complicated.

The house of Orange, which governs today, originated in Germany, from the town of Nassau in Hesse. It got its name from the town of Orange, in southern France, which Count William of Nassau-Dillenburg inherited in 1544. This same aristocrat, together with Count Egmont, threw himself into the 80-year war of independence, or Dutch Revolt, which the Spanish-controlled Netherlands conducted against its colonial ruler. The seven northern provinces were victorious. Forming the Republic of United Provinces of Northern Netherlands, they elevated William of Orange to the status of governor. After a period spent under Napoleonic rule, the Oranges were appointed to the role they had had before – kings – at the Congress of Vienna in 1815.

Johan Maurits was the royal Prince of Nassau-Siegen. He endeared himself to his Dutch relations as the savior of Calvinism in his territory, and entered their service. Initially a field marshal, he was then appointed Governor-General of the Dutch colonial territories in Latin America, in what is now northeastern Brazil, with the capital at Recife. Johan Maurits encouraged scientific and artistic documentation about the land and people which is of extraordinary cultural and historical significance today.

He had a house built in the Hague in preparation for his return from the New World. The architects were Jacob van Campen and Pieter Post; their style was known as Dutch Classicism, an aesthetic that looked to the Renaissance architecture of Palladio and early French Baroque. The Hague was the seat of government in the Net-

herlands. In 1822, the Royal Cabinet of Paintings moved into Johan Maurits's palace.

A total of 400 works

Today, this is the second biggest national art gallery after the Rijksmuseum, and it pursues a similar objective: first and foremost, to exhibit important artists from the Golden Age. The aim is not unrestrained expansion, impossible for reasons of space alone, but special exhibitions take place regularly. They attract international attention and are devoted to subjects whose connection to the museum's own collections is sometimes tenuous at best. European exhibition organizers' favorite occupation at present is showing cross-sections of cultural history, drawing out parallel motifs or simply illustrating unusual subjects. Amongst its 400 pieces, the Mauritshuis possesses some masterpieces of Dutch art

that are not restricted to the art of the Golden Age, but also show the before and after. Overall, the collection can be broken down into five themed categories: histories, portraits, landscapes, still lifes and genre paintings.

Biblical idylls

The Mauritshaus has something special to offer in each of these sections. The historical paintings, for example, are not historical representations in the academic sense, but rather biblical or ancient mythological themes, whereby the Bible was used less for its religious message than for its narrative value. The *Garden of Eden at the Fall* is an idyll with two unashamedly naked bodies, a wealth of animals, and greenery. The artists are Jan Breughel, from the famous dynasty of painters, and Peter Paul Rubens.

Both were Flemish. The relationship between Flanders, now in Belgium, and the Netherlands was as close as it was conflict ridden. They spoke a common language, but clashed over differing religious beliefs. Belgium's freedom from the kingdom of the Netherlands came about as a result of a popular uprising in 1830. There have always been, close cultural ties, between Dutch and Fle-

mish. The great Dutch Baroque paintings came into the inheritance of the great Flemish painters during the Renaissance, a fact confirmed by works in the Mauritshuis. Among the landscape artists whose work hang in the Hague are Jan van Goyen and Willem van der Velde, the creator of dramatic seascapes, and above all, Johannes Vermeer, who painted a famous view of his home town, Delft. Vermeer also painted what is perhaps the most famous painting in the museum, *Girl with a Pearl Earring*. The depiction of a young girl, smiling half shyly, half flirtatiously, out of the picture, the subject of a novel and a movie, is an icon in European art. The Mauritshuis promptly adopted it as its logo. The picture is as famous as *The Anatomy Lesson of Dr Nicolaes Tulp*.

This other group painting, by Rembrandt, which is as famous as *Night Watch*, shows a male corpse being dissected by a Dutch anatomist. What was still a forbidden practice at the time of Leonardo da Vinci, on whom Rembrandt based his chiaroscuro painting technique, became an accepted medical practice one hundred years later, worthy of demonstration, just as Rembrandt painted it.

Two world-famous works in the collection: *The Fall: Adam and Eve in Paradise*, painted jointly by Jan Breughel the Elder and Peter Paul Rubens (above left), and Johannes Vermeer's *Girl with a Pearl Earring*, from 1665 (above right).

A museum since 1822: the splendid Mauritshuis in The Hague (below).

Modern and Old Masters

The **BOIJMANS VAN BEUNINGEN MUSEUM** in **ROTTERDAM** holds 120,000 objets d'art

North Sea
THE NETHERLANDS
● Amsterdam
○ Rotterdam

ADDRESS:
Museumpark 18-20,
Rotterdam

OPENING TIMES:
Tues.-Sun. 11 am to 6 pm

INTERNET:
www.boijmans.
rotterdam.nl

PUBLIC TRANSPORT:
Subway, tram or bus to
Eendrachtsplein stop

OTHER ATTRACTIONS:
Kunsthal Museum,
Museum of Architecture

Alfred Sisley's *Orchard in Spring* (1881) is an example of the Pointillist variation on Impressionism (below left).

Pop-Art cult artist Claes Oldenburg created the *Soft Washstand* installation (below center).

Rotterdam, the second biggest city in the Netherlands, lies on the Nieuwe Maas, a branch of the Rhine delta. Its port is the biggest in the world: around 200,000 inland and oceangoing ships load and unload there every year. Rotterdam is famous for transfer and processing of crude oil. The gigantic site along the Nieuwe Maas is divided into several port sections, where 300,000 people, almost half the city's population, work.

It was this extraordinary economic potential that lead Adolf Hitler's Germany to launch a major offensive against Rotterdam in May 1940. Large parts of the city center and port were devastated. Together with the Basque town of Guernica and Coventry in Great Britain, the city of Rotterdam and its civilian population fell victim to carpet bombing.

Experimental arena for architecture

Burnt-out Rotterdam was rebuilt. A couple historic buildings remained undamaged, such as the Witte Huis (White House), but most had to be rebuilt. The city, backed by its considerable wealth, mainly derived from the port business, was eager to avoid building haphazardly and heedlessly. It called on the services of reputable architects, creating a community that can be regarded as an experimental arena for contemporary architecture.

Modern architecture tends to be cold. The center of Rotterdam suggests generosity and functionality combined with subtle sterility and aesthetic redundancy, but the ambition and creativity that made the reconstruction possible and continues to promote it is far from exhausted. Rotterdam, the Cultural Capital of Europe in 2001, is visibly concerned with modern architecture and contains museums that deal with architecture and the history of architecture. The oldest museum is named after its most important contributors, Boijmans and Van Beuningen.

Gift of 1841

The roots of the Boijmans Van Beuningen Museum lie in the art collection left to the city in 1841 by the wealthy Rotterdam lawyer, Frans Jacob Otto Boijmans. It was housed in the historic Schielandhuis, but much was lost in a fire of 1864. The lost items were replaced by acquisitions and private donations. In 1935, the collection moved to a new building constructed by Rotterdam architect Van der Steuer.

The collection increased greatly in 1958 as a result of a donation by industrialist Daniel George Van Beuningen. He came from a highly regarded family of entrepreneurs and became wealthy at an early age as a result of his commercial and shipbuilding activities. He expressed his interest in art by his purchases of individual pieces; he also acquired foreign collections and thus created a comprehensive collection with some important works by masters such as Rembrandt and Rubens, Jan van Eyck and Pieter Breughel the Elder. He acquired one of the latter's most important works, *The Little Tower of Babel*. Van Beuningen died in 1955. Three years later, his art collection moved to the Boijmans Museum, known since as the Boijmans Van Beuningen Museum.

The Van der Steur building was in urgent need of expansion, attaining its current form in 2003. The architects were Belgians Paul Robbrecht and Hilde Daem. The extension not only created additional exhibition space, but also resulted in an impressive sculpture garden. The new wing of the building, with its almost 407 foot glass facade, mainly exhibits contemporary art.

Source of Surrealism

The international fame of the Museum, with its 120,000 exhibits, relies predominantly on classical and very modern art. There is a small but fine selection of works by Paul Cézanne, Claude Monet and Eduard Munch. The Surrealists are heavily represented by

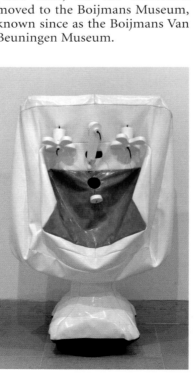

René Magritte, Max Ernst, Man Ray and Salvador Dalí. The Museum possesses paintings and drawings by Dalí as well as the *Dalí News*, the newspaper produced by the artist on his own account. (He was a money-grubber, earning himself the nickname, Avida Dollars.)

Works by Hieronymus Bosch and Breughel the Elder reveal in whose footsteps the Surrealists followed. Magritte's works in the collection emphasize Dutch and Flemish participation in the Surrealist movement.

Modern art otherwise placed more emphasis on figurative experiment and abstraction, exhibiting the work of Vassily Kandinsky and Karel Appel. German Neo-Expressionists are represented by Georg Baselitz and Salomé. Alongside the classic Surrealist, Marcel Duchamp, one finds the prominent installation artists, Joseph Beuys and Bruce Nauman; other modern Americans include George Segal, Donald Judd, Richard Serra, Andy Warhol and Claes Oldenburg.

The Museum has achieved some fame with its special exhibitions. It possesses a beautiful collection of modern designs and art books, shows films and organizes programs for children.

The Little Tower of Babel, a masterpiece by Pieter Breughel the Elder, was created between 1563 and 1568 (above).

View of the Museum building where the Boijmans Van Beuningen collection can be seen (left).

Munch's fear of life

OSLO dedicated an entire museum to the work of EDVARD MUNCH

ADDRESS:
Tøyengata 53, Oslo

OPENING HOURS:
June to August:
Daily 10 am to 6 pm,
September to May:
Tues.-Fri. 10 am
to 4 pm,
Sat. and Sun. 11 am
5 pm

INTERNET:
www.munch.
museum.no

PUBLIC TRANSPORT:
All subway lines
running east from the
center, stop Tøyen.
Bus 20 and 60 to
Munch Museum.

OTHER ATTRACTIONS:
Vigeland Sculpture
Garden in the
Frognerpark, National
Museum

Norway's greatest painter has exhibited his life's work here: the Munch Museum in Oslo.

From time to time, he distanced himself from his homeland, yet throughout his life, Edvard Munch (1863–1944) used Norway as his retreat. He spent the last twenty-eight years of his life in a manor house on the outskirts of Oslo, where he drew up the will that led to the foundation of the Munch Museum. He bequeathed to the city of Oslo, without any reservations, his entire estate consisting of around 1,100 paintings, 4,500 drawings and watercolors, 18,000 graphic works and 6 sculptures. In addition, there were stones and plates for lithographs, woodcuts and etchings as well as an extensive collection of notes, books, photographs and other documents. Later, as a gift from his sister, more paintings and drawings as well as Munch's extensive correspondence were added. The bequest is thought to be the biggest collection ever bequeathed by an artist to his hometown.

Love, loneliness and death

"My paintings are not to be sold, but major sketches and studies that need a museum," he once wrote in a letter that, together with the bequest, made it clear that Munch wanted a museum of his own, even though he never expressly requested it. In 1946, two years after his death, the Oslo city authorities decided to build a Munch museum. However, it was another seventeen years before it was ready to open, on 29 May 1963, one hundred years after the artist's birth.

Munch's biography provides once and for all the explanation for his painful examination of loneliness, love and death. Edvard Munch was born in Loten on 12 December 1863, the second child of Dr. Christian Munch and his wife, Laura Cathrine. But barely five years after his birth, Munch's mother died. His favorite sister, his brother and his father also died young. He himself suffered from illness all his life and worked all these experiences into his paintings, in *The Sick Child and The Dead Mother*, for instance. "Fear has accompanied me, ever since I have been able to think," he once said. And elsewhere he gave reasons for his choice of subject matter: "I paint not what I see but what I have seen."

His decision to become a painter was made early in life. In 1880, he enrolled in an art school, but soon left. In the city now known as Oslo and later in Paris, he socialized with avant-garde artistic circles and lived a life of excess, by turns in Norway, Paris, Nice and Berlin. He developed a "private" set of symbols, provoking frequent scandals. With his paintings in flaming red, strident green, hazy blue and deep black, he created a style that made him one of the most important precursors of Expressionism. After a nervous breakdown in 1909, he returned to Norway as an internationally recognized artist and eight years later, settled on the estate of Ekeby, where he died unmarried in 1944. The last self portraits, showing him approaching death with a face marked by defiance and loneliness, hang in the Museum.

The intention behind the series of pictures to which he gave the title, *Frieze of Life*, was to paint the people who figured in the various sections of his life. Many of the paintings can be found in the Museum and have titles like *Dance of Life, Death and the Maiden, The Scream* and *The Kiss*. The painting, *At Roulette*, portrays the artist's experiences in the casino while the theme of *Vampire* is the relationship between man and woman, which he felt was painfully complicated. A man is entwined in the red hair of a woman as if by the arms of an octopus, a helpless victim of her embrace.

Glimpse into the abyss

The theme of love is recurrent, even in the painting of the *Madonna*, which shows a naked woman with a red halo. However, pictures painted by Munch in Åsgårdsstrand, his holiday destination for many years, show us another side of him. *Two Girls with Blue Aprons, Boys Bathing* and the picture *Girl on the Bridge* convey both joie de vivre and irony.

Munch's relationship with his fiancée, Tulla Larsen, is recalled by *The Death of Marat*, which he painted in 1907. Depicting the aftermath of a quarrel, during which Munch inadvertently shot himself in the finger, he portrayed himself as the bleeding Marat and his beloved as a silent, white woman. The self portrait, *Nocturnal Wanderer*, is also a glimpse into the abyss of his soul.

Munch painted several versions of many of his pictures, the pain-

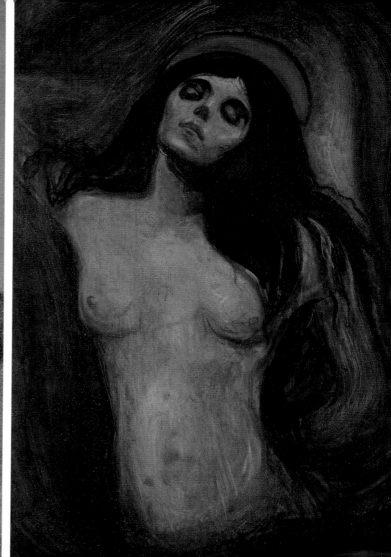

ting, *Puberty*, for instance. Later he also produced woodcuts, lithographs and etchings of important themes. The Munch Museum has an extensive collection of his graphic art, which reveals his outstanding talent in this area.

The Museum was designed by the architects, Gunnar Fougner and Einar Myklebust, winners of a competition between 50 architects. They were inspired by Henry van de Velde and made the building fit harmoniously into the difficult terrain of Oslo's Tøyen district. The Museum – a skeleton construction of concrete and steel, its visible surfaces clad with artificial stone slabs – has 12,400 square feet of exhibition space on a single floor. From the start, the intention was that it should be arranged so that all the interest would be focused on the pictures. As the building quickly proved to be too small, an extension was added that today houses the graphics department and the library, among other things.

The Tøyen district was not randomly chosen as the site for the Munch Museum. It was the southern part of the city, the home of workers and soldiers that fascinated Munch. After all, he wanted "to paint living people, who breathe and feel and suffer and love."

Four of Munch's major works show how the artist fluctuated between fear and joy: *The Scream*, 1893, *Young Girl on the Shore*, 1896, *Madonna* (1893-1894) (above, left to right) and *Two Girls with Blue Aprons*, 1904-1905 (below).

From Dürer to Leonardo, Rembrandt to Holbein

The **VIENNA ALBERTINA** has the biggest collection of prints in the world - the museum itself is a work of art

ADDRESS:
Albertinaplatz 1,
Vienna

OPENING TIMES:
Do. - Di. 10 - 18 Uhr,
Thurs.-Tues. 10 am
to 6 pm,
Wed. 10 am to 9 pm

INTERNET:
www.albertina.at

PUBLIC TRANSPORT:
Subway, Lines U1, U2,
U3, U4; Tram, Ring road
routes 1, 2, D, J;
Citybus, Route 2a

OTHER ATTRACTIONS:
Modern artists' quarter
Kunsthistorisches
Museum

Prince Albert Casimir of the house of Wettin was born in 1738, son of Augustus III, the Elector of Saxony and King of Poland. In 1766, he married Austrian Archduchess Marie Christine, favorite daughter of Empress Maria Theresa. Apart from the principality of Teschen, previously part of the Austrian Empire and now Cieszyn in Poland, he also received an extraordinary dowry in cash. Successively, he was Governor of Hungary, Governor General of the Austrian Netherlands and finally Imperial Field Marshal. From 1795, he lived in Vienna.

He moved into the Tarouca Palace on the Augustinerbastei, which he renovated and extended. Parts of the abandoned Augustinian abbey were also integrated into the palace.

He is mainly famous for building up a comprehensive collection of graphic art, whose origins date back to 1776. Albrecht and his wife were staying in Venice and acquired a thousand works of art from the Genoese diplomat, Giacomo, Count Durazzo. The *Discorso Preliminare* that accompanied them was equal parts deed of establishment, classification system and declaration of intent. The collection was intended to promote education and morality, not image and enjoyment, an idea which was very progressive at the time.

For education and morality

Albrecht continually expanded his art collection. His various political roles gave him the opportunity and money he acquired through marriage gave him the necessary purchasing power. The acquisition of 800 drawings owned by the princes of Ligne was significant, as was exchanging some prints for drawings from the imperial court library collection. This is how the collection of works by Albrecht Dürer, assembled by Habsburg Emperor Rudolph II, came into his possession. Today, it comprises 139 watercolors and drawings and is thus the biggest private collection of Dürer graphics in the world.

A couple of years before his death, Albert willed his collection to be entailed, meaning that it could no longer be sold. Albert's descendents concerned themselves only with maintaining and increasing the collection, which continued to be housed in the rooms on the Augustinerbastei.

After the monarchy collapsed, everything passed into the ownership of the republic which merged the collection of drawings with those from the court library copper engraving gallery in 1920: a good 500,000 folios, including the once famous collection belonging to Prince Eugene of Savoy.

The collection now comprises more than 70,000 drawings and watercolors in addition to more than 1,000,000 prints. They date from all the important periods of art between late Gothic and modern. Apart from Dürer, there are folios by Leonardo, Raphael, Michelangelo, the elder Holbein, Rembrandt, Van Dyck and many more.

Resplendent state rooms

The Albertina regularly organizes major temporary exhibitions, which attract enormous public interest, almost overwhelming in the case of the major Dürer exhibition at the end of 2003, when the renovated rooms in the Albertina were reopened.

The palace suffered damage in the last days of the Second World War as a result of Allied bombing, which also affected the nearby state opera building. It is only now that the state rooms over the Augustinerbastei can be seen in their full splendor – the name "Albertina" not only stands for a great art collection, it also stands for a building of architectural importance.

Built on the Roman remains, the walls stand on the last remaining vestige of the city fortifications which the Emperor ordered demolished in 1857. In 1745, court architect Emanuel Teles, Count Sylva-Tarouca, asked permission of Empress Maria Theresa to convert the royal planning department, housed on the fortification dating from the second half of the 17th century, into a palace for himself. In this form it came into the possession of Prince Albert. The additions and renovations by Vienna's greatest post-Baroque master builder, Josef Kornhäusl, turned it into an important Classical building in the Vienna Old Town, otherwise primarily characterized by Baroque architecture.

Today, the Albertina comprises 215,000 square feet. There are several large exhibition halls, historic state rooms with sculptural adornments and the museum facilities necessary for researching and conserving the collections. The complex unites four distinct architectural styles – the Baroque Tarouca Palace, the Classical additions, the Augustinian abbey, dating from the late Middle Ages, and the underground extensions.

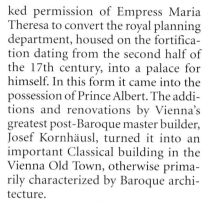

Egon Schiele's *Semi-nude Girl Reclining*, 1911, is one of the Austrian artist's most famous works (left).

The Albertina graphics collection specializes in works from the late Middle Ages and the early Renaissance. Among the highlights are Michelangelo's pietà study, *Mary with the Dead Christ*, 1530 to 1540 (below left), Dürer's *Young Hare*, 1502 (above center), and Leonardo's *Saint Peter*, 1495 (below center).

An important Classical building: the Albertina on the ancient Augustinerbastei (below right).

Habsburg collection

The KUNSTHISTORISCHES MUSEUM in VIENNA is graced with a large collection of Brueghels,

ADDRESS:
Maria Theresien-Platz, Vienna

OPENING HOURS:
Tues–Sun 10 am to 6 pm
Thurs. 10 am to 9 pm

INTERNET:
www.khm.at

TRANSPORT:
Subway, Lines U2 and U3.
Tram, Lines D and J

The collection contains works dated before 1800: Pieter Brueghel the Younger painted the calendar scene, *Winter Landscape*, in 1601 (above right); Lucas Cranach the Elder's *Man of Sorrows* dates from 1515 (above left); J.L. David's painting, *Napoleon at the Great St. Bernhard*, is one of the last works bought by Emperor Franz Joseph I (below left).

In the high Middle Ages, calendar paintings, based on an ancient tradition reaching back into antiquity, represented a way for artists to address secular themes. At first, they came only in the form of miniatures in books. The Duc du Berry's *Book of Hours* is world famous. Pieter Brueghel the Elder produced several large-format paintings on this theme between 1565 and 1566. He divided the calendar year into six sections, one panel for each, and depicted people at their seasonal activities. A particular color scheme dominates each panel, symbolizing a particular activity: green for hay-making, yellow for the corn harvest and snow white for winter. The autumn painting, depicting cows returning home in the evening, is dominated by ochre. The cattle, painted in various colors, seem tempted to break away and graze, but are prevented by a youth with a long, wooden stick. A man on a white horse, evidently the herdsman, rides behind the herd, accompanied by a second youth. The sky is gloomy. The landscape is composed of steep rocks rising above a river valley. The herd has probably spent the summer in an Alpine pasture, which does not exist in the landscape of Dutch polders. But Pieter Brueghel was well-travelled and knew Italy, Switzerland, Austria and France and the customs of their people. The clothing of the three figures suggests mountain folk. Brueghel thus departs from

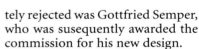

his usual portrayals of Flemish people, as is the case with *The Huntsmen in the Snow* and his panel depicting early spring. Three of the panels hang in the Kunsthistorisches Museum in Vienna. They were originally produced as part of a continuing frieze of pictures, but Brueghel's works very soon became desirable collectors' pieces, so the frieze was taken apart. One of the panels was lost and the two remaining panels are housed in Prague and New York City.

Semper designed the building

The Vienna calendar paintings are part of a total of 12 Brueghel paintings owned by the Museum. They were originally part of the Habsburg art collection, but in 1860, Hapsburg Emperor Franz Joseph I, trailing behind the monarchs of other nations, decided to allow his subjects to view the paintings. Four Viennese architects were commissioned to design an art museum. The site for the expansion of the city, following the demolition of the old city walls, was designated by Franz Joseph. The four architects were chosen because each had designed admirable buildings for the imperial capital. However, the proposals of all four were rejected by the jury. The only one of the four whose ideas were not comple-

tely rejected was Gottfried Semper, who was susequently awarded the commission for his new design.

Originally from Germany, Semper had designed the opera house in Dresden. He had also been involved in the 1848 Revolution, together with his friend, Richard Wagner. Like Wagner, he was forced to flee. He spent 16 years as a professor in Zürich. When the Emperor summoned him to Vienna in 1871, he was almost 70 and had clearly distanced himself from his youthful revolutionary impulses.

Semper was a virtuoso master of Post-Classical building in the style known as Historicism, though he preferred the Italian Renaissance. The Kunsthistorisches Museum is decorated in the manner of a building from the time of Filippo Brunelleschi. The dome originated from an idea by architect Carl von Hasenauer whose original plan had been rejected by Franz Joseph. At any rate, Semper appropriated

aspects of Hasenauer's plans and collaborated with their creator. The other buildings by Semper in the city were also the result of such collaboration.

Painted ceilings in the Museum

All did not go as smoothly as planned. Hasenauer and Semper did not particularly like one another and frequently argued. In 1877, Semper left Vienna. Two years later, he was dead and Hasenauer completed the project. The Kunsthistorisches Museum formally opened in 1891.

It is a prestigious building: massive, sumptuous and somewhat gloomy. It can be seen from the Hofburg, on the other side of the ring road, and is separated by a small square from the Naturhistorisches (Natural History) Museum, which is the same size and of a similar design by the same architect. The magnificent decoration is continued inside, with carvings

and painted ceilings by Hans Makart, Gustav Klimt and other artists.

The art displayed represents a variety of movements and epoques. The most recent work dates from the year 1800. Dutch art is shown side by side with Italian, German, French and Spanish painting from several centuries. Albrecht Dürer, Hieronymus Bosch and Giuseppe Arcimboldo are represented alongside Brueghel the Elder. Many of the works can be credited to a particularly artistic and acquisitive member of the house of Habsburg, Renaissance ruler Rudolf II.

Exchange exhibitions take place regularly, on extremely varied themes, including Goldsmiths' Work from Ancient Persia and Prague Mannerism. The Museum is also responsible for collections of Egyptian and Classical antiquities, the Hofburg treasure chamber, the Lipizzaner-Museum and the objets d'art from the palaces of Schönbrunn and Ambras near Innsbruck.

Gottfried Semper conceived the Vienna Kunsthistorisches Museum in the style known as Historicism (below).

Cracow's glory

Poland's most famous **ART MUSEUM** is located in the former royal castle on the Wawel

Baltic Sea

Warsaw
POLAND
Cracow

ADRESSE:
Wawel 5, Cracow

OPENING HOURS:
The Wawel Hill:
April to September
daily 6 am to 8 pm,
October to March 6 am
to 5 pm
The Museum:
daily 9:30 am to 3 pm
The individual
exhibitions have
different and constantly
changing opening hours

INTERNET:
www.wawel.krakow.pl

PUBLIC TRANSPORT:
Tram, bus, electromobile,
horse-drawn cab

OTHER ATTRACTIONS:
Historical Museum,
Jagiellon Library

View of the former royal palace on the Wawel, in which the Art Museum is currently located (below left).

Cracow, Kraków in Polish, is one of the most beautiful cities in Europe. Sadly, its charm and beauty are not widely appreciated. At any rate, the city can easily stand comparison with Prague and Avignon. It has a similarly long history and the same wealth of historical buildings.

From the 11th to the end of the 16th century, it was the capital of Poland, at a time when the country was a major European power and attracted craftsmen, merchants and artists from many parts of the continent. Warsaw later took over the function of capital city. Until recently, Cracow Cathedral remained the burial place of Polish rulers. The country itself was responsible for its political decline, ending in partition. Disunity and intrigues among the Polish elite more or less invited the neighboring states to interfere in Poland's domestic affairs.

Conversion to a museum

Cracow and southern Poland came under Austrian rule for 150 years. Unlike the regimes of Russia and Prussia (or Germany), it was relatively mild.

When Poland once again became an autonomous state, Cracow engaged in a bitter cultural battle with Warsaw. During the German occupation after 1939, one of Hitler's most bloodthirsty officials, Hans Frank, ruled the city. The notorious Nazi extermination camp of Auschwitz lies just outside the city. Cardinal Wojtyla held the post of archbishop of Cracow before he became Pope John Paul II.

Cracow has a castle complex, the Wawel, built on a rock on the bank of the Vistula. Important monuments and art treasures are gathered there and, with almost

two million visitors a year, it is by far the most popular museum in Poland.

The complex began as a Romanesque castle. Excavations have uncovered the remains of various buildings dating from before the year 1000. A chapel, the Adauctus Rotunda, which had been completely integrated into the palace, has survived from that period. During the 14th century, it was extended into a Gothic fortress, which later became a splendid Renaissance castle. As with other magnificent European buildings, some of the architects came from Italy. Their names were Francesco Fiorentino and Bartolomeo Berecci. Great devastation was caused by fires – particularly in the north wing, which was rebuilt in the Baroque style, again designed by an Italian, Giovanni Trevano.

The result is an imposing castle complex enclosing an inner courtyard between four wings of unequal lengths. It is in the shape of an irregular pentagon and edged by arcaded walks. Four towers of different heights and shapes are built into it.

At the time when the castle was used as a royal residence, it was arranged in such a way that the workrooms and storerooms were on the first floor, the second floor housed the royal chambers and the state rooms were on the third floor. However, now that the palace is used as a museum and has been converted for the purpose, all this can only be imagined.

Painted state rooms

There are three different exhibitions on view. The first presents the crown jewels and the armory. There are four rooms containing the royal insignia and other objects of national significance, including the coronation sword dating from around 1280 and an 11th century silver chalice as well as jeweled weapons and miniatures. The five rooms of the armory house military equipment from several centuries.

The most important exhibition covers the royal chambers and leads through all three floors. There is the Senators' Hall, designed by Giovanni Trevano, and the six prestigious state rooms, known as the Tournament Hall, Military Parade Hall, Ambassadors' Hall, the Zodiac, the Planets and the Battle of Orscha. They take their names from the friezes on their

walls, series of paintings beneath richly decorated coffered ceilings. The painters were German and included the Nuremberg artist, Hans Dürer, brother of the celebrated Albrecht Dürer.

The most renowned of the state rooms is the Ambassadors' Hall, because of the wood carvings on the coffered ceiling: 30 heads out of an original 194 remain. The carvings are an artistic rarity, known as the Wawel heads. The Senators' Hall was used for balls and opera performances and has an orchestra gallery. The Brussels tapestries hanging here are remarkable and very valuable.

The furniture is also valuable. Old Polish chests and Baroque furniture from Gdansk are on show. Among the paintings displayed are

E ABVLAT CV DEO CVI DEVS FVTVRV APERIT
VVIV ARCAMO? SERVATRICEM FACERE IVBET·GEN·VI·

God speaking to Noah is the title of the tapestry that hangs in the former Senators' Hall of the castle. The tapestry, made of wool and silk, is Brussels work from around 1550 (above).

The coronation sword of the kings of Poland dates from the 13th century. It is the showpiece of the collection (below right).

The picture of the angel by Simone Martini comes from the late Gothic period and was painted between 1300 and 1344. Italian artists played an important role at the Polish royal court (below left).

examples of great Western European art, such as paintings by Giorgio Vasari and Peter Paul Rubens.

The third exhibition is concerned with Oriental art. It shows an exceptionally large collection of Ottoman and Persian weapons, Middle Eastern textiles, carpets and objets d'art. Most of these items have come down from King Jan III Sobieski, who, with his army, came to help the Habsburg Emperor Leopold I deliver Vienna from the Turkish siege in 1683. Jan Sobieski won the battle of Kahlenberg. The Grand Vizier Kara Mustafa was forced to leave his treasures behind when he fled and the majority of them were allotted to Jan Sobieski.

Where Poles celebrate art

The most significant works of Polish art can be seen in **WARSAW'S NARODOWE MUSEUM**

Baltic Sea

Warsaw

POLAND

ADDRESS:
Aleje Jerozolimskie 3,
Warsaw

OPENING TIMES:
Tues-Sun 10 am
to 4 pm
Thurs to 6 pm

INTERNET:
www.mnw.art.pl

PUBLIC TRANSPORT:
Tram, Narodowe
Museum stop

OTHER ATTRACTIONS:
Archeological Museum,
History Museum,
Museum of the
Collections of Jean Paul
II, Wilanów, Old Town
Market, Royal Castle

Bernardo Bellotto was born in Venice and came from a renowned clan of painters famous for their depictions of cities. He took the nickname, Canaletto, from his uncle and, like the latter, he first painted his hometown. Among other places, he later lived and worked in Dresden and Warsaw, where he died. He painted views of Dresden, which aided in the restoration of the historic Old Town that lay in ruins after 1945. Canaletto's views of the city were also helpful when Warsaw, destroyed during the Second World War as well, started reconstruction. Poland has dedicated a special memorial to this artist, who was the court painter to the last elected king before Partition.

His paintings hang in the Narodowe Museum, Poland's national museum. It is located in the heart of old Warsaw, in the Aleje Jerozolimskie. The building does not appear in any of Canaletto's views, however, because it was not built until between 1926 and 1938, according to plans by functionalist architect Tadeusz Tolwiński.

During the Partition era, Warsaw, along with central and eastern

Poland, was subject to the Russian tsars and cultural activities were intended to strengthen national identity. From 1862, the Museum of Fine Art housed 200 paintings, the core of the collection, which merchant Pietro Fiorentini willed to the Warsaw School of Fine Arts. The collection grew, primarily through private donations. It was only in 1922, after Poland's autonomy as a state had been restored, that the public were allowed entry. Both collection and building sustained considerable damage in the destruction of Warsaw ordered by Hitler.

From the Renaissance and Baroque

The damage has long since been repaired and the collection has had new acquisitions added to it. The Museum has the astounding figure of 780,000 items at its disposal: paintings, sculptures, drawings, artifacts and coins. There is an Ancient Egyptian department as well as a section with finds from Mesopotamia, much of which was previously in the possession of the aristocratic Czartoryski family. The-

re is a rich collection of Ancient Greek artifacts. Many pieces of medieval art originate from churches in Gdansk and Lower Silesia. European paintings from the Renaissance and Baroque periods – including pieces by Leonardo da Vinci, Rembrandt, Jordaens and Lucas Cranach the Elder – mostly originated in the private collection of another noble family, the Potocki.

The foreign masterpieces may be more valuable and more highly regarded internationally than the examples of Polish art that are the institution's special pride and which attract particular attention from its domestic public. Out of a total of 7,000 Polish paintings, 400 are exhibited in nine large rooms.

The first focal point is the 19th century, during which Poland was dominated politically the three partitioning powers. The desire for national autonomy expressed itself in revolutionary uprisings and passive resistance. Art was the means by which artists spoke for the people. Nationalist Romanticism dominated: a passionate art, based on Géricault and Delacroix, with his-

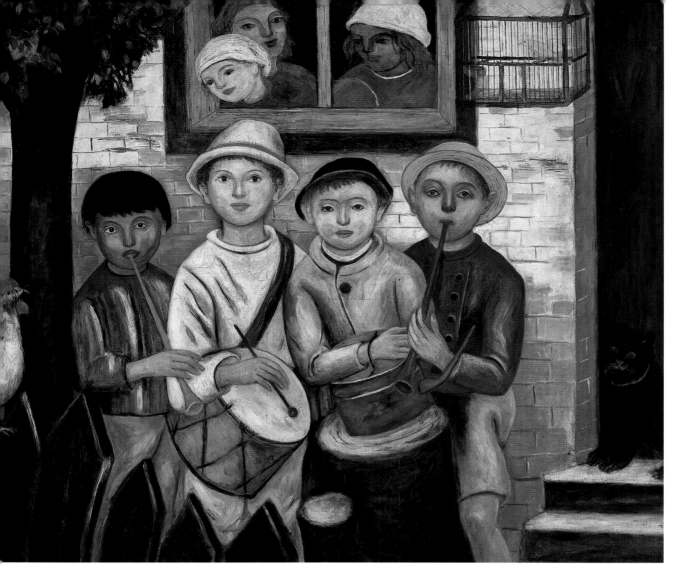

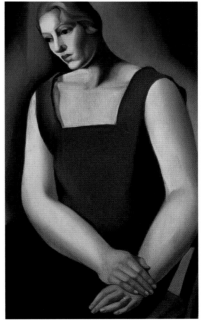

torical and patriotic themes, of which the best known representative is Jan Mateyko.

Of Mateyko's paintings, the Warsaw National Museum shows *The Battle of Grunwald*, depicting the military victory of the Polish army over the Knights of the Teutonic Order in 1410. *Chopin's Polonaise – a Ball in Hotel Lambert in Paris* by Teofil Kwiatkowski (1809 –91) is a paean to the cultural might of the Polish nation, deifying the famous Polish composer, Frederick Chopin.

The National Museum celebrates the reception outside the nation's borders which greeted Polish art on three occasions during the 20th century. Tamara de Lempicka was the only artist to bring the Art Deco style of the 1930s, which had a decisive influence on design, arts and crafts, to painting. Most of her works were painted in Paris and she died in Mexico.

However, from the Polish national point of view, Stanislav Ignacy Witkiewicz, who called himself Witkacy, was a greater artist. He was doubly gifted and is also an extremely important writer, but he was a portrait-painter and all of Polish society during the first republic modeled for him, right up to Marshal Pilsudsky. Among his pictures, the National Museum exhibits *The Fairy Tale*, painted in 1921, a painting of wild movement and intense color – a piece of Polish Fauvism, so to speak.

Poland was the first country in the communist Eastern Bloc to free itself of Stalinist artistic doctrine. Consequently Polish artists were involved in every European and American avant-garde movement, achieving extraordinary status in poster art. Polish posters could be seen all over the world and the National Museum exhibits many of them with great and justified pride.

It started with religious art

The **NATIONAL MUSEUM OF ANTIQUE ART** in **LISBON** has a comprehensive collection of Portuguese art

ADDRESS:
Rua das Janelas
Verdes 95, Lisbon

OPENING TIMES:
Wed–Sun 10 am
to 6 pm,
Tues 2 pm to 6 pm

INTERNET:
www.mnarteantiga-
ipmuseus.pt

PUBLIC TRANSPORT:
Tram or bus, Cais
Rocha stop

OTHER ATTRACTIONS:
Chiado Museum of
Contemporary Art,
Museum of Decorative
Art, Calouste
Gulbenkian Museum

It is virtually impossible not to come across Henry the Navigator in Portugal and its capital, Lisbon. The third son of the Portuguese King, João I, he lived between 1394 and 1460. This man of practical science established the first school for navigators in Europe, promoting improvements in shipbuilding and inventing the caravel sailing ship. He gave considerable thought to a sea route to India. The result was the Portuguese colonial empire, the second biggest in the world for a time. There is a massive monument to Henry the Navigator in Portugal, erected during the rule of the fascist dictator, Antonio Salazar, located on the north bank of the River Tejo in the district of Lisbon known as Belém. A little further upriver is the

National Museum of Antique Art, more commonly known as the Pombal Palace.

The Palace is named for one of its many owners, the Marquis of Pombal, Portugal's most important statesman at the time of Absolutism.

He reformed the education and justice systems, abolished slavery and led the reconstruction of the city after the devastating earthquake of 1755. He occupied the Palace, which was largely spared the effects of the earthquake in 1770. Prior to Pom-

when this was still not enough, the Museum was extended. The last of these measures was completed in 1994.

The Museum now owns 2,200 paintings from the period between the 14th century and 1820. The collection can be divided into seven groups: paintings, sculptures, drawings and graphics, gold and silverware, ceramics, textiles and furniture. Among the usual works of art are items from Africa and the Far East, testaments to Portugal's former colonial empire.

Altarpieces by Nuno Gonçalves

There are a couple of exquisite pieces in the painting collection, including the portrait of *Saint Jerome* by Albrecht Dürer, which the painter himself sold to a customer from Portugal. As far we know, the model was an old man who had reached the fantastic age, for those times, of 93. There are paintings by Lucas Cranach the Elder, Holbein and Velásquez. The Museum owns one of the most famous works by Hieronymus Bosch, *The Temptation of Saint Anthony*. The work consists of three altarpieces showing the pious Egyptian hermit surrounded by hordes of lecherous demons and other lusty, mythical creatures.

The department containing works from four centuries of Portuguese painting receives special attention. The paintings are dominated by religious scenes and portraits. The highlights include altarpieces from the Polytriptych of Saint Vincent, a work by artist Nuno Gonçalves. The sixty or so somber figures that surround the saint include Henry the Navigator – a pale, mustachioed man wearing a black hat, his hands folded in prayer.

Hieronymus Bosch painted the triptych, *The Temptation of Saint Anthony*, around 1500. The three altarpieces are part of the Museum's legendary collection (above).

Albrecht Dürer's painting, *Saint Jerome*, 1521, is also a world-famous German Renaissance work, a *memento mori* (below right).

The external view of National Museum of Antique Art, in the district of Belém, on the north bank of the River Tejo (below left).

bal, the Palace was inhabited by foreign diplomats, at which time the building was still known as the Alvor Palace – named for its builder, Francisco de Távora, the first Count Alvor.

Move to the Pombal Palace

Both the exact year in which it was constructed and the architect remain unknown. What is known is that a building was erected in the 16th century, adjacent to a religious institution and named after Saint Albert of Jerusalem, founder of the order of Carmelite monks. The Alberta monastery was the first Carmelite monastery in the country.

One last remnant, the Alberta Chapel, is now part of the Museum. It is located in the west wing cellar, a lavishly decorated sacred room with a splendid terracotta Nativity by Machado de Castro, the Portuguese Baroque sculptor, on the walls, and many painted tiles, the azulejos ubiquitous in Portugal. It is completely reconstructed. The west wing was only erected in 1930 and at that time, the chapel was nothing more

than an empty space on the verge of ruin. The monastery was abandoned as early as 1834, like many other religious institutions in the country, at the close of a long civil war which ended in a Liberal victory and brought about a radical separation of church and state along the lines of revolutionary France. Countless churches and cloisters were abandoned. Housing and preserving the works of art they contained was now a job for the state. Initially, the collections were housed in the Cloister of Saint Francis, the center of a newly established Academy of Fine Art. In 1869, an exhibition was held.

The decision to move this collection to the Pombal Palace was taken in 1882. Since then it has grown steadily, primarily as a result of donations, most notably by Queen Carlota Joaquina and Armenian oil magnate Gulbenkian, who made great contributions to Portugal's artistic life. The available space quickly became too small. An attempt to remedy the situation was made by transferring parts of the collection to other museums and

Go west, young man!

The NATIONAL MUSEUM in BUCHAREST testifies to a high standard of Romanian art

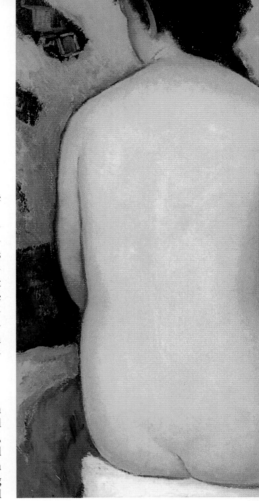

ROMANIA
Bucharest   Black Sea

Mediterranean Sea

ADDRESS:
49-53 Calea Victoriei,
Bucharest

OPENING TIMES:
Daily 10 am to 5 pm

INTERNET:
www.art.museum.ro

PUBLIC TRANSPORT:
Bus routes from the city
center

OTHER ATTRACTIONS:
Museum of
Contemporary Art

Of the images on the tapestries, the Communion of the Apostles is one of the most impressive works (below left).

Why shouldn't art be housed in a royal palace? Since 1948, the Bucharest National Museum of Art has been housed in a former king's palace on the site of the grandiose building that Charles I (1881–1914) of the house of Hohenzollern, King of Romania, built by the French architect, Paul Gottereau, between 1882 and 1885. Here, the artistically minded monarch displayed his collections and adorned his office with a Lucas Cranach and an El Greco, amongst others. Here too, his wife, Elisabeth (known by the stage name of Carmen Sylva), sang in a drawing room furnished with masterpieces of European art.

This palace was destroyed by fire in 1927. Only the great marble staircase withstood the flames. The new building, begun under Queen Marie (1914–38) and completed under Charles II (1930-–40), was seriously damaged by aerial bombing during the Second World War. Nevertheless, it was possible to set up the Romanian National Museum in part of the palace, which opened after the end of the monarchy in 1950, with a statue of Stalin watching over the entrance.

Once again battles raged around the palace during the revolution of 1989. The building was severely damaged and a few paintings irreparably damaged, but it was possible for many of the damaged works of art to be restored as a result of financial donations. The Bucharest art collection has an excellent international reputation.

Royal collection

As early as the first half of the 19th century, there were efforts to build up an art collection in Bucharest, but these efforts remained confined to national art. Acquisitions then extended to European painting under Charles I. The art purchased corresponded to contemporary tastes and included Italian paintings of the 15th to 18th centuries, German and Flemish art and – in accordance with the monarch's preference – Spanish works of art. Charles I made it a condition in his will that his collection should be kept in the country, as the property of the Romanian crown.

The royal collection, which was housed at various sites throughout the country, formed the basis for the establishment of the National Museum in 1948. Important works of art were brought to Bucharest from various other museums throughout the country. Private collections gathered by Romanian intellectuals such as Anastasie Simu, Ioan Cantacusino, George Oprescu and Toma Stelian were an important source. The Museum owes them a debt of gratitude for many works of modern Romanian art.

The department of medieval Romanian art is unique to Romania. More than 9,500 exhibits demonstrate the development of art from the 14th to the 19th centuries, such as the fragment of the fresco, *The Last Supper* (1364–65), and the epitaph, *The Lamentation*, of 1506. Together with numerous icons, the *Four Gospels Book* is regarded as one of the most important works and the Codices are especially valuable. Embroideries, examples of the silversmith's art and precious jewelry are also on display.

Fifteen rooms for Europe

The department of modern Romanian art is impressive proof of the important role Romanian artists played in the 19th and 20th centuries. Some pictures might lead the visitor to believe that he is in a French museum because the art of Nicolae Grigorescu (1838–1907), for example, is so heavily influenced by Impressionism.

More than a hundred of his works are exhibited. Paintings such

as *By the Sea*, which depicts an elegantly dressed woman sitting by the sea, her scarf fluttering in the breeze, parasol put carelessly to one side, are extremely atmospheric. The paintings of Ion Andreescu, Stefan Luchian, Theodor Pallady, Theodor Aman, Georghe Petrascu, Nicolae Tonitza and Stefan Dimitrescu also demonstrate the importance of Romanian artists, who often looked to the west.

The sculptures play a special role. The figures by Constantin Brancusi (1876–1957) are worthy of mention. His bronze statue, *The Prayer*, and the marble bust, *Sleep*, are marked by a very particular style, reminiscent of Rodin's physical language. The collection of Romanian art is completed by an important collection of prints and drawings.

The European Gallery has more than 2,450 paintings exhibited in its 15 rooms. These include works by Antonella da Messina, Boccaccino and Francisco de Zurbarán, as well as paintings by Lorenzo Lotto, Veneziano, Titian and Tintoretto. Jan Van Eyck's *Portrait of a Man with a Ring* radiates great serenity. The stark *Portrait of a Lady* shows a rare side of Peter Paul Rubens. The French Impressionists are also represented by rare works, including Sisley's *The Church in Moret in Winter* and *Camille* by Claude Monet.

Contemporary art has its own home in Bucharest. The gallery, opened in 2004, is located in the monumental palace which was erected by the communist dictator, Ceausescu, and, with a thousand rooms, is bigger than the royal palace. Its massive structure has finally been put to good use.

Nicolae Tonitza's 1928 *Nude with Red Cover* is an impressive work from the modern collection (above left).

The Old Masters collection contains the *Portrait of a Lady*, which Rubens painted between 1606 and 1608, and which is probably the Museum's most famous work of art (top center).

Nicolae Grigorescu is regarded as the Romanian master of Impressionism. His painting, *By the Sea*, was painted between 1880 and 1885 (above right).

Constantin Brancusi called his 1907 figure, *Wisdom of the Earth* (below center).

Once a king's palace: the National Museum in Bucharest (below right).

119

In the name of the poet

The **PUSHKIN MUSEUM** in **MOSCOW** houses "Priam's treasure"

ADDRESS:
12 Volkhonka Street, Moscow

OPENING HOURS:
Tues-Sun 10 am to 6 pm

INTERNET:
www.museum.ru/gmii

TRANSPORT:
Subway, station Kropotkinskaya

OTHER ATTRACTIONS:
Historical Museum

The Museum is a monumental Neoclassical building, opened in 1912 (below left)

Heinrich Schliemann came from a modest family. He was born in Mecklenburg in 1822, apprenticed to a grocer and soon became an extremely successful merchant, traveling abroad often, especially to St. Petersburg. At the age of 44, he began studying archeology in Paris and then traveled to Turkey to search for Troy.

Until then this city, the setting for two epics by the ancient Greek poet, Homer, was thought to be a literary invention. Schliemann trusted the words of the poem and began to dig on the west coast of Asia Minor, where he actually found an ancient complex of buildings under the hill of Hisarlik. Apart from the ruins of nine cities lying in layers, one on top of the other, he found around 8830 objects: drinking vessels, vases, bangles and diadems. The most valuable came to be known as "Priam's Treasure," which consisted of all kinds of gold jewelry and took its name from Homer's King of Troy. Schliemann smuggled his finds out of the country and eventually presented them to the German people. They were accommodated in the Royal Museums in Berlin.

Only copies at first

In 1945, the Red Army conquered East Germany and Berlin. Much of the content of the German museums was looted and taken to the Soviet Union as war booty. It was not returned until years later. The Trojan treasures were never given back. The Moscow authorities denied that they had ever been in their possession. The Berlin museums made do with replicas and copies. Then in 1993, the Russian authorities announced that the Schliemann treasure was in Moscow after all and it was exhibited in Moscow four years later, on the occasion of the 175th anniversary of Schliemann's birth. Since that time, it has been known that the Schliemann treasure was in the Pushkin Museum in Moscow. Nobody knows whether it will remain there or be returned to Berlin or to Turkey, where it was originally found.

At all events, it represents an additional attraction for the Pushkin Museum, one of the great art museums of Russia, second only to the Hermitage in St. Petersburg. It was founded by Ivan Tsvetaev, a professor at Moscow University and the father of the celebrated Russian poet, Marina Tsvetaeva. Towards the end of the 19th century, he had the idea of creating an art museum. Work began in 1898 on the building he envisaged, financed by private patrons of the arts. The architect was Roman J. Klein. He designed a monumental Neoclassical building, which opened in 1912. At first, they exhibited casts of copies of famous works of art, such as the *Knight of Bamberg*, Michelangelo's *David* and the portal of Limburg cathedral as well as Egyptian antiquities, Italian paintings and objets d'art.

Expropriated private collections

The Museum was named after Tsar Alexander III. The name was changed

at the time of the October Revolution to that of Russia's great classical poet and national hero, Alexander Pushkin, although the Museum has no connection with him. The Revolution greatly enlarged the collection by expropriating private collections, including the collections of the exceedingly rich art lovers, Ivan Morosov and Sergei Shchukin, and giving them to the Pushkin Museum. Morosov and Shchukin bought modern French art, as did Sergei Tretyakov, younger brother of the founder of the Tretyakov Gallery. His foreign pieces were also handed over to the Pushkin Museum.

Today, the Museum has a total of over half a million pieces, set out on two floors. The first floor contains most of the antiquities and the earlier European paintings. There is a sarcophagus of a pharaoh and all sorts of finds from excavations in Mesopotamia, Greece, and Rome as well as from the Alexandrian period in Egypt. Among the painters of the modern era represented here are the Italians Perugino, Veronese and Tiepolo as well as a beautiful *Annunciation* by Botticelli. We also have the Spaniards, Velázquez and Zurbarán, as well as Rembrandt and two of the prolific painters of their time, Peter Paul Rubens and

Lucas Cranach the Elder. The latter's *Virgin and Child* of 1525 is a work of exceptional delicacy.

Apart from a few more antiquities, the second floor mostly contains works from the late 19th century and classics of modern art. Ivan Morosov in particular was an avid collector of French Impressionists and Cubists. All in all, the Pushkin Museum's collection of paintings by artists from Monet's circle is the biggest in Russia and one of the biggest outside France.

It includes the famous *Boulevard des Capucines* of 1873, a key work by Claude Monet and one of the great tributes to the Parisian boulevards laid out by the city planner, Baron Georges-Eugène Haussmann. There is a famous nude by Auguste Renoir, dating from 1876, one of Edgar Degas' many depictions of ballet dancers and a beautiful Manet. The Impressionists are supplemented by the French painters who preceded them, from Poussin, Watteau, Fragonard, Corot and Courbet. The Post-Impressionists are represented by Paul Cézanne, Henri Matisse and Pablo Picasso.

Edgar Degas' *Dancer in Blue*, **1890 (above left).**

Claude Monet's painting, *Boulevard des Capucines*, **1873, is considered a key work of Impressionism (above right).**

The collections of Greek and Egyptian antiquities are also among the famous items in the Pushkin Museum. View of one of the exhibition rooms with display cabinets (above).

Russian art history

The **TRETYAKOV GALLERY** in **MOSCOW** is a national museum of Russian art

ADDRESS:
Lavrushinskiy
Pereulok 10, Moscow

OPENING TIMES:
Tues.-Sun. 10 am
to 7:30 pm

INTERNET:
www.mdz-info.de

PUBLIC TRANSPORT:
Tretyakov Gallery:
Tretyakovskaya or
Polyanka subway
station,
New Tretyakov Gallery:
Park Kultury subway
station

OTHER ATTRACTIONS:
The Kremlin, Pashkov
House, Manege, Old
University

Pavel Mikhailovich Tretyakov, born 1832, was a well-to-do Moscow merchant. He inherited a great deal of wealth and derived further income from dealing in textiles. Politically, he was a national democrat and, additionally, he had a weakness for the fine arts. He learned to combine both inclinations by collecting works by the *Peredvishniki*. Peredvishniki means "wanderer." It is a name given to a group of artists founded by painter Ivan Kramskoy. They sought to organize peripatetic exhibitions, promoting art in remote parts of the country. They embraced the Realist style and the content dealt with Russian history, the Russian landscape and everyday Russian life, as well as portraits of Russian people.

Pavel Tretyakov started collecting in 1856. His first purchase was the painting, *The Temptation*, by Nikolai Schilder. His interests expanded to include *objets d'art* from earlier eras, always with a Russian theme. He purchased 18th and early 19th century art as well as icons. He intended to create a gallery of Russian national art. He opened his collection to the public almost immediately. In 1892, he bequeathed the collection, which now comprised 5,000

works, to the city of Moscow, on the condition that it would be expanded. In 1898, he died and was highly honored.

How the collection grew.
Initially the collection was housed in Tretyakov's home in Moscow. It was necessary to extend the house several times until a new building was finally constructed next door. The art collection of the younger Tretyakov brother, Sergei – who owned Russian works like Pavel as well as modern French works – also found a home here.

After 1898, the new building and house were used as a museum by the city of Moscow. The artist and architect, Victor Vasnetsov, designed a Neo-Old Russian style façade which linked both buildings, with construction work continuing until 1902. The city council appointed a committee that commissioned collector Ilya Ostrouchov and Pavel Tretyakov's daughter, Alexandra Botkina, to run the museum.

The collection grew considerably after Lenin's October Revolution. Many items that had been removed from other museums and from private ownership were added to it and the Tretyakov Gallery became a national museum. Paintings were reorganized and rehung; the buildings had to be extended several more times, including in 1926 and 1985. The founder is remembered by a stone monument outside the building, created by Alexander Kibalnikov. The bearded man on the base stares with folded arms into the distance.

The Gallery attracts more than two million visitors a year. They walk past paintings that depict Russian history. One department exhibits mainly icons, the oldest dating from the 12th century and the most famous being *The Virgin* of Vladimir, which formerly hung in Moscow's Uspensky Cathedral and was the template for countless copies, one of which is ascribed to Russia's most famous icon painter, Andrei Rublyov, who lived around

1400. The Tretyakov Gallery owns his *Trinity* icon. Rublyov's contemporary, Theophanes the Greek, who probably painted the *Virgin of the Don* exhibited here, was almost as famous. Boris Godunov was crowned Tsar in front of this icon in 1598.

Historical paintings

The Museum owns numerous works from the 18th and early 19th centuries, including historical and monumental paintings, also painted in other countries during the same period. Russia's most famous artist from the age of Realism, who brought international attention to Russian fine art, was Ilya Repin.

Ilya Efimovich Repin, born 1844, was a trained icon painter. He continued his training at the St. Petersburg Academy of Art, where he later taught and became a member of the Peredvishniki. His art quickly reached an artistic perfection equaling that of Gustave Courbet in France. The Tretyakov

Museum has one of his most famous group paintings, the *Religious Procession in Kursk*, on display.

Marianne von Verefkin was one of Repin's pupils. She moved to Germany with her partner, Alexei Jawlensky. They lived for a while in Murnau, where they met their compatriot, Vassily Kandinsky. All three were pioneers of modern art, which revolutionized fine art from 1910.

The Tretyakov Museum, restricted by Stalinist policy, was unable to show modern art for many years. Now it exhibits paintings by Mikhail Larionov, Natalia Goncharova, Marc Chagall, Kandinsky and Casimir Malevich in the new Tretyakov Gallery, located in another building.

The most famous 19th century Russian painting is Ilya Repin's *Religious Procession in Kursk*, 1883, which is classed stylistically as Russian Realism (above left).

Russia's most famous icon painter is Andrei Rublyov. His *Trinity* from 1411 (below left) is regarded as a masterpiece of icon painting.

Constantly extended: The Tretyakov Gallery building (below right).

The Russian Louvre

The **HERMITAGE** in **ST. PETERSBURG**: home of one of the greatest art collections in the world

ADDRESS:
2, Dvortsovaya Ploshad,
St. Petersburg

OPENING HOURS:
Tues-Sun 10:30 am
to 6 pm; until 5 pm on
public holidays

INTERNET:
www.hermitage-
museum.org

TRANSPORT:
Subway station Nevsky
Prospekt

OTHER ATTRACTIONS:
Peter and Paul Fortress,
Kunstkammer,
Admirality, Smolny,
Taurida Palace

**Part of the Winter
Palace was integrated
into the Hermitage.
View of the facade
from the Neva
waterside (below left).**

Still Life with Curtain
**by Paul Cézanne dates
from around 1895 and
is one of the most
famous still-life
paintings
(below center).**

Tsar Peter I of Russia (Peter the Great) had a city built on the delta where the Neva flows into the Baltic. It was named St. Petersburg after Saint Peter and, of course, after the Tsar himself. Work began in 1703. The Italian architect, Bartolomeo Rastrelli, designed the official buildings for the new royal seat, situated on 44 islands and divided by more than 60 canals. Thousands of forced laborers lost their lives to achieve its construction. At the center was a huge palace complex, the Winter Palace, where the tsars spent the cold season. The building work took a long time and Rastrelli's design was not completed until the reign of the Empress Catherine II (Catherine the Great).

Catherine possessed art collections which she had inherited from her forebears and which she supplemented with her own treasures. They were housed in a part of the palace known as the Small Hermitage. The treasures continued to grow over the years. After a serious fire in 1837, Tsar Nicholas I commissioned the Bavarian court architect, Leo von Klenze, designer of the Alte Pinakothek in Munich, to rebuild the Hermitage completely. The work was finished in 1852 and the Tsar opened the collections to the public.

2.7 million exhibits

After the October Revolution of 1917, the collections were appropriated by the state, which owns them today. Both their installation in a former royal palace and also the size and range of the collections calls to mind the Louvre in Paris. The Hermitage now owns around 2.7 million exhibits, making it one of the most important museums in the world. The immensity of the museum creates a unique atmosphere. Unlike the Louvre, which ceased to be the royal residence long before the French Revolution, the Winter

Palace continued to serve this purpose until 1917. The Hermitage now extends right into the Winter Palace and the exhibits share in the tsarist pomp, which, always more overwhelming than that of other courts, was bought at the expense of enormous poverty for the general population. Among these splendid interiors are the Jordan staircase and the parade halls, a visit to which is included in the visitors' program to the Hermitage.

Right next to these are rooms containing Russian art objects. The remaining sections display Italian, Spanish, Flemish-Dutch, German, French and English painting from the end of the Middle Ages to the 20th century. There are artifacts from Greek and Roman antiquity, oriental, prehistoric and – one of the museum's specialties – a collection of Scythian objects. The horsemen of Scythia were distinguished by their great skill in making gold

jewelry, which is not the only precious metal treasure in the museum! Peter the Great's crown jewels are also on view, as is the collection of pieces from the workshop of Carl Fabergé. This Russian jeweler of Huguenot descent, also famous in Western Europe, was a favorite at the Tsarist court.

Fabergé's porcelain eggs

Modeled on the goldsmith work of Johann Melchior Dinglinger of Dresden, who was purveyor to Augustus the Strong, Carl Fabergé and his brother, Agathon, put together a magnificent collection. Their Easter eggs became particularly famous – richly decorated pieces made of gold and enamel which could be opened to reveal the tiny, meticulously made models contained inside. The tsars' courts were the main customers in Russia for such items and the imperial family and their courtiers liked to give them as presents.

As for sculpture and painting, it must be said that there is scarcely a great name in the history of art which is not represented here. Among them is the famous Madonna of Simone Martini, assumed to depict the Laura idolized in the sonnets of Petrarch. One of Leonardo's

most famous paintings, the *Madonna Litta*, can be seen in the Hermitage, as well as Caravaggio's homoerotic *Lute Player* of 1595. The museum owns a notable collection of Rembrandts, El Grecos, Goyas and the greatest stock of pictures by the Romantic landscape painter, Caspar David Friedrich, is also to be found there.

Modern art can be found on the third floor. As with the Pushkin Museum in Moscow, many of the French Impressionists and Cubists housed at the Hermitage come from the two wealthy Moscow collectors

from pre-Revolutionary time: Ivan Morosov and Sergei Shchukin. There are also sculptures by Auguste Rodin and many works by Paul Cézanne, Pablo Picasso and Henri Matisse. The rooms are relatively small. Before 1985, such paintings were hidden rather than shown and people were careless about labeling them. People were only allowed to appreciate the significance of such works after the official Stalinist art policy was finally shelved.

Homage to Peter the Great, founder of St. Petersburg: Jean-Marc Nattier's *Portrait of Peter I* (above left).

Paul Gauguin's South Sea painting, *Three Tahitian Women*, 1899, is especially well known (above right).

Dutch painting is represented in the Hermitage by Rembrandt's *Danae*, among others (below right).

The stages of Russian history

In **ST. PETERSBURG**, the **RUSSIAN MUSEUM** presents the history of Russia, reflected in her painting and sculpture

ADDRESS:
4 Inzhenernaya Street,
St. Petersburg

OPENING HOURS:
Wed-Sun 10 am
to 5 pm
Mon 10 am to 4 pm

INTERNET:
www.hermitage-museum.org

TRANSPORT:
Subway station Nevsky
Prospekt

OTHER ATTRACTIONS:
Academy of Art,
station Vitebsk

The Russian Tsar Alexander I was at first a follower of the Enlightenment. However, after he conquered Napoleon, he created the ultra-reactionary Holy Alliance.

Alexander's younger brother, Mikhail Pavlovich, on the other hand, was married to an artistic wife. Between 1819 and 1825, Mikhail Pavlovich commissioned the Italian-born architect, Carlo Rossi, to build him a palace in the style of a country mansion in the Russian capital, by the Griboyedov Canal, a branch of the Neva. The courtyard behind a high wrought-iron fence borders the Square of

the Arts. On the garden side, there is a magnificent loggia. During the builder's lifetime, musical evenings were presented here, under the direction of the celebrated Russian pianist, Anton Rubinstein.

Nicholas II was the last Tsar to rule in St. Petersburg. His grandfather, Alexander III, was assassinated and several attempts were made to assassinate his father. Nicholas II was very strict in matters of internal policy. He was anti-liberal, anti-Semitic and pan-Slavonic. His pan-Slavism prompted him to found a Russian museum in 1898. It was to be located in the Mikhailovsky Palace, which had to

be converted for the purpose. Aside from the vestibule with the parade staircase and the "White Room," all the interior architecture fell victim to the new purpose. An extra section was also added, named the Benois Wing after its designer. The collection housed in the palace was assembled largely by Nicholas's father, Tsar Alexander III.

Chronological arrangement
The collection has been considerably enlarged since and today contains around 400,000 items. It is the second largest collection of its kind in the country, after the Tre-

arrival at the Museum because of the repressive nature of Stalinist art and cultural policies, implemented by Andrei Zhdanov when the city was known as Leningrad. Yet St. Petersburg, where the Russian avant-garde artists gathered in the early 20th century, made an enormous contribution to the artistic revolution, second only to Paris. Stalin and Zhdanov condemned modern art as formalism, bourgeois and hostile to the people and their interests. The protagonists were forced to change their style, go into exile abroad or become anonymous.

Kasimir Malevich was one of the victims of Stalinist repression. The Ukrainian painter, born in Kiev, was first influenced by the French Impressionists and Expressionists, before turning to Cubist-inspired simplification. Finally, under the name of Suprematism, a concept he himself invented, he began to use the simplest of geometrical forms. The Russian Museum has his 1915 *Red Square on White Ground* and the 1916 *Black Cross on Red Oval*. His forced return to the figurative took place 15 years later as a result of persecution and psychological pressure. His *Female Worker* from 1933 meets all the naturalistic-heroic demands of the Zhdanov artistic doctrine.

Masterpieces of Russian painting: an icon dating from 1475 shows Saint George and the Dragon (above left).

Kasimir Malevich's 1915 *Red Square* has become a classic of abstract painting (above right).

Karl P. Brullov's picture, *The Last Day of Pompeii*, 1833, is a major work of Russian historical painting (center right).

View of the main entrance to the Museum, with a monument to Russian poet and national hero, Alexander Pushkin in the foreground (below right).

tyakov Gallery in Moscow, which serves the same purpose. The arrangement is strictly chronological. There are ten sections in all: Icons, Paintings, Sculpture, Drawings, Prints, Old Russian Arts and Crafts, Applied Art, Folk Art, Coins and Modern Era works.

Among the icons is the *Angel with the Golden Hair*, which dates from the 12th century, is undeniably Byzantine in origin and impresses the viewer with its expression of intense sorrow. There are icons depicting Saint Peter, Saint Paul, the prophet Sophonias and the Purification of Mary by Andrei Rublev, the great genius of Russian icon painting.

The emancipation of Russian painting from orthodoxy took place in the 17th century, later than in the rest of Europe. Western influences and ideas sparked the transformation to secularism and the results can best be seen in portraits painted during the period.

Ivan Nikitin painted a portrait of Peter the Great, on show in the Russian Museum in St. Petersburg, in the same manner that Fyodor Rokotov painted Catherine the Great almost a hundred years later. Both portraits are typical of the meticulously crafted, and usually very flattering, works commissioned by the royal courts and by the wealthy, bourgeois families of Europe.

Avant-garde suppressed

Realistic landscape painting, exceedingly popular in the 19th century, began in Russia with Simon and Silvester Shchedrin, around the same time as in Denmark and France. Karl Brullov's *The Last Day of Pompeii* is a typical example. Genre painting of the Biedermeier period culminates in the paintings by the genius Ilya Efimovich Repin, who lived in St. Petersburg for many years. His superb portraits of the writer, Leo Tolstoy, and the composer, Alexander Glazunov, are housed by the Russian Museum.

Modern Russian art was a late

A shrine to Swedish art

The **NATIONAL MUSEUM** in **STOCKHOLM** documents Swedish art

ADDRESS:
Södra Blasieholmshamnen, Stockholm

OPENING HOURS:
Tues and Thurs 11 am to 8 pm, Wed, Fri-Sun 11 am to 5 pm

INTERNET:
www.national-museum.se

TRANSPORT:
Subway station Kungsträdgården

OTHER ATTRACTIONS:
Antikmuseum, Moderne Museet, Liljevalchs Konsthall

The woman has a gentle smile on her face. Her hair is curly and powdered grayish white. Over it, she wears a black veil, which also hides her right eye and cheek. In her right hand she holds a closed fan. She wears patterned gloves that only reach her knuckles, leaving her fingertips free. Her dress is *à la Boulognaise*, following the fashion of the time, which originated in the city of Bologna in Italy.

The picture dates from 1768. The person portrayed, Marie-Suzanne Giroust, was a pastel well-known French artist. When her portrait was hung in the Paris Salon, philosopher Denis Diderot called it "very piquant." It was painted by her husband, Alexander Roslin. Roslin had lived in Paris since 1752, but he was born in Sweden. He came from Skåne (Scania) and received his artistic training in Karlskrona and Stockholm.

In 1745, he went to Bayreuth and then traveled to Italy. He was soon sought after as a portrait painter by the European aristocracy. In France, he kept in close contact with François Boucher and, while influenced by Boucher's Rococo art, Roslin preserved his own personal style and his coloration is more powerful and his expression more intense.

He specialized in individual and group portraits. In St. Petersburg alone, he painted a hundred portraits of important figures of science and the nobility, including the Empress Catherine II. He

from Rembrandt, now hangs in the National Museum in Stockholm, alongside Roslin's *Lady with the Veil*.

The Museum is the greatest institution of its kind in Sweden. The core of it is due to King Gustavus Vasa, who set up a picture gallery in Gripsholm Castle in the 16th century. The collection was enlarged with plunder from Europe during the Thirty Years' War and with pictures bought by Queen Christina during her travels in Italy. Carl Gustaf Tessin, the Swedish ambassador in Paris during the 1740s, collected French Rococo painting of the highest quality and donated them to the collection. King Gustavus III, an enlightened and educated ruler, eventually decided that his art collection should be placed in the care of the Swedish state after his death, paving the way for the foundation of the Royal Museum in 1792. In 1866, when the present building – a historic palace in the Neo-Renaissance style – was erected, its name was changed to the National Museum.

Frescoes by Carl Larsson

Magnificently carved and adorned with all the pomp of the epoque, the National Museum is built on a magnificent site on the southern tip of the Blasieholmen peninsula opposite the royal castle, from which it is separated by an arm of the Strömmen. Among the paintings and sculptures, which now number around 16,000, there is a respectable collection of international art from the late Middle Ages to French Impressionism. The Museum also owns 245 exquisite early Russian icons, but Swedish art remains the center of attention.

The staircase is adorned by six large frescoes by Carl Larsson. Born in 1853, he lived for a time near Fontainebleau, learned from the Impressionists and is now considered the father of Swedish monumental painting. His murals in

the Museum reproduce scenes from Swedish cultural history. In 1897, Larsson's contemporary, Anders Zorn, probably Sweden's best-known painter, painted *Midsummer Night's Dance*. Couples in national costume sway under an open sky, traditional, reddish-brown Swedish houses and a maypole can be seen in the background. The painting is an important example of both Swedish art and national consciousness. Zorn, a very busy and well-traveled man for his time – he visited the United States as well as Russia – began as an Impressionist and later became famous as a portrait painter. In his more mature years, he turned to national Romanticism.

A special wing of the Museum is devoted to Swedish arts and crafts from the end of the Middle Ages through the present day. It is here that the roots of Scandinavian design –acclaimed throughout the world – can be found.

Among the internationally known Swedish painters represented here are Carl Larsson, whose painting, *Catching Crayfish*, dates from 1894 (above left), and Alexander Roslin, whose picture of his wife, *Lady with a Veil*, dates from 1768 (above right).

Writer August Strindberg was also a famous painter in Sweden. His *Sunset* was completed in 1892 (below right).

The National Museum building with its Neo-Renaissance facade stands close to the water (below left).

returned briefly to Stockholm, where he painted Carl von Linné (Linnaeus), among others. *The Lady with the Veil* is his most popular work.

Roslin and Pilo

Roslin was the first significant Swedish painter outside his own region, along with his contemporary Pilo, who also spelled his name Pihlou. Pilo, of Polish descent, was born near Nyköping and was a craftsman before studying at the Stockholm Academy of Art. He went on to become a teacher at the Academy and a painter at the royal court in Copenhagen. When political conflict arose between Denmark and Sweden, he returned to his homeland.

In 1772, King Gustavus III, famous commander in the Great Northern War and son of Charles XII, began his reign in Stockholm. Gustavus commissioned Pilo to paint his coronation. The artist reluctantly agreed. His unfinished picture, filled with figures and with chiaroscuro effects borrowed

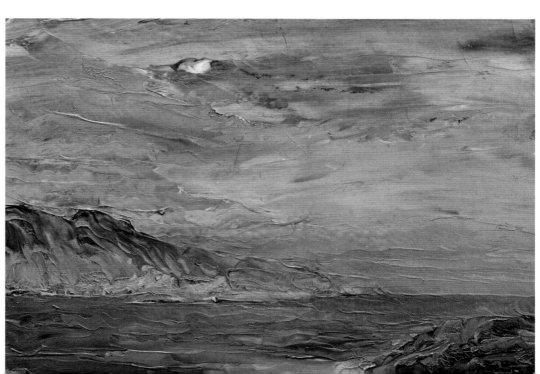

Art promoted by the people

BASLE, the Swiss city on the Upper Rhine, has always had rich patrons. A museum in the Humanist tradition

Basel
Bern ● SWITZERLAND

Ligurian Sea

ADDRESS:
St.-Alban-Graben 16,
Basle

OPENING TIMES:
Museum of Art:
Tues-Sun 10 am
to 5 pm, Museum
of Modern Art:
11 am to 5 pm

INTERNET:
www.kunstmuseum-
basel.ch

PUBLIC TRANSPORT:
Tram,
Kunstmuseum stop

OTHER ATTRACTIONS:
Museum of Antiquities

The Upper Rhine city of Basle, located in the triangle of land where Switzerland, France and Germany meet, is proud of its Humanist past. At the end of the Middle Ages, it was a center for printing, a technique only recently discovered. The great Erasmus from Rotterdam lived and taught here. It is difficult to conceive of Humanism separated from art and aesthetic references and because of this connection, Basle also became a center for the fine arts.

One of the great dynasties of painters from the last years of the Middle Ages, the Holbeins from Augsburg in Germany, worked in the city, as did Konrad Witz from Rottweil, Urs Graf from Solothurn, Switzerland. Matthäus Merian, coppersmith and father of artist Maria Sybilla Merian, came from Basle and the tradition continued down to Arnold Böcklin, from Basle, one of the so-called Deutschrömer, or German-Romans, who acquired a considerable reputation in his day as a painter of themes rooted in antiquity.

Throughout the ages, the city was very proud of its artists. There were always families who patronized them, purchasing and collecting their works. The families were not members of noble houses, as was predominantly the case elsewhere in Europe, but burghers. Basle was a bourgeois city. One of these enthusiasts was Basilius Amerbach. He lived from 1533 to 1591 and was the nephew of a famous printer and the son of a lawyer who was a close friend of Erasmus. He owned a private collection of some 50 paintings, a bundle of drawings and graphic works as well as a large library and all kinds of ethnographic items.

After his death, it seemed as though the complete collection would go to the Netherlands. Professors at the University persuaded the city to purchase Amerbach's collection. The purchase was completed at the exorbitant price, for those days, of 9,000 Reichstaler, or Rix dollars. The city paid two thirds and the University the rest. In 1671, the Amerbach art collection was moved

to the "Zur Mücke" house, close to the Münsterplatz, and made accessible to the public. Basle is convinced that it can lay claim to the first public museum of art ever in the history of culture, despite all assertions to the contrary by France and her Louvre.

Refuge for "degenerate art"

The Museum was complemented and expanded by new acquisitions, including, in 1823, a collection accumulated by the Basle lawyer, Remigius Faesch, during the early 17th century. The space available for displays and storage had long since become too small. In 1849, the Museum moved to a bigger building in the Augustinerstrasse. Further gifts, including donations of Dutch Old Masters, brought further expansion. Several canvases by Konrad Witz were purchased from the margraves of Baden, with the active assistance of wealthy Basle families. A legacy left by an art dealer provided a fund used primarily to acquire works of art from Swit-

zerland. In 1936, the Museum moved again, this time to the St.-Alban-Graben, its present home. The Neoclassical building is the work of architects Rudolf Christ and Paul Bonatz. In the years after the First World War, interest in modern art grew, aided by events in Hitler's Germany, where museums were obliged to get rid of avant-garde works of art regarded as "degenerate," which were then offered for sale on the international market.

Plebiscite on Picasso

The pharmaceutical manufacturer, Raoul La Roche, donated his collection of Cubist art as a foundation. An insurance company provided funds for the purchase of abstract Expressionist pieces. In 1967, there was a veritable plebiscite on the acquisition of two Picassos at the state's expense – the vote went in Picasso's favor. Now Basle's collection of modern art is one of the biggest in the world.

In 1980, the Museum opened an annex intended solely for modern art from 1960. The collection started with a piece on loan from Count Guiseppe Panza di Biumo of Milan, which came with one condition attached – that a suitable exhibition hall should be found for it. A derelict 19th century paper mill was purchased; architects Wilfrid and

Katharina Starb restored it and added a new wing, creating the Museum of Modern Art. Once again, the construction costs were covered by a private donation.

Basle remains unique in its efforts to safeguard art from the Upper Rhine dating from the late Middle Ages and Renaissance and the Museum is particularly proud of the Holbein dynasty's work: that of brothers Sigmund and Hans as well as that of sons Hans and Ambrosius. Hans Holbein the Younger was one of the most extraordinary portrait painters in the history of art, finally entering the service of King Henry VIII of England, part of the house of Tudor, as a court painter.

He first spent several years in Basle and, even during his time in London, he returned time and again to the city on the Upper Rhine. Here, he created his series of woodcuts on the theme of the Dance of Death and also produced all kinds of book illustrations. Here, too, he decorated two burghers' houses

with frescoes. The Museum of Art's Holbein collection includes extraordinary pieces: *Portrait of Mayor Jacob Meyer and his Wife*, 1516, *The Dead Christ in the Tomb*, 1521, and a portrait of a certain Boniface Amerbach, dated 1519, whose nephew the Museum has to thank for its existence.

Arnold Böcklin painted his work *Centaur's Combat* in 1873. At the time, the Basle artist was the most famous painter of themes from antiquity (above left).

***Virgin Forest at Sunset* is the title Henri Rousseau gave to his painting created in 1910 (above right).**

One of Switzerland's most important painters is Ferdinand Hodler, who painted The *Dying Patient* in 1915 (center right).

The Neoclassical building that houses the collections is located in the center of Basle at St.-Alban-Graben (below right).

The agent for many artists

Art dealer Ernst **BEYELER** represented many artists.
His collection can be seen in **RIEHEN**, near Basle.

ADDRESS:
Baselstrasse 101,
Riehen/Basel

OPENING TIMES:
Thurs.-Tues. 10 am
to 6 pm,
Wed. 10 am to 8 pm

INTERNET:
www.beyeler.com

PUBLIC TRANSPORT:
Tram, Line 6 or Line 2

OTHER ATTRACTIONS:
Vitra Museum

During his stay in Paris, the young and as yet unknown art dealer, Ernst Beyeler, often skipped lunch. With the money he saved, he preferred to buy, hot off the press, prints of Toulouse-Lautrec, who fascinated him. He then used works by the French artist to finance one of his exhibitions in Basle, the first of many. Over the course of more than 50 years, Beyeler became one of the best known art dealers and collectors in the world.

The little town of Riehen in the corner where Germany, France and Switzerland meet now has a museum where visitors can see the collection of Ernst and Hildy Beyeler, comprising of 200 works. The Italian, Renzo Piano, used elegant restraint in his design for a 417 foot long, 115 foot wide, low rise building, which blends carefully into an extensive landscaped park and combines nature, space, light and art.

In the beginning was the gallery

There was no art in the Beyeler family house because five children had to be brought up on a railway clerk's salary. Ernst Beyeler was mad about art and took his inspiration from the artistic spirit of the city of Basle. While he studied, he worked in an antiquarian bookshop that also dealt in prints and he took over the little shop after the owner's death. In 1951, he transformed it into a gallery and started to hold summer exhibitions. From the very start, he looked for "big" names, made close contact with museums and bargained with prominent art dealers from all over the world. Thanks to the charismatic personality of the "curator in the guise of a dealer," he made contact with many artists, with whom he maintained friend-

ships for many years – most notably Pablo Picasso, Mark Tobey and Alberto Giacometti. As Picasso's sole dealer, he was allowed first choice of his works at the studio in Mougins.

The obvious highlight of the Beyeler Collection is thus the works by Picasso, but the collection should be seen as a reflection of the life of the collector couple. The paintings hung or stood in the Beyelers' house and were ultimately so "tried and tested" that despite temporary financial difficulties, the Beyelers did not put them up for sale. Finally, the collection became so extensive that a plan to create a museum for them was devised. After a trust was established in 1982, Riehen was chosen as the location because the Beyelers wanted to exhibit the works in a rural environment, distinct from Basle with its municipal museums.

The Museum is like an airplane wing, according to Beyeler after it opened in 1997, with a service corridor at its side to act like a barrier against traffic noise. The massive glass roof makes the building look like it is floating and the skin made from porphyry, a reddish volcanic stone from Argentina, is reminiscent of ancient monastery walls. The roof is supported by four parallel walls which divide all the internal space into twenty-two lengthy rooms. Daylight shines through the white, plate-glass roof so that the pictures always appear slightly different, depending on the light. The tranquil picture is completed by a floor of pale French white oak.

When you enter the Museum, you almost feel you have received a personal invitation, which is due first and foremost to the nature of the collection. The impression of a private collection, however, is suggested by the panoramic gallery

that covers the whole west front like a narrow conservatory.

Focused on individual works

The Beyelers felt a connection with classic modern art, a period which extends from late Impressionism to early Minimalism and Action Art in the Beyeler Foundation. There are few exceptions, such as exhibited works by Baselitz and Kiefer.

One peculiarity of the collection is that pictures or sculptures were collected as conscious, individual acquisitions and not as oeuvres by artists. As a result of the couple's direct contact with the artists, representative groups of works have still come about, however, by Pablo Picasso, Joan Miró, Henri Matisse, Wassily Kandinsky, Piet Mondrian and Paul Klee, for example. There is also a considerable collection of Mark Rothko's color block painting. Individual works of art such as Vincent Van Gogh's *Wheatfield with Cornflowers*, Claude Monet's *Water Lilies*, *Madame Cezanne in a Yellow Armchair* by Paul Cezanne and *Joseph Beuys* by Andy Warhol are fascinating.

Ernst Beyeler also collected African and Oceanic art, but instead of showing it in isolation, it is deliberately placed next to works by Western artists Miró and Picasso in an exciting dialog with a different culture.

Finally, the Foundation is not supposed to be just a treasure trove. It is intended that temporary exhibitions and a dynamic permanent collection should continue what the collection made possible – an artistic debate supported by genuine enthusiasm.

The name of England's most famous contemporary artist is Francis Bacon. He painted *In Memory of George Dyer* in 1971 as part of a triptych (left).

Still Life with Pears is the name given by Nicolas de Staël to this work from 1953 (below right).

The Museum design by Renzo Piano blends perfectly with the rural environment (below center).

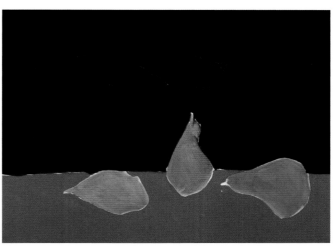

Swiss art history

The **KUNSTHAUS ZÜRICH** uniquely documents
the development of Swiss art

ADDRESS:
Heimplatz 1,
Zürich

OPENING HOURS:
Tues-Thurs 10 am
to 9 pm,
Fri-Sun 10 am to 5 pm

INTERNET:
www.kunsthaus.ch

TRANSPORT:
Tram or bus, stop
Kunsthaus

OTHER ATTRACTIONS:
Graphics collection
of the ETH, Haus für
konstruktive und
konkrete Kunst,
Kunsthalle Zürich,
Museum für Gestaltung

Alberto Giacometti was born in 1901 in a small village called Borgonovo in Grisons, Switzerland. His artistic talent, evident at an early age, was unsurprising since his father, Giovanni, was a well-known Impressionist painter and his godfather, Cuno Amiet, was a renowned Swiss artist, associated for a time with the German Expressionist movement and the group, *Die Brücke*. Alberto's younger brother, Diego, also continued the family tradition by becoming a famous designer.

Giacometti studied in Geneva and Rome. In 1922, he went to Paris, where he remained for the rest of his life. He left the city only during the Nazi German occupation of France, 1940-1944. In Paris, Giacometti continued his studies with sculptor Emile-Antoine Bourdelle, a pupil of Rodin. Later influenced by Cubism and Italian Futurism, he experimented with the abstract. He even briefly joined the Surrealist movement. But he remained original and a work from the peri-od, *Palace at Four in the Morning*, already shows one of those emaciated figures with disproportionately long limbs that later became his trademark.

A stage for Giacometti

In 1945, Giacometti had not exhibited for 12 years and only worked for himself. He was associated with Pablo Picasso and mingled with the Existentialist circle surrounding Jean-Paul Sartre and Simone de Beauvoir. Under the influence of Sartre's philosophy, he sculpted wasted figures, mostly human, but sometimes animals as well, with cracked surfaces. The scultures made Giacometti famous. His paintings show a preference for blue and gray tones and emphasize the isolation of the individual as well as a tendency towards gloomy and forlorn dematerialization. Giacometti's art has been labeled an aesthetic response to recent world events, particularly the Second World War. His emaciated figures evoke Auschwitz and Hiroshima.

At the same time, his models were also friends and relations. Giacometti lived to the age of 65 and died in his native Grisons.

By far the biggest collection of his work is to be found in the Kunsthaus Zürich. Some he donated personally, others were later presented by his family. Here, you can trace Giacometti's entire development as an artist, from the very beginning to his late works. The exhibits, 72 sculptures, 17 paintings, and 62 drawings, take up one whole floor of the gallery. The sculptures stand next to and behind one another, some menacingly large and some tiny, all emaciated and forlorn. It is an oppressive, unforgettable sight.

Switzerland's contribution to the history of European art is not inconsiderable. It begins with the late Gothic art of the 15th century Zürich artist known as the Master of the Pinks, who always signed his biblically-themed works with a red or white carnation – hence the name by which we know him today.

Zürich was one of the hubs of the Reformation, which abhorred imagery. Swiss painting fell victim to the movement and was not revived until two hundred years later, with Salomon Gessner, who was not only an influential writer, but also a respected landscape painter and etcher. One of Gessner's contemporaries was Johann Heinrich Füssli, whose Classical–Romantic art appears surprisingly fresh and modern. As Henry Fuesli, he acquired a considerable reputation in England.

Once the city for the avant-garde

The most important Swiss painter at the end of the 19th century was Ferdinand Hodler. His art, which varied between Realism and Symbolism, sometimes shows traces of Fauvism. With the founding of the Cabaret Voltaire in the Niederdorf in Zürich in 1916, Dadaism took over, along with the avant-garde movement which inspired both the Surrealists and the Swiss artist, Paul Klee, as well as the "Zürcher Konkreten" group, whose best known representatives are Max Bill and Richard Paul Lohse. Bill's influence continued into the most recent times, where the witty Pippilotti Rist represents Swiss modernism.

The aim of the Kunsthaus Zürich is to collect and exhibit the works of Swiss artists. The development of this institution has taken more than two hundred years. In 1787, a sociable group of artists and art lovers met regularly in the city on the Limmat. They founded a gallery, whose profits went toward financing an art collection of their own. Among the earliest purchases were gouaches by Gessner. In 1812, they acquired a "Künstlergüetli" (a small art gallery), which was

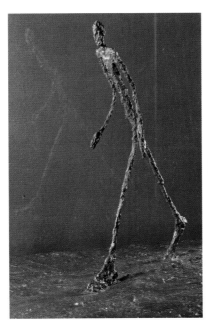

enlarged with an annex in 1847. By about 1900, the space had become far too small. Architect Karl Moser designed a building which opened in 1910 and had to be enlarged in 1925, 1958 and 1976.

Today, Kunsthaus Zürich contains one of the great art collections of Switzerland, with works dated from the late Gothic period to major Dutch and Italian artists as well as the Impressionists. It also houses the biggest collection of works by Edvard Munch outside Norway.

Idleness or the Source of Evil was the title given by Giovanni Segantini to his 1897 painting (above left).

A woman's depression is the theme of Johann Heinrich Füssli's painting, *Silence* (above right).

The Kunsthaus Zürich has the biggest collection of works by Alberto Giacometti in the world. The artist's bronze figure from 1949 is entitled, *Man crossing a Square* (below left).

The front entrance of the museum (below right).

Art exhibition on the Sava

MOCAB in BELGRADE documents the art of the former Yugoslavia and the Serbia of today

ADDRESS:
Usce Save BB, Belgrade

OPENING TIMES:
Wed.-Mon. 10 am
to 6 pm

INTERNET:
www.msub.org.yu

PUBLIC TRANSPORT:
Bus: Route 60

OTHER ATTRACTIONS:
National Museum,
Museum of Applied Arts

Unlike other states subjected to the communist single-party system after the Second World War, Yugoslavian art largely escaped social realism. After Tito's break with Stalin in 1948, instead adopting modernism as its lingua franca, art was freed from the restrictions of socialist reality and was now supposed to "promote artistic freedom and self-reflection," in the words of artist and author Miodrag B. Protić. In the 1950s, he launched the project for a contemporary art museum in Belgrade and became its first director.

The Museum started in 1958 with the Modern Gallery, founded in 1958, which occupied temporary premises until the new building on the left bank of the Sava was ready for occupation in 1965. The building, designed by architects Ivanka Raspopovic´ and Ivan Antic´, is regarded as one of the most successful examples of post-Second World War architecture in Belgrade.

The southern Slavs' artistic world

Through its exhibitions and new acquisitions, the Museum promoted the idea of a "Yugoslavian artistic territory" as part of a universal concept of modern art. The Museum thus represented socialist Yugoslavia internationally, but it also publicized its openness and its progressiveness to the rest of the world.

After the collapse of the federal state of Yugoslavia and its division into new states, the collection of 20th century Yugoslav art developed into a unique regional collection. MoCAB is an important destination for students of 20th century Yugoslav art because it comprehensively documents the art and culture of the Yugoslavian nations from the start of the 20th century. Even before the "southern Slav" state was founded in 1919, the first Yugoslavian art exhibition had been held.

The Expressionist paintings of its founder, Nadežda Petrović, one of Serbia's most important artists early in the last century, form the starting point for a tour of MoCAB. The Museum exhibits important works by a series of Slovenian, Croatian and Serbian artists from the pre-First World War period, who were influenced by Impressionism, Symbolism and Expressionism: Rihard Jakopić, Emanuel Vidović, Miroslav Kraljević, Mališa Glišić and Miloš Golubović.

The multifaceted artistic scene after the First World War and the founding of Yugoslavia, a conglomeration of the Serbs, Croats and Slovenes, is comprehensively represented in the Museum's collection – initially by artists influenced by French Cubism or German Expressionism who experimented with new Abstract ideas: Ivan Radović, Jovan Bijelić and especially Sava Sumanović, one of the most influential and mystifying artists of his generation.

The tour continues with works by artists who embraced widely differing themes, such as social criticism, the dark side of the human psyche, coming to terms with middle class values or the life of the working class. These artists belonged to groups such as Zemlja in Croatia or Zivot in Serbia. The collection also focuses on Surrealist artists and poets with ties to the artistic scene of the time in Paris.

Avant-garde in the 1920s

Perhaps the most exciting part of the MoCAB collection displays the work of various Yugoslavian avant-garde movements of the 1920s,

which were either branches of international movements such as Dadaism or independents like the Zenithists under the leadership of Ljubomir Micić, editor of the journal, *Zenith*, published in Belgrade and Zagreb.

Micić was involved in lively exchanges with the most radical artists in Russia, France, Germany and Czechoslovakia. His movement combined radical political ideas with Constructivist tendencies, represented by the works of Jo Klek and August Cernigoj.

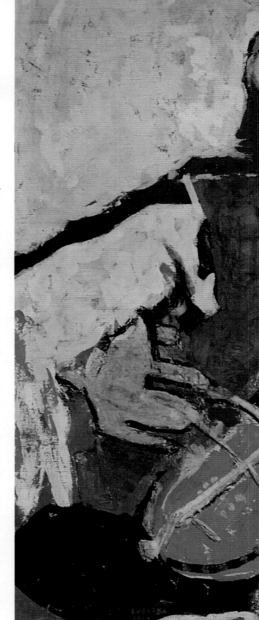

The Museum's new building was erected in the 1960s (below left).

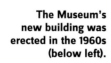

The second part of the MoCAB collection of paintings is devoted to art after the Second World War, especially the paintings of Petar Lubarda, Gabrijel Stupica, Zora Petrović, Mića Popović, Josip Vaništa, Julije Knifer, Bora Iljovski and Rodomir Damnjan as well as sculptures by Olga Jevrić, Vojin Bakić and Ivan Kožarić, among others. Yugoslav art of the 1950s and 1960s is characterized by highly versatile modern forms of expression, yet as early as the 1970s, the focus switched to "new techniques," such as concept art, performance art and video. MoCAB has always brought important and innovative artists to Belgrade, dramatically enhancing the institution's image. Yves Klein, Gutaj, Robert Smithson, Jan Dibbets and Barry Flanagan – to name just a few – exhibited in Belgrade in the 1970s and 1980s. In the 1990s, the Museum stagnated because the Museum's supra-Yugoslavian and international orientation was brought to a stop under the regime of Slobodan Milošević. Reorgani-

zation commenced after 2001, with an intensification of international perspectives. At the same time, however, MoCAB has made a point of exhibiting the work of contemporary Serbian artists.

Four examples of the development of art in the former Yugoslavia from MoCAB's collection in Belgrade: Petar Lubarda's *Guslar*, 1952, named after the traditional single-stringed instrument from the Balkans (above left); Milena Pavlovic Barili's *Self Portrait* (1938); Sava Sumanovic's 1927 *Drunken Boat* (below center); and Bora Iljovski's abstract painting from 1978, *On Black Ground* (below right).

137

Central Europe´s Fringe

The NATIONAL GALLERY in LJUBLJANA documents the role of Slovenian artists in European painting

ADDRESS:
Prešernova 24,
Ljubljana

OPENING HOURS:
Tues.-Sun. 10 am
to 6 pm

INTERNET:
www.ng-slo.si

PUBLIC TRANSPORT:
By city bus

OTHER ATTRACTIONS:
Fužine Castle
(Architectural Museum),
City Gallery

Summer **was the name Ivana Kobilca gave to her genre scene of 1889-1890 that, from the stylistic point of view, is still a Realist work (below left).**

Matej Sternen's picture of a woman, *The Red Umbrella***, 1904, is influenced by French Impressionism (below center).**

Ljubljana is an extremely lively city whose architecture shows traces of many periods, including Baroque and Art Nouveau. It is most particularly marked by the unconventional style of architect Jože Plečnik (1872–1957). Today, Ljubljana is a popular destination for many architectural experts.

However, the city also has a buzzing art scene, as its museums demonstrate. The National Gallery was founded in 1918 and is now the most important art museum in the country, assembling under one roof the biggest collection of Slovenian art from the Middle Ages to the beginning of the 20th century. But it also has a fine collection of European paintings, due to the contributions of many private donors. Several important collections came into the possession of the National Gallery in this way.

The museum consists of three very different buildings. 19th century grandeur and desire for prestige left its mark on the palace-like building erected in 1896. It was once the Narodni dom (National House) and, for a time, it also accommodated a secondary school. In 1911, the National Gallery moved into these grandiose rooms. Right from the start, its aim was to represent Slovenian art as comprehensively as possible.

After spending many years in storage, the Old Master collection eventually found its final home in a new modern building in 1997. In 2001, the two complexes were linked by a glass foyer, a huge futuristic space designed by architects Sadar and Vuga. With its galleries, catwalks and transparent staircases, the Glass Pavilion constitutes a delightful link between different styles and periods. Its broad flight of steps has an almost magical attraction for the visitor.

The tour begins with the Old Master collection. The Italian schools occupy the biggest space, followed by Spanish, French, Flemish, Dutch and Central European painting. There are 155 works on display. Of particular note are Luca Giordano's *Prometheus* and Giovanni Francesco da Rimini's *Madonna with the Christ Child giving the Blessing.* The *Card-players*, painted during the second half of the 17th century by Almenaco Belga – better known as Almanach – is a masterly genre scene.

Among the exhibited works of 20th century artists, Alexej von Jawlensky's *Flowers, Fruits and Jug* and Renato Birolli's *Portrait of the Writer Salvatore Quasimodo.*

Early anonymous masters

Most of the space in the museum is taken up by the Slovenian art collection, beginning with items from the Romanesque period. Many masterpieces of the Gothic era were created by anonymous masters. The most important work of this time is the *Standing Madonna* from 1410, a type of piece widespread in Central Europe and known as the "Beautiful Madonnas." Because of its situation between the Mediterranean, the Alpine region and the gateway to the Pannonian Plain, Ljubljana always paid close attention to European artistic trends.

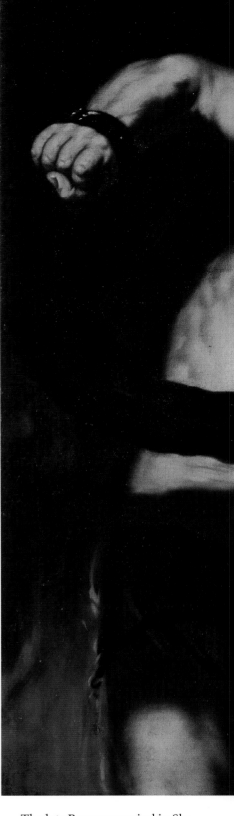

The late Baroque period in Slovenia also produced a great variety of painters. Outstanding among them is the "Quartet" of artists made up of Valentin Metzinger, Franc Jelovšek, Fortunat Bergant and Anton Cebej. Metzinger's *Apotheosis of Saint Francis* and Jelovšek's *Holy Family* are both well worth seeing. Bergant made his reputation as a portrait painter, as did Cebej with his brilliant and colorful images of saints.

Of course, the Biedermeier period also left its mark on a country as bourgeois as Slovenia. It can be seen in the landscape paintings, especially in the atmospheric portraits by Jožef Tominc. The likeness of his father, for example, shows a man on the threshold of old age, whose features reveal both wisdom and resignation. Much of the space

is occupied by the Realists, including the painter, Ivana Kobilca, whose domestic scenes, depicted around the turn of the 20th century, display a highly unique style.

Quartet of Impressionists

A surprise awaits the spectator when entering the early Slovenian Modernist rooms. Slovenian modernism was typified by a quartet of artists. Slovenian Impressionism, which enjoys an international reputation, is striking because of the variety of moods captured by the artists. In addition to Ivan Grohar, whose *Apple Tree* in Blossom is on show, Rihard Jakopič enchants us with his autumn scenes. The landscapes and portraits of women by Matej Sternen and Matija Jama demonstrate a close affinity with the French Impres-

sionists, a relationship which also appears in many Slovenian sculptures influenced by Auguste Rodin.

A very different image of Slovenia is revealed in the Modern Gallery diagonally opposite the National Gallery, a continuation of the museum area. The building, whose architecture is reminiscent of Le Corbusier, houses the biggest collection of modern and contemporary art in Slovenia. For instance, there is a series of self portraits by Ljubljana-born Gabriel Stupica depicting an artist who paints himself as a kind of harlequin. In 1997 and 1998, Jakov Brdar created a sculpture representing a tree bowing down toward the ground, bearing the title, *Preaching to the Birds*. The pictures of Jože Tisnikar, with their alienated faces, are particularly impressive.

Last, but not least, the new art scene in the Modern Gallery is an indication of the awakening that reigns in Slovenia today

One of the major works: *Prometheus* by Luca Giordano (above left).

The *Female Nude* of 1910 by Philip Andreievich Maliavine is particularly fine (above right).

The linking wing and the new building of the National Gallery (below right)

Images of Slovakia

The NATIONAL GALLERY in BRATISLAVA documents the Slovak art world

Baltic Sea

SLOVAKIA
Bratislava

ADDRESS:
Riecna 1, Bratislava

OPENING TIMES:
Tues.-Sun. 10 am
to 5:30 pm

INTERNET:
www.sng.sk

PUBLIC TRANSPORT:
Bus to the bank of the
Danube

OTHER ATTRACTIONS:
Esterhazy Palace,
Galeria Medium

The Madonna and Child **is a work by the Master of the Madonna of Lomnicka (below right). The statue was carved from wood around 1420.**

View of the arcade-lined inner courtyard of the Gallery, called the "Water Barracks" in the vernacular because of its former use and position on the banks of the Danube (below left).

The citizens of Bratislava had finally had enough of the Hungarian troops' ever changing billets and the city council decided to build the soldiers their own accommodation. Of course, a simple barracks would not suffice. In present day Bratislava, city of fortifications and palaces, even a functional building ought to be something special. And so, between 1759 and 1763, a building with four wings was constructed, including a gateway crowned with a tower and three stories furnished all around with arcades. This splendid building on the banks of the Danube, soon a destination for the people taking their afternoon strolls, became known as the "Water Barracks."

The Water Barracks is still there, even if nowadays it accommodates art instead of soldiers. When suitable exhibition space was sought for the Slovakian National Gallery (SNG) after the Second World War, the late Baroque building offered an appropriate setting for exhibitions of Slovak art. A separate department is devoted to European painting as well. Today works by Carracci, Breughel the Elder, Batoni, Rodin, Kokoschka, Picasso, Vasarely and many other artists can be seen. The Gallery was opened in 1950. Between 1969 and 1977, a modern extension was added. In 1990, the SNG acquired the Esterhazy Palace as an exhibition space for applied art, design and architecture from 1900 to 1955. Paintings from eight centuries continue to be exhibited in the Baroque water palace.

Gothic is regarded as Slovakia's most distinct and striking stylistic period, with altar pieces and wooden statues – especially from eastern Slovakia – testifying to great artistry and craftsmanship. Names such as Master Martin and Master Paul are representative of the Zips School, which was at the forefront of painting and sculpture. The various statues of the

Virgin Mary, such as the *Madonna from the Banska Bystrica Area* and the *Madonna of Ruskinovce*, are particularly impressive. Those who see the *Crescent Moon Madonna III of Kremnica* are moved by her facial expression. The art of wood carving reached Slovakia from Burgundy, via southern Germany, with other influences coming from Saxony and Silesia.

The Paul Troger School

The Baroque period is particulary empasized at the Slovak National Gallery, especially the pupils and imitators of the best known Austrian Baroque artist, Paul Troger, whose paintings such as *Christ being Comforted by the Angel* and *The People of Israel crossing the Red Sea* should be mentioned. The Palko family, which originated from Silesia, also played a stylistically decisive role. In *The Cock Fight* by Jacob Bogdan, you can almost hear the creatures hissing and crowing as they await the start of the fight, feathers raised. A death-bed painting showing the deceased Balthasar Horvath-Stansith has a stark beauty. It was painted in the last third of the 17th century by an unknown Slovak artist.

Domain of the portraitists

The 19th century also assumes particular importance in the art of Slovakia. An artistic celebrity of European significance was Ladislav Medňansky (1852-1919), who mostly lived abroad, but occasionally visited the family estates in eastern Slovakia and at the foot of the Tatra Mountains. His landscape painting, *Evening in the Meadow*, has captured the hour of dusk in a masterly way. The artist baron sought connection with ordinary people. His painting, *Old Man seated in a Chair*, is imbued with the melancholy of a life slipping away.

The 19th century was also the domain of the portrait painters, as the collection proves with impressive pictures by Peter Michal Bohún and Jozef Hanula.

Slovakian art took a different direction again in the 20th century and artists were guided increasingly by the movements emanating from Paris and Prague. Together with Mikuláš Galanda and Imrich Weiner-Král, it was mainly Ľudovít Fulla who made a decisive contribution to the

development of the graphic art in Slovakia. His painting, *Madonna with Angels*, is proof of the influence of folk art, but also clearly reveals that he had encountered the ideas of Kandinsky, Klee, Chagall and Picasso.

And if the 1960s were characterized by the restrictions of a communist government, they still had their fruitful moments. Artists such as Albín Brunovsky, Rudolf Fila and Alojz Klimo adopted the West's new forms of representation and painter Juraj Bartusz showed in his work that, even in difficult times, Slovak humor was a powerful weapon which oppressors should never underestimate.

Between 1900 and 1914, the Slovak painter, Dominik Skutecky, visited a hammer mill in Banska Bystrica several times. The study above left shows a worker eating.

The Crucifixion scene (above right) is testament to the high standard of sacred art during the Gothic period.

In the National Gallery's European department, one highlight is the child portrait by the English artist, Raeburn (below right).

Secretive being

The work of Surrealist **JOAN MIRÓ** can be viewed
in a museum dedicated to him in **BARCELONA**

ADDRESS:
Parc de Montjuic, s/n,
Barcelona

OPENING TIMES:
Tues- Sat 10 am to 7 pm
(Oct-June), 10 am
to 8 pm
(July-Sept), Thurs 10 am
to 9:30 pm,
Sun. and public
holidays
10 am to 2:30 pm

INTERNET:
www.bcn.fjmiro.es

PUBLIC TRANSPORT:
Metro station Paral-lel,
then continue by rack
and pinion railway

OTHER ATTRACTIONS:
Picasso Museum,
Frederic Marès
Museum, Antoni Tàpies
Foundation

The Joan Miró
Foundation museum
building designed by
Josep Lluís Sert reflects
elements of ancient
Catalan architectural
styles (below).

The American art critic, Clement Greenberg, described him as "a short, compact, rather taciturn man in a dark-blue suit. He had a well-shaped, round head with close-cut hair, pale skin, small, regular features, sharp eyes and quick movements. Easily enervated, but at the same time, somewhat aloof in the company of strangers. One asks oneself involuntarily what this bourgeois can have contributed to modern art, the Rive Gauche and Surrealism."

He was speaking about Joan Miró. Miró was 54 years old when Greenberg met him in New York where his gallery owner, Pierre Matisse, son of the famous painter, had sent him. Miró was supposed to create a mural for a hotel, a commission that kept him busy for nine months. His stay there gave him a leg up in the American art world and ultimately led to his establishment as a famous painter.

Greenberg's description of Miró's bourgeois appearance is backed by other witnesses. Miró had been part of the group of Surrealists, whose actions were intended first and foremost to provoke, since 1923. The other members liked to mock the formal Miró, and never completely regarded him as one of their own.

Under the sign of revolt

He was a child from a solid, middle-class family and he was a Catalan. Born in 1893, in Barcelona, he studied art through sheer obstinance. He got by, earning his living in a job he disliked. He held his first exhibition in 1911.

It was the era of great aesthetic revolts and Barcelona was no exception. Miró encountered Cubism and attempted it in paintings that are very distantly reminiscent of Oskar Schlemmer. Other works are influenced by the Fauvists, with landscapes and portraits in the style of André Derain. A meeting with André Breton and Max Ernst, together with the impression made on him by Paul Klee's works, led him to the style of painting for which he is known today.

Confident with tone

One of the first pictures to demonstrate Miró's new confidence is a landscape painted in 1924-1925 (now in the Folkwang Museum, Essen, Germany). Here, we see large areas of solid color, red and blue, occupied by strange objects and diffuse clouds. *The Bill*, from 1925 (National Museum of Modern Art, Paris), in which one of the amoeba-like forms that became his specialty appears, is more consistent. Thereafter, we see tableaux that are sometimes almost overpopulated with strange beings, characters reminiscent of Hieronymus Bosch's dream creations, live, combined with Vassily Kandinsky's lines from the "Improvisations" series.

Miró always stressed that his artistic inventions were based on Catalan traditions – and it was important to him to be a Catalan, not Spanish, artist. An equally tradition, familiar to him from his homeland, was working with fired clay, which is why he started to work on ceramics in collaboration with Llorens Artigas. His textiles too followed a native tradition.

He became one of the most famous artists of Art Moderne. He received masses of awards and honors and made a lot of money. He had his friend, architect Josep Lluís Sert, built a villa with a large studio in Palma, on Mallorca, his mother's native island, where he lived with his family when not in France.

In 1975, Spanish dictator Franco died and eight years before his own death, Miró founded the Miró Foundation at the Center for Contemporary Art Studies in Barcelona. The intention was to bring together a collection of his works and create an appropriate exhibition space for them. The piece of land chosen was located on the northern slope of Montjuïc, the mountain that overlooks the city

of Barcelona, to the south of the harbor. The 1992 Olympic Stadium lies nearby.

The architect was again Miró's friend, Josep Lluís Sert. He created a snow-white building that combined traditional Catalan elements with the functionalism of classic modernity. Extended in 1986 by a structure by architect Jaume Freixa, the result is a generous collection of exhibition halls, a patio and a tower. There is a theatre that can be used for musical events. The Miró Foundation possesses a total of more than 11,000 objets d'art: 240 paintings, 175 sculptures, 9 textile works, 4 ceramics, 8,000 drawings and almost

a complete collection of printed works. It is the second biggest collection of the painter's works after the Miró Museum on Mallorca. The works have been made available by the artist's family and other collectors.

A star as a logo

A tour leads visitors past sculptures as different in form and expression as they are in materials and past intensely colored paintings. Populated by secretive beings, sometimes they seem cheerful, sometimes threatening, sometimes obscene – or all three. They undeniably originated in the dream worlds of Surrealism.

Women and Birds at Sunrise (1946) is a rather somber collection of eyes, hands and hairy objects before a grayish-yellow sky with red sun. *The Gold of the Azure* (1967) shows a sky-blue ball and a pair of hominid figures on a golden-yellow ground.
Miró's customary logo, which was at the same time his signature, a star consisting of eight fine strokes, appears here three times.

Surrealist dreams: *Collage-Drawing* is the title of this work from 1933 (above).

Joan Miró in a photo dating from 1967 (below right).

The museum as art

The **GUGGENHEIM** in **BILBAO** is a masterpiece of Deconstructivism

ATLANTIC OCEAN
Bilbao
Madrid
SPAIN
Mediterranean Sea

ADDRESS:
Avenida ¨
Abandoibarra Et. 2,
Bilbao

OPENING HOURS:
Opening hours:
Tues-Sun 10 am
to 8 pm

INTERNET:
www.guggenheim-bilbao.es

PUBLIC TRANSPORT:
The city center is so small and clearly laid out that the best way to get about is on foot. It is also possible to use the subway trains.

OTHER ATTRACTIONS:
Museum of Fine Arts,
Vasco Museum

The photo below left shows a full view of the Guggenheim Bilbao. The torso to the right of it, created in 1948, is by the Spaniard Eduardo Chillida. Chillida is one of the most famous figures in modern Spanish art.

The Guggenheims are a dynasty of American entrepreneurs who became rich during the Industrial Revolution of the 19th century. The dynasty was founded by Meyer Guggenheim, who emigrated from Switzerland and amassed a fortune, initially as an importer and then as the owner of mining companies.

His son, Daniel, who continued the business, started to collect art and established a foundation. His brother, Salomon Robert, who also worked for the family firm, proved decidedly radical in his artistic interests. He was interested in modern art and established the Salomon R. Guggenheim Foundation to promote abstract art in 1937.

The foundation opened a museum in Manhattan in 1939, moving to another building, designed by Frank Lloyd Wright, in 1959. Of all the clan's art collectors, Salomon's niece, Peggy, was the most determined. In 1938, she opened a gallery in London, which formed the basis for a comprehensive private collection. Furthermore, she was married to the German Surrealist, Max Ernst, for a time. In 1951, her collection went to Venice, to the Palazzo Venier dei Leoni, where it can be seen today.

In the meantime, most of the Guggenheims' art acquisitions were stockpiling in the foundation established by Salomon. Their energy was extraordinary, the art collection acquired by them immense and the financial backing massive. Apart from the museums in Manhattan and Venice, the Guggenheims have annexes in Berlin and Las Vegas, with the number of Guggenheim museums currently totaling six. The most

spectacular, apart from the original Museum in New York, is based in Bilbao. It was completed in 1997 and is the work of architect Frank O. Gehry.

Bilbao, the capital of the Basque province of Biscaya, is one of Spain's most important economic centers. During the second half of the 20th century, the heavy industry based here suffered a crisis that affected the entire city. It turned to new areas of business, including tourism. The Guggenheim Museum is one of the main attractions, standing on the right bank of the Río Nervión, the river that flows through the city, in the New Town.

Like a piece by Chillida
Frank Owen Gehry, born 1929 in Canada and resident of the United States since he was a student, is one of the most important modern architects. He is a supporter of Deconstructivism, a style of architecture that detests right angles and relies, contrary to all visual traditions and apparently to all structural laws as well, on slopes and sharp angles, unexpected curves, domes and plunging lines. Apart from Gehry, other famous proponents are Polish-American Daniel Libeskind, Dutchman Rem Kohlhaas and Iraqi Zaha Hadid. Dispensing with the structural norm requires complicated calculations and necessitates the use of unusual materials, predominantly metals. Libeskind clad his Jewish Museum in Berlin with sheet zinc; Gehry used glass, limestone and titanium in Bilbao.

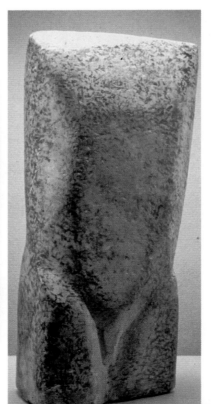

What all Deconstructivist buildings have in common is that they resemble modern plastic art, which is, of course, the intention. Gehry's architecture in Bilbao looks like a massive enlargement of a work by sculptor Eduardo Chillida, some of whose iron plastic art, such as Beserkada XI, can also to be seen in the Guggenheim collection. Furthermore Chillida, whose full surname is Chillida Juantegui, is a native Basque and so belongs in this very special place.

There is no building in the world that fulfills an aesthetic end by merely existing. It must create usable space. Museum rooms are especially demanding with regard to shape, size, display areas and lighting. Gehry succeeds in this extremely well. As with Libeskind's Jewish Museum, the interior architecture relates to and complements the content of the exhibits. Since it is almost exclusively modern art on show in Bilbao, in which Deconstructivism has its

roots, structure and exhibits coincide here. Gehry groups a total of 19 exhibition rooms around a central rotunda, a reference and an ironic nod to the great Andrea Palladio's favorite shape. Some of the rooms are reserved for permanent collections, temporary exhibitions are held in the others. Some modern art has departed from the customary settings and formats, requiring whole rooms, or indeed constituting rooms. Sol LeWitt designed the existing walls and thus made them his own.

Reference to Peggy Guggenheim

The Guggenheim Bilbao concerns itself with the latest trends in the modern aesthetic, preferably abstract, so Anselm Kiefer, Jenny Holzer and Richard Serra are all represented. In comparison, the classic modern artists seem almost conventional, but are still impressive: the abstract Expressionism of Jackson Pollock and Barnett Newman, a

beautiful Wassily Kandinsky, *The Blue Mountain*, that dates from his stay in Murnau in Upper Bavaria, and, a wink to Peggy Guggenheim, a famous painting by Max Ernst, *The Attirement of the Bride*, from 1940. The temporary exhibitions too are concerned predominantly, but not exclusively, with modern themes.

The Museum has a restaurant and its chef, Martín Berasategui, is regarded as one of the best in Spain.

The domes of the Museum built by Frank O. Gehry soar impressively into the sky (above).

Richard Serra's *Snake* is one of the most interesting works of art in the collection (below right).

The secrets of Salvador Dali

The master of Surrealism left behind a museum in FIGUERES, Spain which is a work of art in itself

Even the former town theater in Figueres makes a Surreal impression. On the roof, golden nymphs spread their arms wide like wings, as if they are about to take flight immediately into the bright sky above the nearby Costa Brava. There are also lifesize statues – which appear to be balancing loaves of bread a yard long on their heads – to be admired alongside the temple-like frontage. Three tall doors lead beneath into a many roomed work of art that Salvador Dali (1904–89) bequeathed to the world as a place where "my spirit will live on after my death:" the Dali Theater-Museum, half theater, half museum.

The artist always felt an emotional tie to the northern Spanish city of his birth. He was baptized in the neighboring church and, at 14, he had his first exhibition of paintings in the theater foyer. He admired the classical architecture from the middle of the previous century, the suggestion of columns, the elegant salons. He was sad that in 1937, during the Spanish Civil War, a great fire reduced the splendor to the bare foundations. When the municipal government decided to erect a museum dedicated to the town's most famous son in the early 1960s, Dali insisted that the theater ruins be included in the design of the building.

Love of the theater

Under his guidance the ruined site was transformed into a memorial to Salvador Dali, a "world center of Surrealism." The external facades were rebuilt in the old style, complemented by Surreal elements. Inside Dali ensured high, bright rooms with perfect exhibition spaces. As early as the opening in 1974, the Theater-Museum was able to offer a veritable treasure trove of works by Dali. Others were added later from his estate and as a result of acquisitions, including *William Tell and Gravida* (1931), *Laurence Olivier as Richard III* (1955) and *The Apotheosis of Dollar* (1965).

The Theater-Museum, administered by a foundation established by Dali, now possesses more than 4,000 paintings, sculptures and other exhibits from all the master's creative periods. The crowd of visitors is enormous. Around 800,000 people, many of whom have very little interest in art, arrive each year. "The simple people love secrets," Dali once said, "and they find these in my paintings." There are the famous clocks that ooze like ripe Camembert above branches. Elephants walk on stilts, crutches support a huge nose, a landscape picture is reflected in a silver bottle as a naked woman.

Dali's theater backdrop, *Allegory of Death*, which shows a gigantic human torso with a fractured skull and a tunnel leading through the breast into the darkness, takes up almost the entire back wall of the former stage. A three-dimensional work of art awaits the visitor in a room with a red sofa shaped like bow lips, a nose-shape fireplace, two wall paintings and a canopy of blonde fibers. If one looks through a glass lens, the interior merges to form a portrait of the Hollywood actress Mae West (1892–1980). In the courtyard, formerly the theater parquet, Dali's old Cadillac is parked as a work of art, with a big, strapping statue of Esther by the Viennese artist, Ernst Fuchs on the radiator. Inside, plastic plants rear up out of torn upholstery. The foyer is adorned by a room-height nude, viewed from the back, which Dali painted of his wife, Gala, who was 12 years older than he. When viewed from a considerable distance, the beautiful Russian woman's back appears to be transformed into a portrait of the former American president Abraham Lincoln.

The beautiful swan

Dali's wife posed with a swan in another painting, *Atomic Leda*, and as Galarina, she is seen with a bared left breast. A ceiling painting by the master shows Gala and Salvador Dali arising from the dead.

Gala Dali died in 1982 at the age of 89 in the fishing village of Port Lligat, the couple's home for many years. Salvador Dali spent his final years in a palace adjacent to his Theater-Museum, which he painted ox-blood red. He died in his birthplace, Figueres, in January 1989 at the age of 84.

ADDRESS:
Plaza Gala y Salvador Dalí s/n, Figueres

OPENING TIMES:
Tues-Sun 10:30 am to 5:45 pm, July to Sept Mon-Sun 9 am to 7:45 pm

INTERNET:
www.salvador-dali.org

HOW TO GET THERE:
Figueres is close to the motorway. Nearest airports Gerona and Barcelona.

OTHER ATTRACTIONS:
Dali's home in Port Lligat, the Gala Dalí Castle Museum-House.

The Palace of Figueres, where Salvador Dali once lived, is adjacent to the Museum. Palace and Museum building, formerly a theater, were decorated by Dali in a Surreal manner (left).

The Mae West Room (below), in which Dali satirized the attraction of the Hollywood actress, is a special attraction. The sofa in the foreground symbolizes her bow lips.

Photographic portrait of the artist in his declining years (right).

147

In the artists' park

The PRADO in MADRID focuses on Spanish art

ADDRESS:
Paseo del Prado s/n,
Madrid

OPENING TIMES:
Tues-Sun 9 am to 7 pm

INTERNET:
www.museoprado.es

PUBLIC TRANSPORT:
Subway Line 1, Atocha
station and Line 2,
Banco station

OTHER ATTRACTIONS:
Royal Palace, Royal
Monastery of the
Discalced (Barefoot)
Carmelites

During a visit to Spain, Edouard Manet, France's greatest Realist and an important trailblazer for Impressionism, wrote to his colleague, Henri Fantin-Latour,

"Dear friend, I regret that you cannot see Velázquez with me; how great would be your joy since this journey is worth it for him alone. The artists of all schools that surround him in the Prado and whose outstanding works are exhibited appear amateurs beside him. He is the greatest painter of all time. He has not just amazed me, but enraptured me."

Diego Velázquez (1599–1660) was a grand master of Spanish Baroque. His productivity was extraordinary and the diversity of his themes was considerable; he was court painter to the Spanish royal family and supplied the ruling dynasty with historical paintings as well as depictions with religious content. Most noteworthy of all are his portraits, which combine rtistic delicacy with an unerringly sharp eye. His paintings of court dwarves and the maids of honor, *Las Meninas*, have no equal in any age.

Ill-favored royal family

It was only one and a half centuries later that this skill was revived with the paintings of Francisco Goya, also a court painter. The massive portrait of the Spanish royal family, whose stupendously ugly faces are depicted without flattery, is as spectacular as his portraits of Maya, clothed and naked, and – above all – his print series depicting scenes from the Spanish War of Independence, *The Executions of Third May* and the *Disasters of War*. They, like the Diego Velázquez painting admired by Manet, are to be found in the Prado Museum, Madrid. The word *prado* means 'meadow.' The name is derived from the park, the Prado de

San Jerónimo, where the building was erected in 1785.

The history of the collection starts in the 16th century. The Spanish kings of the house of Habsburg began to collect art. Spain had just risen to be the mightiest empire in the world through Columbus's discovery and the Conquistadors' raids that generated a steady stream of riches from the New World. The Crown acquired whatever was available on the international art market. Charles V, his son Philip II and his successors, including Philip IV, a distinguished collector, all ordered and commissioned works of art.

Purchases were made first and foremost from countries with whom a good political relationship existed, such as Flanders and Italy, which is how works by Pieter Brueghel the Elder and Hieronymus Bosch's *Garden of Earthly Delights* were acquired. Bosch's somber, demonic masterpiece of Flemish Mannerism reached Madrid alongside works by Rogier van der Weyden, Anthony Van Dyck, Jacob Jordaens and Peter Paul Rubens. The court bought Albrecht Dürer and Hans Memling. It collected Italians such as Titian, Fra Angelico and Raphael.

At the same time, one artist above all, El Greco – who was not Spanish born, as his name suggests – helped Spanish art achieve the global status it deserved. Alongside him were the other great Baroque masters such as Luis de Morales, Francisco Ribalta, José de Ribera, Francisco de Zurbarán and Bartolomé Esteban Murillo. The tradition continued right to the present day. Both Pablo Picasso and Salvador Dalí were native Spaniards.

View of the Prado's entrance façade. The Museum is regarded as an architectural masterpiece of Spanish Classicism (below).

Rooms for individual artists

Today, Spanish art created between the 12th and 19th centuries dominates the Prado collection. As far as the history of the building is concerned, the architect was Juan de Villanueva. He was an important Classicist and designed the Plaza Mayor and the Palace of Justice in the capital. The works of King Ferdinand VII and his Queen, Isabella, were decisively promoted. The building opened in 1819 as the Museum of the Royal Collection of Paintings and Sculptures. The Museum became the Spanish National Museum in 1868.

Since then, the collection has expanded continuously. Soon space in the Villanueva building was scarce, so it was extended. 19th century art had to be housed in the Casón del Buen Retiro. From time to time, parts of the Museum were obstructed by scaffolding, but now all rooms are again accessible. The exhibits in the 100 rooms are arranged according to national highlights or, in the case of the great Spaniards, by individual artist. The present collection contains some 8,600 paintings, one seventh of which are on display.

The Good Shepherd by Bartolomé Esteban Murillo is just one of the Museum's attractions (above left).

El Greco's *Saint Sebastian* is impressive proof of the artist's skill at expressive depiction (above right).

Edouard Manet was fascinated by Velázquez's painting, *Bacchus or The Topers* (below).

149

Fleeing fascism

MADRID made the Palacio de Villahermosa available for the **THYSSEN-BORNEMISZA COLLECTION**

ATLANTIC OCEAN

Madrid

SPAIN *Mediterranean Sea*

ADDRESS:
Paseo del Prado 8, Madrid

OPENING HOURS:
Tues-Sun 10:00 am to 7 pm

INTERNET:
www.museothyssen.org

TRANSPORT:
Subway Line 1, station Atocha u.
Line 2, station Banco de España

OTHER ATTRACTIONS:
Museo Nacional de Artes Decorativas, Museo de la Real Academía de Bellas Artes de San Fernando

Camille Pissarro also embraced Impressionist themes in his 1896 *Orchard in Éragny* (below left).

The most famous portrait of King Henry VIII of England was painted by Hans Holbein the Younger (below right).

The Thyssens were one of the great German industrial dynasties. August Thyssen founded an iron-rolling mill in Duisburg in 1867. Later, he acquired mining companies and metal-processing factories, subsequently owning one of the biggest iron and steel groups in the Rhein–Ruhr area. August's son and heir, Fritz Thyssen, distinguished himself by being an early supporter of Adolf Hitler. He later fell out with the dictator, which earned him a long stay in a concentration camp.

His younger brother, Heinrich, was more interested in art than Nazism and invested his inherited wealth in an art collection, thus continuing a tradition begun by his father, who had acquired a number of sculptures, including some by Auguste Rodin. In 1907, Heinrich Thyssen married Hungarian Baroness Bornemisza de Kaszon, whose name and title he took one year later, when he had himself adopted by his father-in-law.

Gallery on Lake Lugano

The first home for his growing art collection was Schloss Rohoncz. In 1937, when Adolf Hitler – whom his brother so much admired – was about to annex the republic of Austria, he moved to Castagnola in Ticino, Switzerland with his family and collection of paintings. He was supported by his son, Hans Heinrich, born in 1921. It was Hans Heinrich who first opened the collection to the public in the Villa Favorita on the shore of Lake Lugano.

His father, Baron Heinrich, died in 1947. The collection began to split up as a result of various inheritance claims. Hans Heinrich succeeded in buying everything

back and extending it with new acquisitions, particularly modern art works, which had previously been underrepresented. Eventually, he owned around eight hundred paintings, making it the second biggest private art collection in the world.

Baron Hans Heinrich von Thyssen-Bornemisza married Spanish woman, Carmen. In 1992, their joint collection went to Madrid, originally as a loan. It was kept in the Palacio de Villahermosa in the Plaza de Cánovas del Castillo, a classical building from the early 19th century converted by Antonio López Aguado, a pupil of the architect, Juan de Villanueva, who designed the Prado.

Rafael Moneo was the architect charged with overhauling and converting the palace for its new purpose. He chose not to change the facade with the Doric columns of the portico or its stone and brick walls and created several floors of austere exhibition rooms. The pieces were arranged chronologically, with the oldest paintings hung on the top floor and the most recent on the lowest.

As you come in, the first thing you see is a more than life-size double portrait. It shows the Thyssen-Bornemisza couple and is considered utterly devoid of any artistic merit. What follows is frankly extraordinary for admirers of the Old Masters or modern art lovers. The Museo Thyssen-Bornemisza complements the the Prado and the Museo National Centro de Arte Reina Sofía, in the best possible way by showing important examples of 20th century art and by not restricting its selection of modern artists to artists of Spanish origin.

From the castles of Europe

One of the oldest paintings is by Duccio di Buoninsegna. In his *Christ and the Samaritan Woman*, the Sienese painter, a genius of the Italian late Gothic period, combines the techniques of Byzantine icon painting with the aesthetics of his contemporary, Giotto; the result is a surprising impression of modernity, similar to what we get from the painting of the Fauves and the German Expressionists. The collection includes works by Jan van Eyck. Hans Holbein the Younger is represented by his famous portrait of his employer, King Henry VIII of England. There are works by Hans Memling, Hans Baldung Grien and

Metropolis (1916–1917),
by the German artist
and satirist, George
Grosz, is a masterpiece
of German Expressio-
nism (above).

View of the Palacio
de Villahermosa,
in which the Thyssen-
Bornemisza Collection
can be seen
(below right).

Lucas Cranach the Elder. Italian
art is splendidly represented by
Titian and Caravaggio.

The high proportion of more
recent German art is due to the
Thyssen family's German origins.
There is an exceptional painting by
Caspar David Friedrich and many
works by members of the two
groups of artists, "Die Brücke" and
"Der blaue Reiter." Contemporary
artists include Americans such as
Edward Hopper and Robert Rauschenberg.

Part of the Thyssen-Bornemisza Collection, a total of 72 paintings and 8 sculptures, has been
kept in the monastery of Pedralbes
in Barcelona since 1992. Meanw-

hile, extensions to the Museo Thyssen-Bornemisza in Madrid are
being considered. Two plots of
land close to the Palacio de Villahermosa have been acquired and
the plan is to increase the exhibition area by 86,000 square feet.
The competition to develop them
was won in 2000 by a group of
architects led by Manuel Baquero.

Guernica! Guernica!

Picasso's painting is one of the 20th century's most renowned works of art and hangs in **MADRID'S QUEEN SOFÍA MUSEUM**

ADDRESS:
Santa Isabel 52,
Madrid

OPENING TIMES:
Wed.-Mon. 10 a.m.
to 9 p.m.,
Sun. until 2.30 p.m. only

INTERNET:
www.museoreina-
sofia.es

PUBLIC TRANSPORT:
Subway, Atocha station

OTHER ATTRACTIONS:
Museum of Art
Siglo XIX

Something unusual took place in the United Nations' New York headquarters in early February 2003. A large tapestry was spirited away for the occasion of the appearance of US Secretary of State Colin Powell, who was defending the decision of the United States government to intervene militarily in Iraq. Shortly thereafter, the US intervened, overthrowing a bloody dictator, destroying many civilian facilities and igniting a civil war that would cost the lives of tens of thousands of people.

The tapestry, a gift from American businessman Nelson Rockefeller, is a reproduction of a famous anti-war painting by Pablo Picasso, Guernica. The title echoes the name of a small Basque town to the east of Bilbao.

There was also foreign involvement in the Spanish Civil War, which started in 1936 with a military putsch led by General Franco against the republic. Volunteers from many countries fought on the Republican side;

the Fascist dictatorships of Italy and Germany backed Franco. Hitler sent the military contingent of the Condor Legion, whose air forces attacked Guernica on April 26, 1937. They carpet bombed the town, causing serious damage and costing many lives. It was the first major action of its kind against the civilian population of a country at war and it became the pattern during the Second World War, foreshadowing the bombardments of Coventry and Rotterdam, Dresden and Hiroshima.

A World's Fair was held in Paris in 1937. The 56-year-old painter, Pablo Picasso, who was born in Malaga but lived in France, was asked to design Spain's pavilion. In response, he created the painting, *Guernica*. He spent five weeks painting it and presented it to the public on July 12, 1937.

Black, white, and gray
It is one of the most renowned painting of the 20th century, impressive

for its scale alone, almost $11^1/_2$ by 26 feet. The color scheme is also unusual. Picasso, a genius with color, limited himself to shades of black, white and gray.

The destruction of the Basque town is not depicted in a naturalistic style, but by using strange pictograms and symbols. There are human heads across the entire width of the canvas, men's heads, those of women, that of a child. The faces show presentiment, fear, confusion, pain, agony and rigor mortis. There are detached limbs. Hands grasp objects. A horse screams in its death throes. A bull, a symbol that Picasso liked using for General Franco at the time, stamps calmly through what is happening. The artist depicts everything using the special technique, collage, that characterized his style in the 1930s. The painting made its point. It was not just professional art critics who were impressed. There is a well-known anecdote about a se-

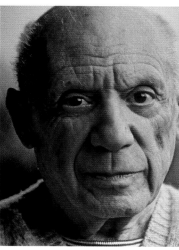

In *Guernica*, Pablo Picasso (photo above) depicts a town of the same name bombed by the German Fascists. *Guernica* came to symbolize the bestial dstruction of the Second World War.

nior SS officer who stood before the painting and asked the artist, "Did you do that?"

"No," the artist replied, "you did."

The Spanish Civil War ended in 1939. Franco won and set up his dictatorship. It ended with his death in 1975 and it is a historical paradox that King Juan Carlos I, whom Franco himself named as successor, immediately brought about a return to democracy. His wife, Queen Sofía, regarded it as one of her duties to promote the Museum for contemporary Spanish art that existed in Madrid, even if the existence was a shadowy one. The Museum has born her name since 1988.

Guernica, on loan to the Museum of Modern Art in New York until 1981, came home to Spain and found a home in the Queen Sofía National Museum of Modern Art's Picasso Room. It hangs there with his numerous preliminary studies, alongside other works by the artist from different periods.

Spain in the world of modern art

The Museum's origins date back to the end of the 19th century. At that time, contemporary Spanish art was promoted at the University of Madrid's campus, but was restricted to temporary exhibitions. When a collection was put together, the search began for a suitable building.

It was found in a Baroque hospital complex dating from the time of King Philip II, which had subsequently been converted many times until, at the end of the Franco era, it was once again used as a hospital. It escaped the threat of demolition by being elevated to the status of a national monument.

The extremely functional exhibition rooms mostly display Spanish art of the last hundred years, starting with Impressionist and Post-Impressionist artists relatively unknown abroad, such as Joaquín Mir and Dario de Regoyos, before turning to the impressively large number of Spanish artists who were important to the international avant-garde movement, from Juan Gris to Juan Miró and Salvador Dalí. There is a Sculpture Room, where the most prominent representative is Eduardo Chillida and Antoni Tàpies has a room to himself. The Museum does not forget to place Spanish avant-garde in its international context, which spans Jean Arp, via Alexander Calder, to Mario Merz and Donald Judd.

View of the front entrance to the Queen Sofia Museum (below).

A modern paradise

The **CZECH NATIONAL GALLERY** in **PRAGUE** comprises Czech Impressionism, Expressionism and fine Bohemian art

North Sea

o Prague

CZECH REPUBLIC

ADDRESS:
Staroměstské nám. 12, Prague

OPENING TIMES:
Tues.-Sun. 10 am to 6 pm

INTERNET:
www.ngprague.cz

PUBLIC TRANSPORT:
Both royal palaces are only accessible by foot; the Trade Fair Palace can be reached by metro.

OTHER ATTRACTIONS:
Museum of Czech Cubism, Alphonse Mucha Museum

František Kupka is one of the best known Czech artists of the 20th century. His graphic design, *The Way of Silence* (below left), combined elements of Symbolism and Art Nouveau.

Paul Gauguin's self portrait, *Bonjour Monsieur Gauguin (Good Morning Mr Gauguin)*, 1889, is considered an early Expressionist work (below right).

When Soviet communism dominated Eastern Europe and Joseph Stalin's anti-modernist view of art was more or less binding in most countries, Prague was regarded by art lovers, at least those from the former German Democratic Republic, as a paradise on earth. Several rooms on the Hradcany contained work by all the gods of classic modernism, including Georges Seurat, Pablo Picasso, Georges Braque, Fernand Léger and Henri Matisse.

The pictures had once belonged to Vincenc Kramář, an early 20th century Czech art historian and one of the first collectors of French avant-garde in Central Europe. Today, the collection is no longer to be found on Hradcany, but to the north of Letná Hill, in the Trade Fair Palace near the Baumgarten.

The building, purpose built between 1925 and 1928, is regarded as exemplary architecture from the first Czechoslovakian republic. Outwardly rather simple and easily confused with a factory building, its interior surprises visitors with its clear layout and perfect lighting. Everything the National Gallery has to offer in the way of art and crafts from the 19th and 20th centuries is housed here.

Homage to the Czech Republic

First come artists and sculptors from early in the reign of Emperor Franz Josef II. They produced portraits, landscapes and historical paintings which differ little from the art created in Vienna at the same time. However, the rising Czech nationalist movement pro-

foundly influenced fine art, literature and music. Many Czech artists considered themselves spokesmen for the Czech people.

However, it was not until the Art Nouveau period that Czech art truly achieved its aesthetic independence. Many important Austrian architects of the period were natives of Bohemia and Prague possesses extraordinary Art Nouveau architecture, especially on Wenceslas Square in the heart of the city. Alphonse Mucha, an Art Nouveau graphic artist, came from Bohemia, but made his name in Paris.

František Kupka, one of the pioneers of abstract art, became Czechoslovakia's best known 20th century artist. Born in 1871, he went to Paris at 21 years of age and stumbled into the poet, Guillaume Apollinaire, who made up the Orphinist Circle together with Francis Picabia and Robert Delaunay. Picabia and Delaunay were known for paintings without subjects, based on Cubism. Kupka's gift was only recognized after his death in 1957. *Amorpha – Fugue in Two Colors* of 1912, his first painting without a subject and his most famous, hangs in the Trade Fair Palace. Other Czech avant-gardists were Otto Gutfreund, Josef Gočár and Pavel Janák. They painted or

built in the Cubist style and also created Cubist artifacts.

The National Gallery in the Trade Fair Palace provides exhaustive information about all of them. It always introduces the corresponding applications in design and the industrial forms that parallel the free arts. It shows developments through to the present day, right up to Jíří Kolář who died in 2002 and whose exquisite collages have won a reputation internationally.

Palace of old art

The Trade Fair Palace in Prague contains the Modern department of the Národní Gallery, the Czech Republic's National Gallery. Another building, the Sternberg Palace located on the Castle Hill right next to the Archbishop's Palace holds the collection of older art. It is a beautiful, late Baroque building erected around 1700.

The attached garden is famous. The Sternbergs, to whom the palace belonged, were typical of the charismatic, noble Frankish families spread across half of Europe and who achieved influence, wealth and power in old Austria. The branch of the family concerned here is the Sternberg-Manderscheids. Their most important scion was Caspar Maria von Stern-

berg, born 1761. A highly educated man originally destined for a career in theology, he resigned all his spiritual roles in 1806 and devoted himself to Bohemian culture. He then became director of the Bohemian National Museum, a further artistic stronghold in the city on the Vltava.

From Rembrandt to Dürer

The items in the Sternberg Palace represent by far the biggest collection of art in the Czech Republic. The collection stands on an equal footing with other great museums in Europe and America in terms of renowned artists and antiquities as well as Russian icons. The Italians are represented by Sebastiano del Piombo, Tintoretto, Bronzino and Tiepolo. The elder Breughel hangs there alongside Rembrandt Harmensz van Rijn, Peter Paul Rubens, Anthony Van Dyck, Jacob Jordaens, Gerard Terborch and Frans Hals. Among the Germans are Lucas Cranach the Elder and Hans Holbein the Elder. *A pièce de resistance* is *The Feast of the Rosary*, painted by Albrecht Dürer in 1506.

One of the most beautiful pieces in the collection of Old Masters is the icon, *Mary and Child*, the work of an unknown Bohemian master, created around 1400 (above).

View of the National Gallery. It was originally a trade fair hall (below).

Bohemia's art gallery

The CASTLE GALLERY in PRAGUE houses a small but valuable collection of Czech paintings

North Sea

Prague

CZECH REPUBLIC

ADDRESS:
Obrazáma Pražského
Hradu, Hradcany,
Prague

OPENING TIMES:
Mon.-Sun. 10 am
to 6 pm

INTERNET:
www.hrad.cz

HOW TO GET THERE:
The streets of Prague
Old Town are narrow.
The route up to
Hradcany is best tack-
led on foot.

OTHER ATTRACTIONS:
Saint Vitus Cathedral,
Strahov Monastery

**B. Spranger titled his
painting in the Oriental
tradition: *Hercules and
Omphalé* (below left).**

**The painting, *A Gallant
Situation* by N. Grund
(above left), is fully in
keeping with the style
during the age of
gallantry.**

In 1526, Bohemia's crown fell to the Habsburgs. The first Austrian ruler in Prague was Franz I and his son and successor was Maximilian II. It was the age of the Reformation and Counter-Reformation. Jan Hus had carried the reformed faith to Bohemia, which remained an area of constant dispute between the estranged Christian Churches.

Emperor Maximilian II's son and successor was Rudolph. He was intelligent and educated, but also ill, mentally as well as physically. He remained unmarried and proved largely uninterested in politics. His passions were science and art and he was interested in alchemy and astronomy. He preferred to reside in Prague and during his reign, the city flourished as never before. The scientific minds that he gathered around him at court included Danish astronomer Tycho Brahe and his pupil, Johannes Keppler, who built the first astronomical telescope and discovered what are known as Keppler's Laws.

Many of Rudolph's predecessors had already been patrons and collectors, including Emperor Maximilian I, who brought the Italian Mannerist, Giuseppe Arcimboldo, to his court. Rudolph continued the tradition, purchasing paintings by Pieter Breughel the Elder, with their powerful and gloomy depictions of carnal lust and the atrocities of war. His art

collection was by far the biggest in Europe at a time when assembling art galleries was a popular activity for princes. Prague, an architectural masterpiece, became a lavish treasury for paintings, sculptures and *objets d'art*.

Art robberies during war
Rudolf II died in 1612. He was succeeded by his brother, Matthias, a papist zealot, who plunged the country into the Thirty Years' War, which started in Prague when two imperial councilors were forcibly ejected from a castle window (Defenestration of Prague).

Even after the war ended, Bohemia remained an area of military unrest. Rudolph's art collections suffered as a result and many pieces were lost. The core remained intact, however, and can still be seen in the royal castle at Hradcany. The collection was topped again by the ruler who followed

Matthias. He was the second Ferdinand and also the emperor whose radical response to the Reformation started the Thirty Years' War. Appointed emperor-in-waiting by Matthias, his childless predecessor, during the latter's lifetime, he was already wearing the Bohemian royal crown in 1617. The fanatical Catholic, brought up by Jesuits, persecuted Protestants wherever they appeared in his kingdom. Less well known is that he was an equally obsessive art lover and collector, who contributed to preserving the treasures collected by his predecessors.

When the Thirty Years' War ended in 1648, Swedish troops plundered the collection, stealing almost everything. Ultimately, what has survived to this day – in spite of battles, plundering and other disasters –is classed by current travel guides as small, but precious. It is housed in the Castle Gallery,

located in the inner castle courtyard, the first being known as the Courtyard of Honor, the addition to the palace buildings carried out by Empress Maria Theresa between 1756 and 1774, to the west of and right next door to the Archbishop's Palace. The gallery building was comprehensively restored inside during the 1960s by architects František Cubr and Josef Hruby and reopened in 1965.

A Czech Raphael

There are around 70 items, including many masterpieces of European art by artists such as Hans von Aachen. This Mannerist, born 1552 in Cologne, finally reached the court of Emperor Rudolph II after many detours and was appointed court painter. Together with Arcimboldo, he embodies what is known as Rudolphian Mannerism. In his case, this means a technically perfect, frequently extremely complicated style of painting. After Rudolph's death, Han von Aachen then entered the service of Matthias, whose portrait he painted. His likeness hangs in the Castle Gallery, next to Titian's *Young Women at her Toilet* and works by Peter Paul Rubens and Paolo Veronese.

Furthermore there are examples of genuine Bohemian art, by Jan Kupecky, for example. The child of Protestant parents who had fled to Slovakia to escape persecution, he was born in 1667 and traveled widely in Europe. He studied in Italy, where he was inspired by Caravaggio, but Dutch influences in his work are also unmistakable. Finally, he became a popular portraitist.

Another Czech Baroque artist was Karel Škréta. He too came from a Protestant family, but converted and became a prolific painter of religious pictures. He earned the nickname the "Czech Raphael." His place, and that of Kupecky, in the Castle Gallery mark the beginnings of independent Czech art.

The best known painting in the Prague Castle collection is Titian's painting, *Young Woman at her Toilet* (above right).

View of the wing in which the Castle Gallery is housed (below right).

Museum of the two seas

The **TOPKAPI PALACE** in **ISTANBUL** houses art treasures from 470 years of Ottoman rule

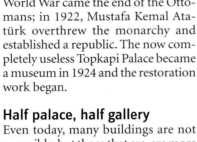

ADDRESS
Topkapi Sarayi
Sultanahmet, Eminonu
Istanbul

OPENING TIMES:
Wed-Mon 9 am to 5 pm

INTERNET:
www.ee.bilkent.edu.tr/
history/topkapi

HOW TO GET THERE:
On foot through the
Old Town

**ANDERE OTHER ATTRAC-
TIONS:**
Hagia Sophia

The towers, domes,
and minarets of the
Topkapi Palace are
unmistakably in the
tradition of Old Byzan-
tium (below left).

Since Islam prohibits
the representation of
figures, artists develo-
ped ornamentation
until it reached the
peak of perfection.
Ceramic tile varies the
flower shapes with the
greatest subtlety
(below right).

Mehmet II, known as Fatih or 'conqueror,' captured Constantinople in 1453 and the Byzantine Empire came to an end after more than a thousand years. Constantinople became Istanbul and was the capital of Ottoman capital until well into the 20th century. The Turks' first steps towards Europe were by no means the event of 1453; they had already occupied the Balkans for two hundred years and, prior to Istanbul, they had made Edirne in Thrace, once called Adrianopolis, their home.

Mehmet II wanted to make his imperial mark in the conquered Byzantine metropolis, so he built a palace, planning it almost immediately after the capture. Building work began in 1462 on a spit of land which provided views of both the Straits of Bosporus and the Sea of Marmara. Previously, an olive grove and a weapons store had stood on the site. The Topkapi Palace covered an area of 7,500 square feet and was surrounded by a defensive wall almost nearly 1 mile long, with several gates. "The ruler of two seas," another of Mehmet's nicknames, promulgated a body of laws, in Turkish *kanunname*. They determined the administrative mechanisms and thus the structure of the Palace as well.

The Palace remained the Ottoman rulers' residence in subsequent centuries and almost all of them changed or extended the site. Sometimes fires and earthquakes raged, which led to rebuilding and new designs. A city within a city – a labyrinth of corridors, domed pavilions, minarets, walls, fountains and squares – arose.

The last Sultan to live in the Topkapi Palace was Abdulmecid I, who died in 1860. The Ottoman Empire which had once controlled vast expanses of the eastern Mediterranean was in decline. The massive Palace

stood largely unused and began to fall in disrepair. With the end of the First World War came the end of the Ottomans; in 1922, Mustafa Kemal Atatürk overthrew the monarchy and established a republic. The now completely useless Topkapi Palace became a museum in 1924 and the restoration work began.

Half palace, half gallery

Even today, many buildings are not accessible, but those that are, are more than comprehensive. Topkapi Palace is reminiscent of the Hermitage in St Petersburg and the Louvre in Paris because it combines Palace, treasury and art gallery. The other two museums are part of the Christian European cultural tradition, however. The Topkapi Palace is an Islamic building. Islam did not produce an architectural style common to all the countries that have followed it, but the sites of religious practice, the mosques, have the same basic structure and function in common and the Koran's prohibition of images is largely followed. But art in the various Arab countries is very distinct and the Turks are not Arabs. The unique characteristics of the Topkapi Palace are a result of the Eastern Roman-Byzantine tradition, which left its mark on the Ottomans, regardless of the Islamic religion.

It is easy to pick out partial architectural matches between Orthodox churches in Greece and the Topkapi Palace's pavilions, but the fact remains that this was an Islamic ruler's residence. One of the complexes of buildings is the harem, where the women of the court lived: the sovereign's mother, his wives and their children. They were served and watched over by female slaves, mainly dark skinned eunuchs.

By the way, being the son of a ruler was no fun. Killing them was a

popular pastime, for fear of their possible desire to seize the throne at a later date, which is why the rulers' sons preferred to make their escape in good time.

Administration of the government was in the hands of viziers in other parts of the Palace. Another section of the building was given over to the janissaries, the Ottoman army elite, which occasionally rebelled, threatening the power of the ruler.

The art of ornamentation at its peak

The museum exhibits contain the imperial treasure, quite extraordinary in scope and preciousness. It includes equipment, weapons, jewelry and furniture, much of which is made from precious metals and set with gemstones. There is a collection of porcelain and calligraphies. The Koran's prohibition of images led to a highly refined art of ornamentation, in textile design for example, throughout the whole Islamic world. The museum exhibits a wealth of samples in the form of the sultans' robes from several centuries. In the end, the prohibition on images was circumvented or undermined, firstly in Persia, by the use of miniatures in books. The Topkapi Palace possesses 13,000 of these alone.

The Koran's prohibition on images was circumvented time and again by the miniatures used to illustrate books. The miniatures above show representations of Noah's Ark and the Flood (above left) and a Dance of the Dervishes (above right).

The miniature (left) shows craftsmen and merchants in the bazaar.

A Hungarian artists' castle

THE NATIONAL GALLERY in BUDAPEST is home to eight centuries of Hungarian art

HUNGARY
Budapest

Adriatic Sea

Mediterranean Sea

ADDRESS:
Castle Palace
Buildings B, C, D,
Budapest

OPENING TIMES:
Tues.-Sun. 10 am
to 6 pm

INTERNET:
www.mng.hu

PUBLIC TRANSPORT:
Bus 16 from Erzsebet
Square, castle bus from
Moszkva Square, cable
railway from
Clark-Adam Square

OTHER ATTRACTIONS:
Hotel Gellért with the
Turkish bath, Heroes'
Square

The former royal
palace, where the
National Gallery now
exhibits its treasures,
lies high above the
banks of the Danube.
View from the Chain
Bridge to the complex
with the central cupola
building (below left).

The National Gallery is Budapest is housed in a former royal palace. Only in Budapest could you enter a museum by cable railway. The cable railway at the Chain Bridge has carried passengers up Castle Hill since 1870 and it is the second oldest cable railway in Europe. Note the elegant interiors of the three compartments, each of which can carry eight people.

From the plateau in front of the Hungarian National Gallery, there is a commanding view of the city, the Danube River and the bridges that imperiously span it. All in all, Budapest is on a slightly grander scale than most other eastern European cities, especially the Castle Palace, which has been home to the Hungarian National Gallery since 1975.

Construction commenced under Bela IV (1206–70), who built a fortified castle on the hill that falls steeply to the Danube. Under Ludwig I (1326–82), the seat of government was moved from Visegrad to Buda, entailing development of the castle into a Gothic palace. After several reconstructions, the Hapsburgs erected a three-winged Baroque castle complex, in which the governor of Vienna resided after Hungary was annexed to the Austrian Empire. It assumed its present form between 1899 and 1905, when two majestic wings and a central cupola were added.

Commissioned by nobility and Church

During the Second World War, the palace was almost completely destroyed. It reopened after 1955, albeit in a somewhat simpler form. The Ludwig Collection of Contemporary Art, the History Museum and the National Library are housed here. More than eight centuries of Hungarian art are exhibited in the National Gallery, the main wings and central cupola.

On the second floor, there are three high quality departments. The former throne room contains 13 winged altars from the 14th to 16th centuries, most of which originate from Upper Hungary. The former ballroom shines with the gleaming gold and brilliance of the colors. The *Visitation of Mary* altarpiece, signed by a master using the initials M.S., is regarded as a masterpiece because of its particular composition and the modern representation of the scenery.

The former master bedroom is also used for art. It now houses Baroque paintings, most of which were produced by foreign artists on behalf of the Church. The Hungarian nobility also commissioned works, however, and had themselves depicted in grand settings, as demonstrated impressively by the portrait of *Ferenc Rákóczi II* by Adám Mányoki.

Hungarian artists were especially active in the 19th century, producing important painters. One dominant art form was the large format histori-cal painting, of which names such as Bertalan Székely (*Women of Eger*) and Viktor Madarász (*Mourning László Hunyadi*) are representative. Additionally, many artists addressed themselves to bourgeois Romanticism too and, like Miklós Barabás in *The Arrival of the Daughter-in-Law* and József Borsos in *Young Maids after the Ball*, took middle-class daily life as their theme. In the second half of the 19th century, open-air painting paved the way for a gradual turn toward Impressionism. In *Picnic in May*, Pál Szinyei Merse created a painting full of merriment and brilliance.

In Munkácsy's salon

It is a little gloomy in the room devoted to Mihály Munkácsy and László Paál, but it suits the paintings, which frequently use a dark color palette and take melancholy nature as their theme. Munkácsy, in particular, is regarded as a "Goethe" of painting in Hungary. Time and again, he painted the broad, dry expanses of his homeland, but also concerned himself with

Mihály Munkácsy is regarded as the most important Hungarian artist of the 19th century. His portrait of the violin virtuoso and composer, Franz Liszt, is a masterpiece of romantic Realism (above left).

The painting *Girl with Cage*, painted by Jözsef Rippl-Rónai in 1892, has echoes of Art Nouveau. The artist lived in Paris for a long time (above right).

Between Romanticism and Impressionism: *Picnic in May* by Pál Szinyei Merse was painted in 1873 (below right).

, such as in his large for-
g, *The Last Day of a Con-*
n. On the other hand,
y sculpture is characteri-
icism and the longing for
armony, best demonstra-
n Ferenczy's *Shepherdess*
of the Fine Arts).
ian art of the early 20th
nexpectedly versatile. Ká-
zy's *Morning Sunshine*
magic of the moment, as
Derkovits' *Bridge in Win-*
ert Berény's *Celloist*. More
ry art can be found in the
. With works such as Erz-
r's *Sisters* and Béla Kon-
s of Mechanical Flight,
nts of the dawning of a

New England's heritage

The MUSEUM OF FINE ARTS in BOSTON has a big collection of American art

ADDRESS:
465 Huntington Avenue, Boston

OPENING TIMES:
Sat.-Tues. 10 am
to 4:45 pm,
Wed. - Fri. 10 am
to 7:45 pm

INTERNET:
www.mfa.org

PUBLIC TRANSPORT:
Subway: Green Line,
E Train to Museum
of Fine Arts or Orange
Line to Ruggles

OTHER ATTRACTIONS:
Shipand Museum,
Isabella Stewart
Gardner Museum

The street in Boston on which the city's biggest museum is located has been christened "Avenue of the Arts." Like so many other things in the intellectual capital of the United States, the name is certainly stylish.

Everything in Boston is different from the rest of the United States, where people look suspiciously and a little enviously toward New England. In 1620, the Puritans landed on the Cape Cod peninsula, close to Provincetown Harbor, and launched the European occupation of North America. A couple of the Pilgrim Fathers set up home in what is now Boston, founding a city clearly influenced by both worlds: the New World, with its heart set on a democratic society, and old Europe with its wealth of culture. The Museum of Fine Arts is characteristic of this twin ideal. It was pointedly opened in 1876 on the one hundredth anniversary of American independence and placed great emphasis on American art from the very outset. The European art collection is still splendid, however, and contains works by many great names.

Many paintings were donated to the MFA by private collectors, but the citizens also spent hard cash to build up the famous collections.

Emphasis on Asia
As in many European museums, art begins here with the ancient cultures, and the institution has an exquisite collection of Egyptian art.

Sarcophagi stand in the gloom, gold masks gleam, costly jewelry glitters in the half light and one gets a real sense of the extent to which life in Ancient Egypt revolved around death. Greek art is represented by important exhibits, such as ancient bronze figures, vases from Athens and rare terracotta statuettes. In addition to many other exhibits, the Roman art department possesses frescoes from Pompeii. Furthermore, there is a comprehensive collection of Oceanic art and rare objects from Nubia (an ancient region of northeast Africa, now covered by parts of Egypt, the Sudan and Ethiopia). The MFA star-

ted collecting Asian art as early as the 19th century. Today, it possesses the most valuable collection of Asian art under one roof in the world.

The English, Spanish, Dutch, French and German exhibits in the European collection cover painting from the 7th to the 20th centuries, and the names read like a parade of stars: Titian, Veronese, Tintoretto, Rubens, Velázquez, Murillo, and many more. Rogier Van der Weyden's *Saint Luke Madonna (Saint Luke Drawing a Portrait of the Virgin)* and Rembrandt's self portrait, *The Artist in his Studio*, are particularly valuable.

Copley and Stuart
The collection concentrates on 19th-century landscape painters, represented by J.M.W. Turner, Jean-Francois Millet and the Impressionists. With more than 30 paintings, the MFA has one of the biggest Claude Monet collections outside Paris, including the bizarre female portrait *La Japonaise (Camille Monet in Japanese Costume)* which, like Pierre-Auguste Renoir's *Dance at Bougival,* evokes the pleasures of French artistic circles.

The visitor enters into a completely different world on approaching American painting. The MFA's first American painting was *Elijah in the Desert* by Washington Allston, soon to be followed by portraits from the colonial era. Since then the collection has grown to more than 1600 works, the most impressive of which are exhibited in the renovated first floor of the Evans Wing.

The two most important early American artists, John Singleton Copley (1738–1815) and Gilbert Stuart (1755–1828), are represented by numerous works, including Copley's picture *Watson and the Shark* and Stuart's *Washington at Dorchester Heights.* Of the artists who painted in New England in the second half of the 19th century, the cosmopolitan John Singer Sargent stands out alongside William Morris Hunt and Winslow Homer. Sargent's painting, *The Daughters of Edward Darley Boit,* is one of

the most popular paintings in the MFA. John Singer Sargent also designed the rotunda and the impressive staircase. The new American artists of the 20th century are represented by Edward Hopper, Georgia O'Keeffe and Jackson Pollock.

Contemporary art has been integrated too. Since 1971 there has been a big department of contemporary art with 500 paintings, sculptures and works of photographic art. The exhibits include names such as Kiefer, Baselitz, Richter, Clemente and Rothenberg.

The fact that visitors don't get lost in the MFA, despite its size and splendor, is due to the almost homely atmosphere. Piano music rings out during a lunchtime recital. Smartly dressed society ladies serve tea in the Gallery, for a small charge which is donated to the Museum. Very English, and yet American through and through. This is Boston.

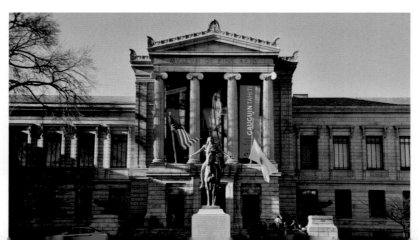

The main entrance to the Museum of Fine Arts in Boston with the neighboring old wingd building (below left).

A reminder of the fate of the Native Americans: Albert Bierstadt painted Indians near Fort Laramie in 1859 (above).

One of the high spots among the 18th century paintings is Jean-Antoine Watteau's *The Prospect: View through the Trees in the Park of Pierre Crozat.* Watteau painted this picture around 1718.

Chicago's masterpieces

The **ART INSTITUTE** in **CHICAGO** made American art history by favoring modern art

ADDRESS:
111 South Michigan
Avenue, Chicago

OPENING TIMES:
Mon–Wed, Fri. 10:30 am
to 4:30 pm,
Thurs 10:30 am to 8 pm,
Sat and Sun 10 am to 5
pm

INTERNET:
www.artic.edu

PUBLIC TRANSPORT:
Subway: Green Line, to
Adams/Wabash
Bus: Route 3 to
Adams/Michigan

OTHER ATTRACTIONS:
Chicago Museum
of Contemporary Art,
Field Museum
of Natural Science

The Chicago Art
Institute's Neoclassical
portal with roaring
lions (below).

Visitors to the Art Institute of Chicago must first stare a roaring lion in the face. Edward Kerney's bronze sculptures of 1894 stand on tall sockets flanking the flight of stairs up to the Neoclassical facade of the Art Institute. These lions have become the emblem of one of the United States' greatest encyclopedic museums of art, which lies in the heart of Chicago, Illinois, two blocks away from Lake Michigan.

Visitors pass through revolving doors to reach the majestic entrance hall, where a big double staircase guides visitors up into the Institute's galleries. The fanlight was designed by Frank Lloyd Wright and bathes the entrance area in flattering daylight.

Ground-breaking exhibition
The Institute was founded in 1879, initially as the Chicago Academy of Fine Arts. It still houses one of the most highly regarded academies of art in the country, whose pupils include Georgia O'Keeffe, Claes Oldenburg, Grant Wood and Walt Disney.

In 1882, the name was changed to the Art Institute. Even at this early stage, the generous foundations created by two art lovers turned the Institute into a Mecca for artists. In 1890, Charles L. Hutchinson, the first President of the Institute, and patron Martin A. Ryerson donated parts of the Demidoff Collection of Old Masters, acquired at auction, including paintings by Frans Hals, Meindert Hobbema and Rembrandt van Rijn.

Constructed in 1893 by the Boston architects' practice of Shepley,

Rutan and Coolidge, the Beaux-Arts building guarded by the lions first served as the venue for the World's Columbian Exposition on the 400th anniversary of the discovery of America. Immediately afterwards, in December 1893, the Art Institute and its steadily growing collection moved in.

In 1913, the Museum split the art world with a ground-breaking exhibition, the Armory Show. Critics were shocked by European avant-garde painting and sculpture, largely unknown in middle America. Yet the Art Institute's visionaries stood their ground, purchased numerous works from the exhibition and thus established an outstanding Modern art collection.

In 1924, art collector Bertha Palmer donated one of the most important collections of Renoirs, Monets, Degases and Manets to the Art Institute, including four versions of Monet's *Wheatstacks*. In 1925, the Museum was given Helen Birch Bartlett's collection that contained the most famous work by George Seurat: *A Sunday Afternoon on La Grande Jatte*. The Impressionist and Post-Impressionist works became the Art Institute's biggest attraction.

The breadth of the collections increased constantly; visitors were to be shown cultural items and objets d'art covering 5,000 years of human history, from antique statues to Bauhaus architectural models. A second complex of buildings was opened in 1924. Today, some 300,000 exhibits are displayed in 273 galleries covering around 172,000 square feet.

"Masterpiece of the Week"
Chicago exhibits an impressive collection of American masters, including *The Child's Bath*, the best-known painting by the Impressionist, Mary Cassatt. Two further examples of classic American art, Grant Wood's *American Gothic* and Edward Hopper's *Nighthawks*, serve as magnets, drawing the public to the 16 galleries that also show numerous masterpieces by Georgia O'Keeffe.

A further jewel in the Collection can be seen in the Bergman Galleries – the Surrealist art cubes by Joseph Cornell.

All the major representatives of the post-war movements are there, including Willem de Kooning, Jackson Pollock, Robert Rauschenberg, Mark Rothko, Lucian Freud, Frank Stella, Ellsworth Kelly, Andy Warhol, Kiki Smith and Chuck Close.

The superb collection of contemporary art also houses the biggest collection of works by Gerhard Richter in the United States. *Christa and Wolfi* and *Woman Descending the Stairs* shimmer there before the visitor's eyes.

A particular feature is the Kraft Education Center, with an interactive exhibition for children. The Art Institute demonstrates its user-friendliness for adult visitors as well. In addition to daily guided tours, there is the "Masterpiece of the Week," a 30-minute viewing of a cultural delight, at midday. This approach and the big "blockbuster" exhibitions have led to the Art Institute having the biggest membership – 140,000 – of any museum in the world.

Modern masterpieces on display in the Art Institute include Edward Hopper's painting of solitude, *Nighthawks*, completed in 1942 (above) and George Seurat's Pointillist work, *A Sunday Afternoon on La Grande Jatte*, dated 1884-6 (below).

Gurus of modern art

The **MENIL COLLECTION** in **HOUSTON** is one of the great collections of modern art

ADDRESS:
1515 Sul Ross, Houston

OPENING TIMES:
Wed–Sun 11 am to 7 pm

INTERNET:
www.menil.org

PUBLIC TRANSPORT:
Visitors are recom
mended to hire a car
because public
transport is almost
nonexistent in Houston.

OTHER ATTRACTIONS:
Museum of Fine Arts,
Contemporary Arts
Museum, Houston
Center for Photography

*Architect Renzo Piano
designed the main
building in Houston
(below). Several other
buildings in the imme-
diate vicinity
provide additional
exhibition space.*

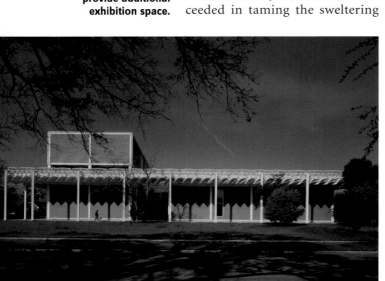

Dominique de Menil wore her fur coats with the lining on the outside because she loved the exquisite feel of the luxurious fur against her skin. Her museum works in exactly the same way. The masterpieces are concealed inside; the museum's facade is restrained and unassuming.

In the 1980s, the native Parisian met Renzo Piano. She chose him to build a museum for her that was supposed to be "big on the inside, small on the outside" – a museum to exhibit the 15,000 works in her art collection in rotation.

Dominique emigrated from France with her husband, Jean de Menil, to Texas in 1941, where the family built an oil empire. The couple invested all their wealth in art; the collection of paintings, sculptures, prints, drawings and photographs is truly one of the most wonderful collections of art in the United States. The Menils made their mark on the city of Houston with their commitment to culture and humanism. They became the patrons of countless artists, artistic institutions and universities and donated nume-rous works of art to the city and its museums, but it was only 14 years after the death of Jean de Menil that their private collection found a fitting home.

The museum, Piano's first building on American soil, opened in 1987. Dominique de Menil wanted natural light in the galleries. Using whitewashed, slat-like "leaves" of ferro-concrete, the architect suc-ceeded in taming the sweltering Texan sun, creating lighting effects that change magically with the time of day.

Free entry to art

The architecture is restrained and elegant; simple materials such as dark brown parquet floors, white steel and light gray wood panels merge unassumingly into the Houston residential district. The neighboring, bungalow-style deta-ched houses are painted in the same pale gray as the museum, their gardens and open spaces ver-dant with tropical vegetation and the gigantic oak trees characteris-tic of Houston, creating an urban oasis that radiates magical peace as one strolls between sculptures by Tony Smith and Michäl Heizer. The architect has not only facilita-ted the dialogue between nature and culture, but also within the museum, by the use of conserva-tory-like inner courtyards.

Almost all the neighboring houses are owned by the Menil Collection; the rents are a source of income to ensure free entry to the museum. Dominique de Menil considered art the artists' gift to the world, a gift that should be accessible to anyone at any time.

Art is the focal point of the Menil Collection; the visitor is almost forced to focus on it. Inti-mate dialogue is possible in the small museum, the gap between antique and modern just a few paces wide. No museum shop, cafe or noise from guided tours det-racts from the selected exhibits that are brought from the store rooms on the second floor on a rotation basis.

The high quality Collection ranks right alongside the famous Phillips, Frick and Getty Collec-tions. It extends from Robert Rau-schenberg's 1962 *Glider* to Rem-brandt's copper-plate etchings; from René Magritte's 1953 *Golconde* to the world's best collections of Byzantine icons. Aboriginal art from Oceania and Africa is present-ed impressively in context with the Surrealists, who were often inspired by the former. The Surrealist collec-tion is surely one of the museum's highlights, not least because an inti-mate friendship existed between the Menils and René Magritte, as well as Max Ernst.

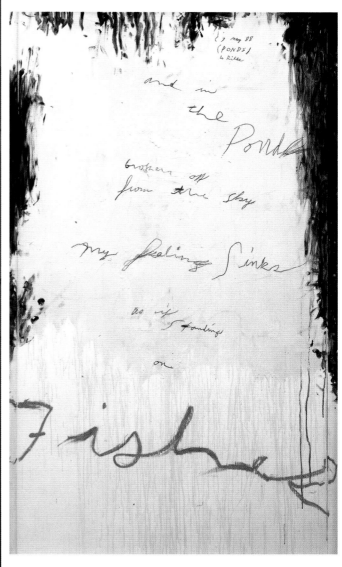

In the 1960s, the de Menils embraced the post-war art movements of Abstract Expressionism, Pop Art and Minimalism. Close personal friendships were also established between the collectors and the artists Jasper Johns, Andy Warhol, Yves Klein and Robert Rauschenberg. Warhol's *Big Campbell's Soup Can, 19 Cents* (1962) and *Lavender Disaster* (1963) adorn the Menil Collection's galleries.

A museum village

In 1995, the Menil Foundation dedicated a separate museum annex to the American contemporary artist, Cy Twombly, with more than thirty works, including the monumental *Untitled (Say Goodbye, Catullus, to the Shores of Asia Minor)* from 1994. The neon tube guru, Dan Flavin, also gets his own exhibition hall, which includes, amongst other pieces, *Monument 1 for V. Tatlin* from 1964.

Back in 1971, the Mark Rothko chapel opened on the site, a place of meditation for all religions that contains 14 of the artist's works. The monumental *Broken Obelisk*

sculpture by American Barnett Newman, master of Abstract Expressionism, stands in solitary splendor before the chapel. Just a few steps take you from its shadow to the door of the Byzantine chapel, the only one in the United States. Dominique de Menil ransomed the 13th century fresco, which had been broken into separate pieces, from art thieves, restored it and installed it in Houston in 1997.

It would not be wrong to say that this is virtually a museum village, whose individual treasures are concealed like treasure chests in the area's luxuriant greenery, just waiting to be discovered.

Despite its variety, the Menil Collection lays no claim to completeness. "The great encyclopedic museums such as the Metropolitan Museum in New York are like a dictionary," enthuses Swiss-born Josef Helfenstein, director of the Menil Collection since 2003, "the Menil is like a poem."

On the American art scene, Dan Flavin is regarded as the neon tube guru. His installation (above center) is called *untitled 1996* and can be seen in Richmond Hall, a former supermarket located on the museum site.

Cy Twombly's calligraphic work, *Fisherman*, contains the words of a poem by the German lyricist Rainer Maria Rilke and appears beneath *untitled 1988*.

Andy Warhol's Pop Art painting, *Double Mona Lisa*, 1963, has become an icon of modern American art and satirizes the most secretive smile in the world (below right).

America's richest museum

The **METROPOLITAN MUSEUM** in **NEW YORK** has the most famous collection of paintings in the United States

If America were the king of the arts, Manhattan would be his head and the Metropolitan Museum his crown – set with innumerable and ancient royal jewels. If you want to get yourself in the right mood for this majestic museum, start your journey in the roof garden, enthroned above the treetops of Central Park with a panoramic view of the Manhattan skyline.

During the summer months, you can enjoy changing sculpture exhibitions here, as well as a drink. Then it's a matter of taking a deep breath and beginning the descent through 50 centuries of the history of art and culture. Two million exhibits of every imaginable kind from all over the world are shown. The tour leads through an Egyptian temple, past suits of armor and Dior dinner dresses to Pieter Brueghel's *Corn Harvest* (1565).

A walk through the history of art

The founders could not have imagined such an encyclopedic collection when they decided in 1870 that New York needed an institution for the history of art. Their collection grew quickly and they commissioned architects Calvert Vaux and Jacob Wrey Mould to build a Neo-Gothic brick building in 1874. Today, the original building is completely surrounded by the many conversions and extensions.

The history of the Metropolitan is synonymous with the history of the donors. It was only through the generosity of individuals that the Metropolitan grew to be the finest museum in the United States. It had a particular stroke of luck in 1901, when Jacob S. Rogers donated seven million dollars. Many masterpieces, such as *Cypresses* (1889) by Vincent Van Gogh, bear the note "Rogers Fund" on their label.

In 1913, Benjamin Altman bequeathed his extraordinary collection of over 1000 works to the Metropoli-

tan, including the *Virgin and Child with Saint Anne* by Albrecht Dürer (1519).

The collection of Horace O. Havemeyer followed in 1929. Advised by the American Impressionist, Mary Cassatt, he bought El Greco's *View of Toledo* (1597) and the foundation of the Impressionist collection with works by Degas, Manet and Cezanne. Classics from Monet to Gauguin in opulent gold frames are on show in the pastel-colored galleries on the third floor, flanked by a sculpture hall, in which a number of sculptures by Rodin point the way to the picture galleries.

Excellent collection of Klees

With over 3000 works, the Metropolitan's collection of paintings is the most valuable outside Europe. This is particularly true of the Rembrandt collection which includes *Aristotle contemplating the Bust of Homer* (1653). The Metropolitan Museum also owns 5 of only 35 paintings by Johannes Vermeer – the big crowd-puller is the *Portrait of a Young Woman* (1660).

The Lila Acheson Wallace Wing houses the 20th century galleries. Opened in 1987, the straight lines of glass and steel architecture are very appropriate to the collection of modern painting. Painted entirely white, the wing forms the perfect backdrop for the brightly colored, large-format masterpieces by postwar artists to be found on the third floor. James Rosenquist, Ellsworth Kelly and Willem de Kooning vie with the fantastic views of Central Park. On the mezzanine floor, the *Ventriloquist and Crier in the Moor* (1923) by Paul Klee calls attention to the excellent Klee collection of Heinz Berggruen. The first-floor galleries are chock-full of goodies representing all the art movements of the early 20th century, including works by Picasso, Braque, Léger, Giacometti, Modigliani, Boccioni, Dalí and Miró.

The American Wing is reached through an enormous roofed garden. The world's finest collection of American art from colonial times through to the early 20th century can be found on its three floors. However, the pictures are hung in the early 19th century manner, frame by frame, almost reaching to the ceiling, rendering some difficult to see. In the middle is Emanuel Leutze's masterpiece *Washington crossing the Delaware* (1851). The outstanding collection of the glass artist, Louis Comfort Tiffany, including *View of Oyster Bay* (1908) can also be seen here.

The Metropolitan has something for everyone – five million visitors a year set its head spinning. But it is worth coming more than once, in order to grasp the richness and uniqueness of this collection.

ADDRESS:
1000 Fifth Avenue at 82nd Street, New York

OPENING HOURS:
Fri and Sat. 9:30 am to 9 pm
Sun, Tues, Wed and Thurs 9:30 am to 5:30 pm

INTERNET:
www.metmuseum.org

TRANSPORT:
Subway Lines 4, 5, or 6 to 86th Street or Bus: M1, M2, M3, or M4 on Fifth Avenue to 82nd Street or on Madison Avenue to 83rd Street

OTHER ATTRACTIONS:
The Cloisters is a branch of the Metropolitan, where you can see an excellent collection of art and architecture from medieval Europe.

The Art Nouveau stained glass window, *Magnolias and Irises*, by American Designer Louis Tiffany (picture on left).

Rembrandt's *Aristotle contemplating the Bust of Homer* is one of the great attractions of the Metropolitan (above right).

Edgar Degas' *Dancer* shows the French artist's talent as a sculptor (below center).

The Neo-Classical facade was designed by architect Richard M. Hunt (below right).

A spiritual temple

Legendary architect Frank Lloyd Wright designed the **GUGGENHEIM MUSEUM** in **NEW YORK**

ADDRESS:
1071 Fifth Avenue
(at 89th Street),
New York

OPENING HOURS:
Sat–Wed 10 am
to 5:45 pm
Fri 10 am to 8 pm

INTERNET:
www.guggenheim.org

TRANSPORT:
Subway: Lines 4, 5,
or 6 to 86th Street. Bus:
Lines M1, M2, M3 or M4
on Madison or Fifth
Avenue

OTHER ATTRACTIONS:
MoMA, Frick Collection

The industrialist Solomon R. Guggenheim was 66 years old in 1927, when he met the German artist, Baroness Hilla Rebay von Ehrenwiesen, who inspired him with her enthusiasm for modern art. In her opinion, "non-objective" art represented the future of pictorial art. Rebay introduced Guggenheim to her friends, and he soon found himself engaged in heated discussions on Abstract art with Robert Delaunay, Albert Gleizes and Wassily Kandinsky. Guggenheim bought pieces like *Composition 8* (1923), one of over two hundred paintings by Kandinsky, which subsequently made his collection famous.

Spiral-shaped Gallery

With charm and determination, Rebay pushed the collector to buy art en masse. Works by Marc Chagall, Rudolph Bauer (her lover), Paul Klee (140 works), Laszlo Moholy-Nagy, Lyonel Feininger, Amedeo Modiglian and Fernand Léger were soon hanging in his drawing room. In 1937, Guggenheim allowed Rebay to convince him of the need for a museum – with her as director. So the Museum of Non-objective Painting was set up in a former car showroom in the heart of town. Joss sticks and classical music created an atmosphere.

Six years later, Rebay commissioned the legendary architect, Frank Lloyd Wright, to build her a "monument," a "spiritual temple." The struggle with the New York authorities went on for 16 years, until the visionary art museum in Central Park was able to open its doors in 1959.

Frank Lloyd Wright's vision for the Guggenheim was of organic forms to break up the rectangular pattern of Manhattan. His revolutionary idea was for people not to have to make any stops while looking at the art. This resulted in a quarter-mile-long spiral-shaped gallery with intimate niches for hanging the canvases.

The cylindrical main complex rises 90 feet high to a glass skylight decorated with leaf-like elements. The big, open rotunda is both unusual and inspiring. Artists like Jenny Holzer and Daniel Buren have integrated it into their works in special exhibitions.

The neighboring Monitor, also based on a circular ground plan and decorated with organic ornamentation, was planned as an office and residence for Hilla Rebay and Guggenheim himself, but now houses the permanent exhibition. In 1982, Gwathmey Siegel & Associates extended the Museum with a concrete-gray, windowless tower that remains modestly in the background, while greatly extending the exhibition and administration areas of the Museum, which is a listed building.

Focus on Expressionism

The collection changed as quickly as the Museum. In 1948, they bought the collection of Karl Nierendorf, who had specialized in Paul Klee and the German Expressionists, among others. A donation from Katherine S. Dreier extended the collection with works by Brancusi, Archipenko, Mondrian and Schwitters.

With the purchase of favorites such as Chagall's *The Fiddler* (1923 to 1924) and Marc's *Yellow Cow* (1911), the way was opened for representational art, which led to Rebay's resignation in 1952.

The new director, James Johnson Sweeney, received a donation in 1963 from Justin K. Thannhauser, who hung his entire collection of Impressionists and Post-Impressionists in the Monitor Wing of the Guggenheim, built especially for the purpose in 1965. Suddenly the Museum was filled with masterpieces by Cézanne, Degas, Gauguin, Manet, Picasso, Toulouse-Lautrec and Van Gogh. The third-floor gallery appears to have been created just for them, with low ceilings and

a teardrop-shape ground plan creating a warm, intimate atmosphere for the gold-framed pictures. Like jewels in a treasure chest, small-format pictures such as Picasso's *Bird on a Tree* (*L'Oiseau*, 1928) glitter on the vaulted interior walls of this gallery.

On the floor above, the Guggenheim has recently returned to its roots and created a permanent gallery for the works of Kandinsky. 20 works at a time from the stock of about 250 are now exhibited in rotation.

Provocative exhibitions

Art lovers also come to see the collection of American Minimalists of the 1960s and 1970s, donated to the Guggenheim by Count Giuseppe Panza di Biumo in 1990. Donald Judd's sharp-edged, geometric works and Dan Flavin's glowing, neon-green *greens crossing greens* (to Piet Mondrian, who lacked green) find a place in the spacious galleries in the tower annex.

Even so, the Guggenheim is cramped for space, so only a fraction of the permanent collection can ever be shown: The galleries in the rotunda and the tower are used exclusively for the most provocative special exhibitions. So no two visits to the Guggenheim are ever the same. Sometimes the usually white walls are covered in brown felt or painted black or covered with cobweb-like installations.

Today, the Guggenheim Foundation is geared to the international scene. The Peggy Guggenheim Foundation, established by one of Solomon's nieces, opened the first branch in Venice in 1979. Other exhibition centers followed in Bilbao, Berlin and Las Vegas.

A revolution in museum building: looking upward from the rotunda at the glass skylight and the spiral exhibition area (above left).

The rotunda designed by Frank Lloyd Wright is also extremely impressive from the outside (above right).

Roy Lichtenstein's *Pop-dog GRRRRRR* is one of the highlights of the Pop Art collection (below left).

Wassily Kandinsky's 1913 abstract painting, *Black Lines*, is a very well-known work from the Guggenheim's Kandinsky collection, which comprises more than two hundred pieces.

MoMA in New York

New York City's Museum of Modern Art possesses
a fine collection of modern art

ADDRESS:
11 West 53rd Street,
New York

OPENING HOURS:
Sat, Sun, Mon, Wed,
Thurs 10:30 am
to 5:30 pm,
Fri 10:30 am to 8 pm

INTERNET:
www.moma.org

TRANSPORT:
Subway: Lines E or V
to 5th Avenue / 53rd
Street; B, D or F to the
Rockefeller Center.
Bus: Lines M1, 2, 3, 4, 5
to 53rd Street

OTHER ATTRACTIONS:
Frick Collection,
Neue Galerie

The view from the sixth-floor balcony is breathtaking, but looking down into the atrium of the Museum of Modern Art is hardly a pleasure for art lovers with a fear of heights. But anyone brave enough is richly rewarded by the sight of Barnett Newman's *Broken Obelisk*, and behind it the mega-version of Claude Monet's *Water Lilies*, 14 feet long.

The MoMA was the first museum ever to be exclusively devoted to modern art. It was founded in 1929 by visionaries Lillie P. Bliss, Abby Aldrich Rockefeller and Mary Quinn Sullivan. Bliss made the first major donation in 1931, including Paul Cézanne's *Bather* (1885). However, the MoMA did not acquire its world-famous collection until the Second World War, when the Nazis sold degenerate art and rich American collectors and immigrants offered their treasures to the Museum. All the same, the Museum has always been a discriminating recipient and only works of the highest quality are accepted.

Grandiose renovations

The Museum of Modern Art turned 75 years of age in 2004 and celebrated its birthday in triumphal manner with grandiose renovations to the building, located in the heart of Manhattan, at a cost of over 650 million dollars. Japanese architect Yoshio Taniguchi redesigned the MoMA, referring back to the original building by Edward D. Stone and Philip L. Goodwin, completed in 1939. The complex had been extended several times, in 1951 and 1964 by Phillip Johnson and by Cesar Pelli in 1984. Taniguchi kept the facade on 53rd Street, but doubled the exhibition area. Philip Johnson's sculpture garden was extended and retained as an urban oasis.

The major collections are now displayed on six floors in glass, granite and aluminum architecture, preserving the black, white and gray coloration with pale parquet flooring. The scale is tremendous and the stylistic impression created by the complex is one of ascetic modernity. A number of floor-length windows allow daylight into the galleries and offer a view of the fantastic Manhattan skyline. Delicate and transparent, the galleries and floors merge into one another. Walkways and bridges create floating states and smooth transitions which provide continually surprising views from unexpected angles – for instance, *The Dance* by Matisse – which are like a wink from the architect, bringing a smile to the face of the visitor. On a sour note: escalators evoke the sensation of an art department store, which is unfortunately emphasized by the extremely high number of visitors, creating a bustling atmosphere.

The extension of the exhibition area means not only that 7,500 visitors at a time can be accommodated in the MoMA, but that there is also room for monumental works like Gordon Matta-Clark's *Bingo* (1974).

Selected from the biggest collection of modern painting and sculpture in the world, which contains 3,200 works, the modern masterpieces from the late 19th century to the Second World War shine in more intimate, enclosed galleries on the sixth floor: Vincent Van Gogh's *Starry Night* (1889), Picasso's *Les Demoiselles d'Avignon* (1907) and Henri Matisse's *The Dance* (1909). The last named hangs, confusingly at first, on the stairs between the fifth and sixth floors. However, the information board tells us that the man who commissioned it, Sergei Shchukin, a collector from Moscow, demanded that the work serve to decorate the staircase.

Art is celebrated

Post-war art is fully documented. All the post-war movements up to the 1970s are represented on the fifth floor. Iconic images of every "ism" can be seen here, as diverse as they are famous: Jackson Pollock's action painting, *One: Number 31, 1950*, competes with Claes Oldenburg's limp *Giant Soft Fan* (1966–7) and Robert Rauschenberg's *Bed* (1955), to name but a few of the top-flight works.

Art is not enough for the MoMA. There is also a helicopter floating in the lobby. Designed in 1945, the Bell-47D1 was known as "Bug-Eye" and was mass produced. Now it is a museum piece. The MoMA also loves its extravagant collection of automobiles. The bright red Pininfarina, Cisitalia 202 GT (1946) has a place in the sun by a fourth-floor window.

Contemporary artists have their place in the high galleries on the third floor. The exhibitions here are changed every nine months so that the rich hoard of masterpieces by Gerhard Richter, Rachel Whiteread, Jeff Koons and younger artists, such as Andreas Gursky, can be displayed in rotation.

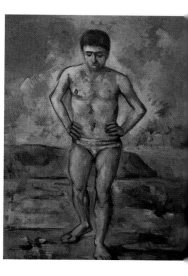

View of the illuminated MoMA building by night with the sculpture garden in the inner courtyard in front (left).

The entrance area of the building has also been modernized (below right).

Among the highlights of the MoMA collection are *The Dance* by Henri Matisse (below center, with a view of the staircase) and *The Bather* by Paul Cézanne (above).

The legacy of the Vanderbilts

The **WHITNEY MUSEUM** in **MANHATTAN** displays the collections of great American patrons of the arts

ADDRESS:
945 Madison Avenue
(at 75th Street),
New York

OPENING HOURS:
Wed, Thurs, Sat, Sun
11 am to 6 pm,
Fri 1 pm to 9 pm

INTERNET:
www.whitney.org

TRANSPORT:
Subway 6, station
Lexington Ave./77th St.,
Bus M1, M2, M3 or M4
to 74th St.

OTHER ATTRACTIONS:
Of the many museums
in New York City, the
following exhibit
modern American art:
Museum of Modern Art,
Guggenheim Museum,
Brooklyn Museum. In
addition, there are
many galleries, some
600 in all, on Madison
Avenue, in the SoHo
and Chelsea districts
and elsewhere.

The Vanderbilts are one of the oldest and most powerful industrial dynasties in the United States of America. Their patriarch, Cornelius Vanderbilt, born in 1794, made his money building steamships and railroads. He was also a successful speculator on the stock exchange and thus became the richest man of his time in the country.

His daughter, Gertrude, born in 1875, is described as highly active and very passionate. In 1896, she married Harry Payne Whitney, himself the child of an extremely rich entrepreneurial family, and they had three children. During a trip to Europe in 1901, Gertrude discovered her penchant for the fine arts and began collecting. In 1931, 11 years before her death, she donated her art collection to the Museum she founded, which was named after her.

A trove of modern art

The Museum continued to buy art in spite of its very small budget. Later, other wealthy patrons joined in, including a Rockefeller, a Hurst and several Lauders. Today, the Whitney Museum has by far the biggest collection of modern American art: paintings and sculptures, graphics, art objects and photographs, totaling around 12,000 works by around 2,000 artists. The Museum is located on Madison Avenue, not far from Central Park and other great museums.

The present building is light and strictly functional. It was erected in 1966 by Marcel Breuer, a former master at the Dessau Bauhaus, who emigrated from Germany in 1934. An extension has since been built, overseen by architect Renzo Piano, who designed the Pompidou Center in Paris together with Richard Rogers.

The international standing of modern American fine art is comparatively recent. It did not become known until the second half of the 20th century. Its development was stimulated by avant-garde artists, such as Marc Chagall and Marcel Breuer, who fled Hitler and became active in American artistic circles. In the wake of the Second World War, the international market for modern art was relatively deserted and the vacuum was filled by Americans.

Great masters of Pop Art

The abstract Expressionism of Jackson Pollock and Willem de Kooning was the first movement which began in the United States and spread throughout the world. Pollock and De Kooning were followed by the great masters of Pop Art: Roy Lichtenstein, Jasper Johns, Claes Oldenburg and Andy Warhol. Since then, almost every artistic innovation has come from North America or been heavily supported by the major gallery owners in Manhattan. For the last three to five decades, the art capital of the world has been New York City, not Paris.

Of course, modeling and painting were going on in the United States before 1945. Jackson Pollock, for instance, was a pupil of Thomas Hart Benton, a Realist, who trained in Paris. The worldwide success of abstract Expressionism and Pop Art also brought its precursors into view outside the United States and made them popular. Georgia O'Keeffe, whose flower paintings and landscapes are influenced partly by Native American and partly by Asian models, and Edward Hopper, whose style of painting, developed from newspaper illustration, expresses the forlornness and loneliness of modern city life, emerged into the limelight.

The Whitney Museum owns and displays outstanding works by O'Keefe, Hopper, representatives of Pop Art and also Arshile Gorky, Franz Kline, Mark Rothko, Frank Stella and Barnett Newman. Gorky and De Kooning were immigrants. America's unique ability to take in immigrants and assimilate them until they become Americans in attitude as well as nationality served American fine arts well.

One artist particular to the Museum is Alexander Calder. The painter, sculptor and graphic artist from Pennsylvania, born in 1898, was an engineer before he decided on a career in fine art. After 1926, he spent seven years living in Paris, where he associated with Joan Miró, Hans Arp and Piet Mondrian. Miró, Arp and Mondrian taught him to trim forms down to the essential and helped him to develop a surrealist tendency. Calder began experimenting with engines and motor activity, eventually creating the mobiles that made him famous.

The Whitney Museum's Calder exhibits include his *Brass Family* of 1927, a wire sculpture of a group of seven artists, and *Calder's Circus*, a circus ring made of different colored materials with figures of all kinds. *Calder's Circus* is a particular favorite with visitors.

Robert Henri (1865–1929) painted the portrait of Gertrude Vanderbilt Whitney posing luxuriantly in 1916 (above).

Edward Hopper's A *Woman in the Sun* depicts modern isolation and loneliness (below).

The Whitney Museum building was designed by Bauhaus architect Marcel Breuer, an emigrant from Germany. The functionalistic building, completed in 1966, has since been extended (below right).

From the jeans generation

The first floor of MOMA'S SAN FRANCISCO collection has been financed by Levis

San Francisco
Washington
U.S.A.

PACIFIC OCEAN
ATLANTIC OCEAN

ADDRESS:
151 Third Street,
San Francisco

OPENING TIMES:
Mon. and Tues. 11 am
to 6 pm,
Thurs. 11 am to 9 pm,
Fri.-Sun. 11 a.m.
to 6 p.m.

INTERNET:
www.sfmoma.org

PUBLIC TRANSPORT:
Bus, Routes 5 to Fulton
Street, 9 to San Bruno
Street, 14 to Mission
Street, 15 to Third
Street, 30 to Stockton
Street, 38 to Geary
Street, and 45 to Union
Street Subway lines,
J-Church, K-Ingleside,
L-Taraval, M-Oceanview,
N-Judah (to
Montgomery Street or
Powell Street stations)

OTHER ATTRACTIONS:
Asian Art Museum,
Fine Arts Museums
of San Francisco

View of the main frontage of SFMoMA: three floors of red brick facade and an "eye of light" high above the entrance.

SFMoMA's fame is due to Levi jeans or, to put it another way, the Fauvist works by Henri Matisse, including the legendary painting *Woman in the Hat* (1905), form the artistic core of the collection at the Museum of Modern Art in San Francisco.

Michael Stein, brother of Leo and Gertrude Stein, an industrialist from San Francisco, and his wife, Sarah, emigrated from the United States to France in the early years of the 20th century. In France, the Steins met Henri Matisse, with whom Sarah developed a close friendship, buying many of his works. After Hitler seized power, the family returned to sunny California with their valuable collection in 1935.

Unfortunately, Sarah's children gambled away her wealth on horse racing and she was forced to sell her beloved Matisses. This is where jeans come into it: Levi-Strauss president Walter A. Haas and his wife, Elise, bought the collection and later gave it to the Museum, "in honor of the Stein family, which brought Matisse to San Francisco."

New Museum building

The first American museum of modern art outside New York opened its doors in the Civic Center's War Memorial Veterans Building in 1935. Its ambitious agenda stressed the desire to introduce the West Coast of the United States to modern art. It held 146 exhibitions in the first two years alone, many of which were on an exchange basis with New York, with which the SFMoMA still has an outstanding partnership today.

In 1985, on the Museum's 50th anniversary, it became clear to its directors that the premises in the Beaux Arts-style Civic Center no longer met the demands of the growing, prestigious collection. In 1988, it was decided that Swiss architect Mario Botta should build a completely new Museum building in downtown San Francisco. On the Museum's 60th birthday, the directors proudly presented a 90 million dollar architectural sculpture, which critics maintained would overshadow the art contained therein. The modernist building exhibits a red brick facade, broken by a round "eye," a sloping zebra-stripe cylinder. The latter serves as a huge skylight for the atrium and ensures natural light inside the

Museum. It is supported there by three slender columns that give the room a religious feel.

The "Piazza," as Botta calls his foyer, is furnished in gray and black, alternately matte and polished granite and birch. The art here includes Sol LeWitt's gigantic, brightly striped *Walldrawings #935+936: Color Arcs and Color Bands in Four Directions*.

Magical light

Mario Botta is a master of lighting. By emphasizing the vertical and the shafts of light in the eye, he creates an upward vortex effect to the art on the third and fourth floor galleries which are windowless and almost exclusively white. Gentle daylight streams through the skylights. The modern works of art glow with magical colors against the very pale parquet floor.

Jeff Koons' statue, *Michael Jackson and Bubbles*, stands out here, a parody in golden yellow porcelain, the material harmonizing with Marcel Duchamps' porcelain urinal, *Fountain*.

The Museum contains an impressive collection of early modern works, including Matisse, as well as Picasso, Braque, Marc and Magritte, but its specialty is postwar American modernism.

The first video artists

The SFMoMA made many American post-war artists world famous. The abstract Expressionists Clyfford Still, Jackson Pollock, Mark Rothko and Robert Motherwell had their first one-man shows here and their epoch-making works are part of the collection. The Museum places special emphasis on local art. It possesses a superb collection of Bruce Conner and Richard Diebenkorn, the most important artists from the San Francisco Bay area. Minimalists Ellsworth Kelly and Sol LeWitt are represented as well and there are masterpieces by Pop-Art icons Robert Rauschenberg and Jasper Johns, such as Johns' *Lands End* from 1963.

San Francisco, close to Silicon Valley, traditionally a place of technological revolution, also gave rise to the first video artists. Even in the early 1970s, Dan Graham was experimenting with the new medium in works such as *Opposing Mirrors and Video Monitors on Time Delay*. Visitors here will also be amazed by flickering installations by Nam June Paik, Mary Lucier and Bill Viola.

The SFMoMA has also proved to be open-minded about the Internet and new art forms associated with it. As early as 1995, it created its own website. The exhibition, "010101 – Art in Technological Times," in which five Internet artists displayed their innovative works, expanded its exhibition space into cyberspace.

Jeff Koons' porcelain sculpture, *Michael Jackson and Bubbles*, a piece of American self irony (above).

Examples of young American painters: Philip Guston's *Blue Light* from a triptych dated from 1975, (above right) and Richard Diebenkorn's *Cityscape I* from 1963 (below right). The latter work, which can be categorized as Neo-Realism, was originally entitled, formerly *Landscape I*.

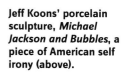

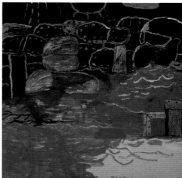

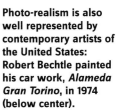

Photo-realism is also well represented by contemporary artists of the United States: Robert Bechtle painted his car work, *Alameda Gran Torino*, in 1974 (below center).

Ellsworth Kelly is a Minimalist. His painting, *Blue Red*, created in 1966, has great luminosity (below center).

Art treasures on the Mall

The NATIONAL GALLERY in WASHINGTON DC
houses many major works of European art

ADDRESS:
National Mall at
Constitution Avenue
between 3rd and 9th
Street NW, Washington

OPENING HOURS:
Mon-Sat 10 am to 5 pm
Sun-11 am to 6 pm

INTERNET:
www.nga.gov

TRANSPORT:
Metrorail: Judiciary
Square (Red Line),
Metrobus: Fourth Street,
Seventh Street,
Pennsylvania Avenue

OTHER ATTRACTIONS:
The Phillips Collection,
National Museum of
Women in the Arts,
Freer Gallery of Art and
Arthur M. Sackler
Gallery, Hirshhorn
Museum and Sculpture
Garden, National
Museum of African Art,
Smithsonian American
Art Museum

**The East Building
of the National Gallery
was designed by the
Amrican architect,
I.M. Pei, in the 1960s.
The H-shape building
mainly houses works
of art from the second
half of the
20th century.**

On the famous National Mall, set among the magnificent buildings in the Smithsonian Museum District, the United States guards its national art treasures.

In the classic American tradition, the collection was originally in private hands. In the 1920s, it occurred to the businessman from Pittsburgh, Andrew W. Mellon, that the United States did not have a single national museum. He set about investing his fortune in first-class works of art and, in 1936, he gave his collection to President Franklin D. Roosevelt on condition that he hand them over "to the American people."

A magnificent building was needed to provide appropriate settings for Mellon's masterpieces, which included works such as Raphael's *Alba Madonna* and Rembrandt's *Lucretia*. The architect, John Russell Pope, who also designed the Jefferson Monument, built a pink marble Neo-Classical temple. The doors were opened to the public in 1941 and, since then, millions of visitors have walked through the rotunda with its black marble Ionic columns into the galleries of the West Building.

A selection of Old Masters

Andrew W. Mellon stipulated that later donations to the collections must be of the same elite quality as his own. The result is one of the highest quality collections in the United States. The West Building houses paintings and sculpture covering art from the 13th to the 19th centuries. *Ginevra de' Benci* by Leonardo da Vinci, the only painting by Leonardo in America, and *Girl with a Red Hat* by Johannes Vermeer smile down from the walls. The selection of masters continues with Giotto, Fra Angelico, Botticelli, Van Eyck, Bosch, Van der Weyden, Grünewald, Bellini and Titian. Rubens and Rembrandt have their place in wood-paneled galleries, which create a setting appropriate to their time. The American galleries house art treasures by Impressionist painter Mary Cassatt as well as Gilbert Stuart, who painted the famous portraits of the first five American presidents.

In the 19th century galleries, Impressionists and Post-Impressionists such as Manet, Monet, Van Gogh, Gauguin, Renoir and Cézanne vie with Degas' wax sculptures for the spectators' attention.

From Moore to Calder

In the 1960s, the West Building needed expanding. The brilliant architect, I.M. Pei, was engaged by Paul Mellon and Ailsa Mellon Bruce, Andrew W. Mellon's children, to design a modern building. This East Building, linked to the West Building by an underground tunnel, has become a "temple of experience" for modern art.

The H-shape facade of the East Building complements the impressive, older West Building with pink marble from the same quarry in Tennessee. Henry Moore's *Knife Edge Mirror Two Piece* was unveiled outside the entrance at the opening in 1978 and escorts the visitor into the five-story building. Ramps, stairs and bridges afford a clear view of all five floors through this atrium and hint at unimaginable distances. The lightness and transparency at the top is playfully emphasized by a specially created piece by Alexander Calder. His huge 1976 mobile, *Untitled*, floats beneath the triangular design of the glass and steel roof.

Few influential artists are missing from the galleries of modern and contemporary art in the East Building. One of the highlights is Joan Miró's *The Farm*, originally owned by Ernest Hemingway, whose wife donated it to the National Gallery after his death.

In 1999, the complex was extended with a new billion dollar donation: the sculpture garden adjacent to the west side of the building. In addition to Claes Oldenburg's *Typewriter Eraser, Scale X*, there are 17 contemporary sculptures draped around a fountain, which becomes an ice rink in winter.

Thus high art merges with popular entertainment. Where else could you twirl and jump in the company of such masterpieces as Magdalena Abakanowicz's *Puellae*?

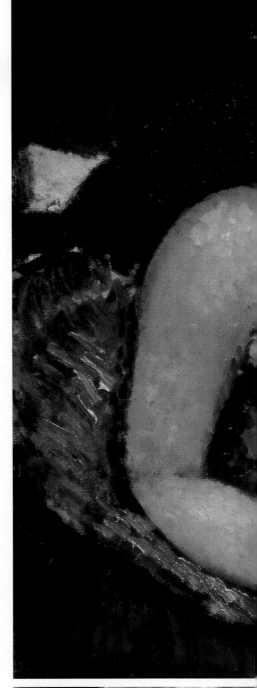

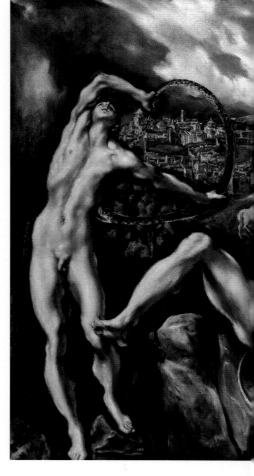

From the collection of the National Gallery: Amedeo Modigliani's *Female Nude*, 1917 (above), El Greco's *Laocoon*, 1610-1614 (below center), *Gray and Silver: Chelsea Wharf*, a harbor scene by James McNeill Whistler, c. 1864-1868 (below center right) and a portrait of an American Indian by George Catlin,1844-1845 (below right).

Art in the old pumping station

The MUSEUM OF FINE ARTS in BUENOS AIRES exhibits a comprehensive collection of modern Argentinean art

ADDRESS:
Avenida del Libertador 1473, Buenos Aires

OPENING TIMES:
Tues.-Fri. 12:30 pm to 7:30 pm, Sat. and Sun. 9:30 am to 7:30 pm

INTERNET:
www.mnba.org.ar

PUBLIC TRANSPORT:
Subway, Pueyrredón station; various bus routes

The Argentinean metropolis's classical museum of art is hidden away in a landscaped park in the Barrio Norte, on the majestic Avenida del Libertador and Avenida Figueroa Alcorta. It is literally just a stone's throw away from the most famous place in Buenos Aires, the Recoleta Cemetery, necropolis for all former luminaries and dignitaries, who seem to be trying to outdo each other in Byzantine splendor. The headstone of national saint Evita Perón is more restrained, however, but is always decorated with fresh flowers. It is not only places for the dead that are expensive and scarce in Recoleta; the apartments in the mighty *fin de siècle* apartment blocks are prohibitively expensive. Recoleta and the Barrio Norte are chic districts.

But we should be talking about the Art Museum and its extremely prosaic past. The centrally symmetrical building, with its wings and pillared front, was nothing more than the pumping station for the municipal waterworks until it was beautified by architect Alejandro Bustillo in 1931, in the imperial style which became the state's architecture of choice under General Juán Domingo Perón a few years later. The monstrous Faculty of Law, which overshadows the Museum from the east, also exemplifies the so-called international fascist style.

Longing for Europe

The Mexicans are descended from the Aztecs, the Peruvians from the Incas and, so they say, the Argentineans are descended from the ships. A longing for Europe, the former homeland, still drives the Argentineans today. The nation is loath to count itself part of Latin America. It is hardly surprising, then, that one always seems to hear an echo of Europe in Buenos Aires, and this echo also sounds in the Museum of Fine Arts.

Art moved into the Buenos Aires pumping station, today the Museum of Fine Arts, in the early 1930s. It contains art treasures from the estates of the incredibly rich Argentinean cattle barons and wheat kings, who, as part of the elite in one of the richest nations in the world, considered themselves connected to Europe.

The municipal authorities of Buenos Aires always measured the city against Paris. However, while the Museum houses the biggest treasure trove of European art of all the Latin American art museums – or so they say in Buenos Aires – the collection of Renaissance and 20th century European masters is comparatively meager.

Sculpture park worth visiting

The Museum includes works by Goya, El Greco, Tintoretto, Tiepolo, Rubens, Zurbarán, Van Gogh, Gauguin, Renoir, Toulouse-Lautrec, Manet, Monet, Modigliani, Dégas, Picasso, Kandinsky, Klee and Miró as well as sculptures by Bourdelle and Auguste Rodin. In 32 rooms, more than 300 paintings wait to be admired. The first floor houses the permanent exhibition of European paintings that starts with El Greco and ends with Klee, Picasso and Rodin and includes a big work by Pollock. The second floor contains exhibits by Argentinean artists and other 20th century works which will give visitors to the Museum an overview of the movements and history of modern Argentinian as well as European art.

20th century Argentinean fine art is not a subsidiary or copy of the European model, but is totally independent and original. It is associated with the names Carlos Morel, Benjamín Franklin Rawson, Prilidiano Pueyrredón, Cándido López, Eduardi Sívori and Ernesto de la Cárcova, who, throughout their lives, confronted a public fixated on European art. Today, these national artists are recognized and duly honored and their work sells for high prices.

The truly original sculpture park is well worth visiting, housing art by Antoine Bourdelle – *The Dying Centaur* – and Lucio Correa Morales among others. Perhaps the most impressive, however, is the *Bust of Balzac*, modeled by Rodin.

Themed exhibitions organized at the Avenida del Libertador on a regular basis are extremely popular. The Museum is superbly complemented by a publicly accessible library of 30,000 volumes. From the Museum, it's just a quick hop over the Plaza Francia to the Recoleta Cultural Center, where you can see modern furniture designs and decorative items. Afterwards, you can also delight in the culinary arts at the museum restaurant.

Spain's Old Master El Greco is represented by his painting, *The Agony in the Garden* (1605-10) (left), and Frenchman Paul Gauguin by *Bathers* (top center).

The Bath (below right) is by Argentinean Prilidiano Pueyrredón.

The Museum building (above right) was constructed in an architectural style associated with fascism.

Supported by steel beams

MASP in SÃO PAULO has the biggest collection of modern Brazilian art

ADDRESS:
Avenida Paulista 1578, São Paulo

OPENING TIMES:
Tues.-Sun. 11 am to 6 pm, Thurs. to 8 pm

INTERNET:
www.masp.art.br

PUBLIC TRANSPORT:
Subway, Trianon-Masp station

OTHER ATTRACTIONS:
Museum of Modern Art in Ibirapuera Park

Spanish artist Francisco de Zurbarán created this transfiguring image of the monk, *Saint Anthony of Padua* (below), in 1627.

Brazil's biggest museum of art's full title is Museu de Arte de São Paulo Assis Châteaubriand, otherwise simply known as MASP.

MASP – on Avenida Paulista, São Paulo's Fifth Avenue – has since become a prime attraction of the biggest dynamic metropolis south of the Equator. The Museum, opened in 1947, lies above the Trianon Park, one of the few oases of green in the concrete desert of São Paulo, which continues to expand. The bustle of commerce rules all around this place – almost all the banks and conglomerates have established offices on Avenida Paulista, where the splendid villas of coffee barons and early industrialists once stood, because Avenida Paulista actually runs up a hill from which you once had a lovely view and fresh air. Both avenue and hill are now completely built up and polluted, but in the boom years of the 1950s and 1960s, when construction of the Museum was being planned on this site, the architects were instructed not to block the view. How might this be possible?

Like a flying elephant

Italian Lina Bo Bardi hit the jackpot in an architects' competition. She proposed a kind of beam, a right-angled solidium, held up at either side just by supports, making it possible to look underneath the Museum to Trianon Park and the city skyline. What looked on paper like an elegant supporting beam construction required completely new technology to build. MASP is the only museum in the world carried like a litter by steel beams that span 243 feet and which have to support a solidium weighing several thousand metric tonnes.

In order to make this beamed construction stand out even more clearly, in 1990, the 3 foot thick concrete supporting beams were painted red so they stand out from the two-story solidium. Two floors of exhibition rooms float above the pilaster; another two are invisible, below ground. Visitors to MASP get the overall impression of a flying elephant.

Customary museum architecture has not been used inside; there are almost no display walls.

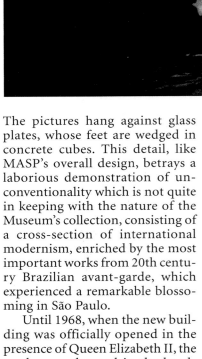

The pictures hang against glass plates, whose feet are wedged in concrete cubes. This detail, like MASP's overall design, betrays a laborious demonstration of unconventionality which is not quite in keeping with the nature of the Museum's collection, consisting of a cross-section of international modernism, enriched by the most important works from 20th century Brazilian avant-garde, which experienced a remarkable blossoming in São Paulo.

Until 1968, when the new building was officially opened in the presence of Queen Elizabeth II, the works were housed in the headquarters of newspaper tsar Assis Châteaubriand, who owned almost half the periodicals in Brazil. Châteaubriand not only had political clout, he also collected anything that fell into his hands. Works by the Paulistan "people eaters," the name given to the modern Late Expressionist movement, could be bought for a few dollars in those days. In the 1950s, works by Brazil's own modern artists started to increase in value, by which time Assis Châteaubriand had long since assembled his collection. He generously donated it to the city of São Paolo, with the proviso that the community should provide it with an appropriate museum.

As we have said, MASP focuses on the modern, but it also exhibits classic European art in its hall, such as the Italian school, with works by Bellini, Mantegna, Raphael, Titian, Tintoretto, Botticelli and Veronese. The French are represented by Delacroix, Manet, Degas, Gauguin, Cézanne, Matisse, Toulouse-Lautrec and Picasso. You will also find classical works by Spanish, Portuguese, Flemish

and English artists – as well as pieces by Hieronymus Bosch, Lucas Cranach and Hans Holbein.

Permanent exhibition of 500 paintings

Visitors come to MASP because of these big names, represented in each case by just a few, lesser known works. But for art-lovers and tourists, an insight into Brazilian modern art is much more interesting because such a complete collection cannot be found anywhere else. Some of these artists' names, such as Lasar Segall, Anita Malfatti and Emiliano Di Cavalcanti, are known internationally as well.

In addition to the permanent exhibition of 500 paintings and pieces of plastic art from its stock of more than 10,000 items, MASP constantly organizes themed temporary exhibitions which are high-

ly regarded much further afield than São Paulo. Workshops, conferences, seminars and a well-stocked library make MASP a well-attended cultural center. At the international level, MASP maintains close ties with the great art

museums in Europe and the United States, and on weekends, its beamed construction shelters antiques dealers who set up shop in its shade.

Emiliano Di Cavalcanti (1897–1976) painted the Five Maidens of Guaratinguetá *in 1930, a masterpiece of modern Brazilian art (above right).*

Paulo Afonso Waterfall, *painted by Frans Post in 1649 (above left).*

One of the boldest modern museum buildings in the world: MASP in São Paulo (below right).

183

In the spirit of the Aztecs

The **ANTHROPOLOGICAL MUSEUM** in **MEXICO CITY** gathers together the most important monuments of Pre-Columbian culture

ADDRESS:
Paseo de la Reforma,
Chapultepec,
Mexico City

OPENING TIMES:
Tues.-Sun. 9 am to 7 pm

INTERNET:
www.mna.inah.gob.mx

PUBLIC TRANSPORT:
Metro, Auditorio or
Chapultepec stations

OTHER ATTRACTIONS:
Museum of National
History, Museum of Art,
Rufino Tamayo Museum

The National Museum of Anthropology is located in Chapultepec Park, on the prestigious Paseo de la Reforma, in the heart of Mexico City. It is the most important museum of ancient American culture in the world and a very good reason to travel to the Mexican capital.

As visitors approach the Museum entrance, they are greeted by a massive stone figure. It is unclear whether this is a representation of an Aztec rain god, but when the statue was brought from a village on Lake Texcoco in summer 1964, transported to its present resting place by special overnight convoy for the Museum's inauguration, longed-for rain arrived over the city and its environs after weeks of drought.

The Museum building was based on plans by the renowned Mexican architect, Pedro Ramírez Vázquez. It's a spacious site with echoes of Pre-Hispanic architecture, reflecting the power of the masses by the particular monumental quality characteristic of Mexico's modern architecture. The entrance hall leads into a massive inner courtyard. Roughly half of it is covered by a roof more than 43,000 square feet, supported by a single central column, down which water pours from the roof in an artificial waterfall. Even after 40 years, this architectural design is extremely bold and elegant.

The exhibition rooms surround the square patio. The first floor contains the archaeological finds, organized according to culture. The generous exhibition of art is complemented by models, large format photos and life-size reproductions of monuments that are difficult to reach or badly preserved in addition to informative wall paintings by contemporary artists. The biggest room opposite the entrance hall is devoted to Aztec culture, which created the foundations of modern Mexico.

An ethnological collection from all over Mexico can be seen on the Museum's second floor, which is linked repeatedly to the first floor by staircases, galleries and lines of sight. Utensils, tools, items of clothing and reconstructed rooms show the differing regional traditions and lifestyles of earlier cultures.

The power of stone

It is impossible to see all the treasures on display in the Museum during a fleeting tour. You simply cannot see everything, you must prioritize. But it is not just the collections of antiquities that are worth a visit. A little detour to the contemporary culture exhibitions on the second floor is also interesting. Most visitors devote the bulk of their time to the Aztec department, the heart of this Museum. Looking from the entrance, the tour starts on the right wing with the culture of Teotihuacán and ends with Mayan art.

The parrot's head from Xochicalco, at the entrance to the Toltec room, dating from around 900 A.D., is a magnificent Pre-Columbian masterpiece. The representation is strange, almost alienating. The monumentality and power of the stone has a strange, unearthly and very immediate impact on the beholder. 20th century sculptors are often inspired by Pre-Columbian work.

The effect that the figure of Coatlicue has on the beholder is even more fascinating, possibly even frightening. This 8 foot high, 15th century Aztec statue – with its severed hands and human hearts, snakes, monsters' heads, predators' claws and skulls – is a demonic powerhouse whose outline forms a human figure. Coatlicue, "serpent skirt," gave birth to the moon and stars, gods and men, animals and plants. She is the primeval mother; in the end, everything comes back to her and she embraces and devours her children: earth goddess, symbol of life and death in one. Her final creation was the sun, which ascended to become Huitzilopochtli, the Aztec god of war and father of the gods. He is the most powerful force to emerge from Coatlicue's womb.

Aztec cosmology as conveyed by the carved stone is still impressive in its harshness and violence. Objects from a display case in the Maya room, on the other hand, from the period between 600 and 900 A.D., have a completely different, almost intimate, human impact. These are terracotta figures from Jaína, depicting priests and priestesses, rulers, ball players, warriors, musicians and men and women from the Mayan elite, similar to ancient Roman art depicting lust for life daily, customs and odinary habits.

The Mayans' message is important. The ancient Indian cultures were not bloodthirsty, primitive, theocratic societies. History is written by the victors – in this case, merciless conquistadors armed with swords and crosses. Perhaps western culture is now advanced and sophisticated enough to listen to and appreciate the voices of the conquered.

The mighty stone figure of Coatlicue with her severed hands. She is regarded as the mother of the moon and stars (above left).

This stone disk, depicting a ball player (above center), is an impressive testament to Mayan culture.

One of the earliest known figures is the representation of the seated god, embodying corn and happiness (above right).

The photo below right shows the main entrance to the Anthropological Museum in Mexico City.

Treasures from Peru

The **MUSEO NACIONAL DE ARQUEOLOGÍA Y ANTROPOLOGIA** in **LIMA** boasts the biggest collection of Inca art

PERU
Lima

PACIFIC
OCEAN

ATLANTIC OCEAN

ADDRESS:
Plaza Bolívar,
Lima

OPENING HOURS:
Tues.-Sun. 9:30 am
to 5 pm

INTERNET:
www.museonacional.
perucultural.org.pe

HOW TO GET THERE:
Taxi, on foot in the
historic city center

OTHER ATTRACTIONS:
Gold Museum, Museo
de Arte de Lima

Peru's most internationally famous museum is without a doubt the Museo Nacional de Arqueología, Antropologia e Historia del Perú, situated on Lima's Plaza Bolívar in the Pueblo Libre area of the city. The building, formerly a country house located outside the gates of the city, once accommodated the two freedom fighters, José de San Martín and Simón Bolívar, in the years before independence.

The modest-looking building has undergone several conversions during the past two centuries and gives no outward indication of the pricelessness of its collections. The Museum, which acquires hundreds of new items every year, is quite literally bursting at the seams. Its few thousand square feet of display space are simply not enough – what the visitor gets to see is just a tiny fraction of the vast collection.

Although the Museum provides a safe haven for valuable finds dating from the pre-Columbian period, most of the more recently discovered archaeological treasures from Peru's past tend to disappear into foreign hands. The country possesses neither the financial nor the human resources necessary to exercise its sovereign rights over the cultural treasures contained within its frontiers.

Grave robbing, a widespread curse

Wherever archeological finds come to light or scientists are seen carrying out a dig, the *huaqueros* or grave robbers will not be far away. They hover like vultures, lying in wait for the burial sites to be left unattended for a moment, at which point they swoop in and plunder the grave themselves. This is hardly surprising, considering the extreme poverty in many areas of the country. Even the remotest village gets wind of what the gringos are prepared to pay on the black market for ancient Inca artifacts. In 1981, pre-Columbian gold jewelry worth five million dollars was even stolen

from the Museum itself. When the thieves were eventually apprehended, only a few items were recovered. What was probably Peru's most famous tumi – a ritual knife depicting a Lambayeque ruler, one of the most valuable finds from pre-Hispanic times – had been melted down in order to extract the gold. Peru is a desperately poor country sitting on a vast cultural treasure which it is incapable of protecting. The Museo Nacional de Arqueología y Antropologia's collections, which have been accumulating for the past 180 years, provide the most opulent display of advanced Indian cultures south of the isthmus of Panama.

No sooner does the unsuspecting visitor enter the lobby than they are met by the giant of Chavín, a creature of ancient American mythology. A mute sentry, the Estela Raimondi guides the visitor into the strange, remote world of these ancient civilizations. One of the main focal points of the Museum, however, is the Chavín col-

lection, comprising the round, demonic stone heads which once decorated temple walls. Many are copies of originals that were lost in a landslide in 1945. The stones raise many questions, one in particular. Were these hideous creatures meant as a warning to the faithful or to scare off evil spirits?

Myths and ceramics

An adjoining room contains one of Chavín's most impressive treasures: the Tello obelisk. Once again, the somewhat baffled visitor is faced with a confusingly complex, mythical creature. It is 8 feet tall and it is conceivable that the influence of drugs might induce a better understanding of it, together with the rituals which once centered around it.

Chavín de Huántar and Condorhuasi, Garagay, Ocucaje, Pucará – the Chavinoid style is represented in various areas all over the country and was undoubtedly the dominant culture between 1200 and 200 B.C. The visitor cannot fail to notice that themes and techniques from that time frequently crop up again in later works.

Other highlights of the Museum include exhibits from the classical coastal civilizations of the Moche, Nazca and Chimú. While clear, stylized drawings and brilliant, natural colors of the Nazca ceramics are cap-

tivating, the effigy vessels of the Mochica and the Chimú who followed them are equally fascinating for their depiction of many different aspects of life.

The people of the Mochica civilization have left us with some extremely lifelike portrait heads featuring dignitaries, warriors, prisoners and musicians as well as sick and crippled people. The faces of people with hare lips and the laughing blind man – dating from the period of the early Middle Ages in Europe – still have the power to move us, even centuries later, despite the strangeness of the figures.

The dark side of life is also evident in the vase records: there are sacrifice-demanding gods, vengeful priests and armed warriors. The face mask desi-

gned with the features of a jaguar is powerfully suggestive and was undoubtedly used for bloody rituals.

Several rooms are devoted exclusively to the Incas. Here you will find a greater number of everyday items than is the case for the older civilizations. After all, this represents recent history. The exhibits consistently feature animal and plant themes while mythology and religion are less in evidence among the conserved paintings. Or were all the Inca's idol images destroyed by the Spaniards in their blind religious zeal?

The Museum's exhibits include some gold masks of mummies. This superb example (above left) was found on Peru's northern coast.

A ritual drawing on textile from the Necropolis of Paracas (above right).

This vessel, decorated with humming-birds, comes from the Nazca civilization (below right).

Relatively modest in appearance, Peru's national museum, home to priceless treasures (below left).

187

Art of dead kings

Splendid finds from the Pharaohs' graves are gathered together in the **EGYPTIAN MUSEUM** in **CAIRO**

ADDRESS:
Tahrir Square,
Cairo

OPENING TIMES:
Daily 9 am to 4:45 pm
Last admission 4 pm,
closed Fri 12 noon
to 2 pm

INTERNET:
www.egyptian-
museum.gov.eg

PUBLIC TRANSPORT:
Subway, Midan el-Tahrir
Metro station,
or minibus

OTHER ATTRACTIONS:
Museum of Islamic Art

Tuthmoses III with incense and water before Amun-Re. The wall paintings date from the 15th century B.C. (below left).

The sculpture of Rahotep and Nefert was created in 3000 B.C. The colorful figures of the married couple are among the most important sculptures from the Ancient Egyptian era (below right).

The oxen's coats are light with dark spots. They are driven by barefoot male slaves carrying long rods. Their upper bodies are naked; only around the hips do they wear skirt-like cloths. Under a canopy supported by colored pillars sits the inspector who supervises the counting of the passing beasts.

This group of figures, carved from wood, plastered and painted, is 4,000 years old.

It forms part of the burial gifts for senior Ancient Egyptian government official Chancellor Meketre, who served the Pharaohs Mentuhetep II and III during the 11th Dynasty and who was buried in Deir el-Bahari. Another of the burial gifts intended for him shows men catching fish – they sit in two green papyrus boats, paddling along; a net with fish caught in it hangs between them.

The most spectacular thing about these burial gifts is that the figures show a great departure from the artistic canon of Ancient Egypt because they depict everyday, not royal, events. There are depictions of physical labor on the walls of burial chambers as well. The formal rules regarding reproducing the human figure are strictly observed: head in profile with eyes to the side, shoulders facing front, hips and legs viewed from the side again – an anatomically impossible position, obviously traditional and painstakingly observed throughout three millennia of Ancient Egyptian culture.

Art at the time of the Pharaohs was funerary art. The Ancient Egyptians believed in life after death. The deceased had to be embalmed for the afterlife and equipped with plenty of burial gifts. The wealthier and more po-

werful the person in life, the more lavish the expenditure post-mortem. The effect of this was most splendid in the case of the rulers, whose graves became extended treasuries which attracted robbers and plunderers, even in Ancient Egyptian times. In many cases, nothing remains but the stone sarcophagus and the wall paintings.

In the Valley of the Kings

Englishman Howard Carter stumbled across the completely untouched grave of boy king Tutankhamen in the Valley of the Kings in 1922. The riches and variety he found there were overwhelming. The 3,500 portable objects were brought to the Egyptian Museum in Cairo, where around half of them are exhibited today. Almost as many items from Carter's find are stored in the depositary, unless they are out on loan or form part of a touring exhibition, which happens from time to time.

The Museum has been in existence since 1858. It was founded by a French Egyptologist, Auguste Mariette. The collection moved several times and was located temporarily at Giza, where the three famous Pyramids and no less famous Sphinx stand. Starting in 1902, it has occupied its present home on the northern edge of Tahrir Square, in the center of Cairo. Long queues of tourist coaches drive past the palace-like structure, unloading their human cargo onto the rather dusty forecourt.

The Museum covers two floors, each crammed full of exhibits. The treasures from the tomb of Tutankhamen are located on the upper floor. They are besieged by visitors, especially the darkened room with the jewelry made from gold and precious stones. The

other big attraction is also located on this floor; the room with the 11 mummies of pharaohs, including the mummy of Ramses III, Ancient Egypt's mightiest and most famous King.

The ground floor displays pieces from three millennia of Ancient Egyptian culture, in almost chronological order, starting with

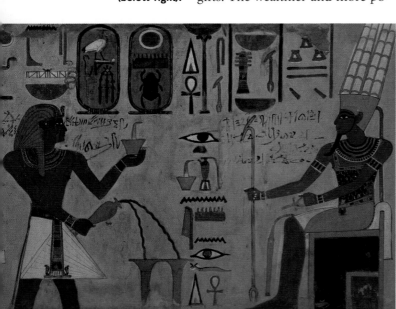

the votive palette from the temple of Hierakonopolis, where all the essential elements of Ancient Egyptian art are united for the first time in bas relief, and leading to the exhibits from the Greco-Roman era, which show the influence of conqueror's art.

There are impressive pieces from the short reign of the reforming Pharaoh Akhenaton, husband of the famous Nefertiti. The King wanted to do away with polytheism and replace it with sun worship. He did not succeed. Either he was unable, or did not want, to set aside the traditional art. The only detectable change is a greater tendency towards everyday representation in art. Akhenaton is unmistakable because of the overly long back of his head, which may have been shaped cosmetically for the sake of fashion, or may be the result of an illness.

120,000 exhibits

The Egyptian Museum has more than a hundred departments. It is absolutely impossible to appreciate all of them thoroughly at a single visit. The total number of exhibits on display comprises 120,000; as many pieces again are held in the depository. After years of fruitless discussions, the Egyptian state is now in the process of building a new, bigger home south of Cairo and near the Pyramids at Giza, for the collection. According to current predictions, it should be ready for visitors in 2010.

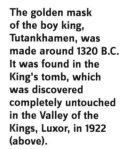

The golden mask of the boy king, Tutankhamen, was made around 1320 B.C. It was found in the King's tomb, which was discovered completely untouched in the Valley of the Kings, Luxor, in 1922 (above).

View of the main entrance to the Museum (below right).

The worlds of African art

The **SOUTH AFRICAN ART GALLERY** has the most important collection of Black African art

ADDRESS:
Government Avenue,
Cape Town

OPENING HOURS:
Tues.–Sun. 10 am
to 5 pm

INTERNET:
www.museums.org.za/
sang

HOW TO GET THERE:
By taxi or hire car

OTHER ATTRACTIONS:
South African Museum,
Castle of Good Hope,
William Fehr Collection

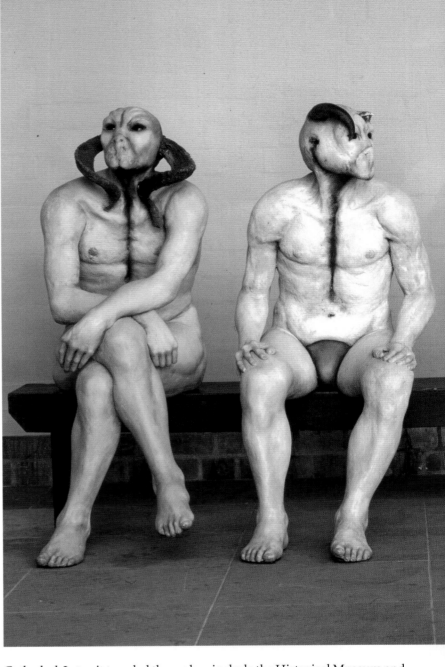

At first glance, it resembles Western art: the Savior with his crown of thorns hangs on the cross, his mother mourns him, one of the Roman soldiers thrusts a lance into his side. However, the Savior in this painting does not have a white skin; he is a black African with the features of a historical person. Albert Luthuli, born in 1898, strove to end apartheid and was persecuted by the white South African government. The freedom movement that had been in existence since 1912, the African National Congress (ANC), chose him as their president. The victim of constant oppression, he won the Nobel Peace Prize in 1960 and died under house arrest in 1967.

Luthuli is not the only person who can be seen in the painting of the Crucifixion. The two Roman torturers have the features of Hendrik Verwoerd, prime minister of South Africa until 1966, and John Vorster, the minister of justice. Both played a significant role in the intensification of the apartheid policy. Verwoerd was also responsible for the massacre of black demonstrators in Sharpeville in 1960.

The persecution of Christ

The South African Art Gallery building (below left) opened in 1930.

Many young African artists use elements of indigenous African painting in their pictures. The painting, Azibuye Emasisweni, was painted by Trevor Makhoba in 1991 (below right).

The picture is called *The Black Christ* and was painted two years after the Sharpeville massacre. The artist, Ronnie Harrison, came from Cape Town. The picture immediately aroused the attention of the Verwoerd government, which did everything in its power to gain possession of it in order to destroy it. The painting was taken out of the country. Ronnie Harrison was arrested and tortured. *The Black Christ* made its way first to London, where it hung in St. Paul's Cathedral. Later, it traveled through England and other European countries. Millions of dollars in donations for the victims of apartheid were contributed.

In 1997, the painting returned to South Africa, "like the prodigal son," said the aging Ronnie Harrison, with great emotion. In the meantime, apartheid had been abolished and the ANC recognized as the strongest political force in the country. Nelson Mandela held office as the first black president.

The picture now hangs in the South African Art Gallery in Cape Town. Located in the heart of the capital, it is one of a number of museums gathered together under one roof, known as Iziko. Others include the Historical Museum and the Michaelis Collection, which contains Netherlandish and Flemish masters of the Baroque, from the period when the Dutch East India Company took possession of the Cape of Good Hope peninsula.

The modern successors to the Dutch colonists form part of the white minority. The British, who seized control of the territory of South Africa with a number of military campaigns, represent another part. Unlike the Dutch Boers, they pursued a relatively liberal course, abolishing slavery and opposing apartheid, which affected not only black South Africans, but also the many Indians in the region. Works of art from all these

ethnic groups compose the National Gallery's collection, which focuses principally on art created in Africa.

Wall and pavement paintings

The history of the institution begins with the South Africa Museum, founded by the British in 1825. At the beginning, it was an ethnological collection, looked after by a Briton named Andrew Smith. After 1871, an art club established a gallery which initially contained only the 45 paintings of its sponsor, Thomas Butterworth Bayley.

The collection grew in the years that followed. A building was acquired and the gallery became government property. The present gallery, a flat white building in the moderate functional style constructed by the architects, Clelland, Mullins and Kendall, opened in 1930. The buildings have been extended many times, most recently in 1991, when the last discriminatory apartheid laws disappeared.

As in most great art galleries there are both permanent and temporary exhibitions, educational activities and numerous publications. The gallery follows the general trends of contemporary art. It participated in the rediscovery of the Bloomsbury Group, formed in London and centering on Vanessa Bell and Duncan Grant, whose significance in the development of modern art in Britain has only been truly appreciated in the last decade. It also took an interest in the famous Anglo-American Pop artist, Ronald B. Kitaj. The main focus remains African art, particularly art of black African origin – that of Trevor Makhoba and Sfiso Ka Mkame, for instance.

Something resembling a common Black African style can be recognized. It is mainly self-taught, finding expression outside the building in the wall and pavement art of the townships and in sculpture and in the animist cult objects of the rural population. Woodcuts are a favorite medium, some colored, often using unmixed paints.

Art that does not deny its origins: Jane Alexander's *Butcher Boys* of 1985-86 (above left) and Ronnie Harrison's *Black Christ* of 1962 (above right) are moving examples of the Black African struggle for human rights.

The art of the Chinese

The FORBIDDEN CITY in BEIJING has been turned into a palace museum accessible to the public

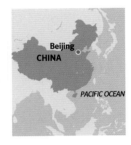

ADDRESS:
Square of Heavenly Peace, Beijing

OPENING TIMES:
Daily 8:30 am to 4:30 pm (until 5 pm in summer).

INTERNET:
www.dpm.org.cn

PUBLIC TRANSPORT:
Subway, Line 1; Bus, Lines 1, 20, 47, 54, 116

OTHER ATTRACTIONS:
China National Museum of Fine Arts

Chinese works of art from antiquity to the present day can be seen in some permanent and some temporary exhibitions in the former imperial residence. The photo (below left) shows the entrance to the Imperial Palace, whose buildings house the exhibitions.

From the 15th century, a moat and a 3 foot high red wall surround the splendid complex of buildings in the center of Beijing that is the Forbidden City. The palace district, measuring just 247 acres, was regarded by the Chinese as the center of the world, holy ground on which only the imperial family and selected servants were permitted to walk. It was only with the end of the monarchy that the taboo of the preceding centuries was overturned. Since then the world and his wife have been free to visit the Forbidden City, now known as the Palace Museum, which shelters unique Ancient Chinese architectural, artistic and craft treasures behind its high walls.

Masterpieces for 24 emperors

The imperial residence, consisting of courtyards and buildings radiating from the center, called *gu-gung* (Old Palace) by the Chinese, was built in the early 15th century after the Ming dynasty moved from Nanking to Beijing. Emperor Yongle designated a long strip of land that was already partly built up as the new palace district. Between 1406 and 1420, a million slaves, around 100,000 craftsmen, and the best artists in the country created palaces, reception rooms, gardens and accommodation for the court on this land. Twenty-four emperors of the Ming and Qing dynasties lived here in succession; the last was child Emperor Puyi, forced to abdicate by republicans in 1911.

Although buildings from the 17th and 18th centuries have shaped the district around the palace,

alongside palaces from the original complex, the overall architectural character of the site has been preserved. The history of Chinese architecture has never been documented as easily and charmingly. External walls, internals walls and slightly bowed roofs glow with the festive red which gave the residence its nickname, Purple City. Glazed tiles in imperial yellow, the white marble of carved stone balustrades and the fresh green of artfully pruned trees provide splashes of bright color.

The most beautiful of the four entrances to the Palace Museum, the Meridian Gate, is crowned by five pavilions. It rises up to the north of Tiananmen Square, the Square of Heavenly Peace. In the imperial era, only the "Son of Heaven," the emperor, was permitted to use the central gate. Now up to 10,000 mortals a day cram through this main entrance to the imperial refuge with its colorful lacquer work and fantastic carvings. Cheerful families are photographed in front of one of the terrifying guardian lions, whose threateningly raised paw symbolizes the ruler's ability to strike people who fail to show respect. Behind the Meridian Gate, the main route leads through two courtyards to a high marble terrace with the famous "Three Great Halls" (*san-da-dien*). Immediately ahead in the first hall

stands the deserted imperial throne on a jacaranda wood dais, surrounded by incense burners and screens with precious inlays and paintings. The throne room dates from the 17th century and is built of wood without a single nail. The roof rests on twenty-four camphor wood pillars. The emperor prepared for his speeches seated on the throne in the smaller, second room. The third hall, originally used for banquets, is now used to exhibit archeological finds and antique works of art.

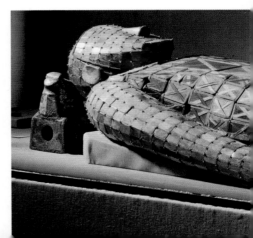

In the Purple Palace

Further palaces full of antiques can be visited in the northern section of the site, where the private quarters of the emperor, his family, his consorts and his concubines were located. The Palace of Earthly Tranquility, painted completely red, is where the imperial majesties of the Qing dynasty spent their wedding nights. The Chinese symbol for double luck (swang-hsi) gleamed out at them from the red. The biggest palace within the private chambers is the Hall of Heavenly Purity, where guests were received and celebrations held. Bronze incense burners engraved with turtles and cranes symbolize a long life.

Although the Forbidden City lost a lot of valuable works of art to plunder and evacuations, the present Palace Museum is still well-equipped with antique clocks with adventurous mechanisms, the finest porcelain, an imperial dinner service made of pure gold and tea services in agate, crystal and white jade. There are gold incense burners and bronze dragons. A ceremonial chain from the imperial wardrobe has been preserved, made up of 600,000 jade, silver and iron disks that took fifteen craftsmen 30 years to thread onto gold thread. It is also possible to see a massive block of jade, which an unknown sculptor carved with a highly contemporary motif: the battle against a terrible flood.

The carriage with the man under a parasol is a bronze from the 2nd century (above right).

The calligraphic scroll, *Prawns*, by Qi Baishi was created in 1952 (above left).

Around 200 B.C., Chinese artisans put together a Han princess's impressive funerary dress of jade plates (below center).

This religious vessel is around 2,500 years old (below right).

Art between two rivers

The treasures of Mesopotamia have been collected
by the **IRAQ MUSEUM** in **BAGHDAD**

ADDRESS:
Rashid Street/crossing
with Shuhada Bridge

OPENING HOURS:
At the time of writing
no public access is
possible

INTERNET:
www.baghdad-
museum.org

The Iraq International Museum was probably the most oft-mentioned museum in the world in 2003. The United States' military intervention in Iraq, which led to the fall of Iraqi dictator Saddam Hussein, came to a temporary end with the occupation of the capital, Baghdad, where the Museum is located.

Immediately before the start of the intervention, there had been urgent calls from academics for the Museum to be protected. But when the American troops moved in, they saw no reason to protect the Museum and, as a result, there were no controls preventing people from breaking into the building. Display cases were smashed; fragments of shattered earthenware piled up on the floors; objects vanished, only to reappear shortly afterwards on the international antiquities market.

Later, two American presidential advisors resigned in protest.

After a deplorable delay, guards were finally stationed outside the Museum. Since then, academics from all over the world have been engaged in the task of producing lists of missing art. The most current news is that the losses may not be quite as terrible as at first assumed, since many items were stored in inaccessible vaults.

Search for lost works

The Museum is currently leading a more or less virtual existence. At the time of writing, the city of Baghdad is still the target of assassination attempts and bombings. The Museum is using many different means, including the Internet, to request support and search for lost items.

Nevertheless, it is still recognized as one of the greatest and most important museums in the world. The variety and the cultural and historical value of its collection are comparable to those of the Louv-

re, the British Museum, and the Near Eastern collections of the Berlin museums.

Compared with those of other countries, the Baghdad collection has one invaluable advantage that nothing else can replace. It is located in the precise area in which the individual articles were originally produced and used. The Iraq Museum in Baghdad has the advantage of complete authenticity.

Present-day Iraq is a political invention of the British. Its geographical heart is the alluvial plain between the Rivers Tigris and Euphrates. Before the British and the Ottoman Turks, the area was ruled by Mongols, Arabs, Greeks, Romans and Persians. Mesopotamia is one of the oldest cultural landscapes in the world. Before the Persians, it was the site of Assyria and Babylon and the kingdom of Sumeria. The earliest Mesopotamian cities, Ur and Uruk – both of which lie to the south of Baghdad

near the present-day port of Basra – are around 7,000 years old and had highly efficient administrative systems at their disposal.

Invention of cuneiform writing

Among the means of guaranteeing this efficiency were instructions and documents, which required knowledge of writing. The Mesopotamians invented and used the cuneiform script, which was written with a stylus on tablets of moist clay. The tablets were then fired. The Iraq Museum has some 80,000 such tablets, which represented an immense fund of cultural and historical information. It is not known how many of these were destroyed or stolen in 2003, but it is thought to be a very large number.

For signatures and also for religious purposes, there were cylinder seals, small stone cylinders carved in intaglio that were rolled over moist clay, leaving behind their impression. The Museum collection also includes a large number of cylinder seals.

The conquerors of Mesopotamia, before and after the Sumerians, were the Akkadians, the Elamites, the Hittites, the Gutians, the Kassites and the Medes. Various great empires were formed, sometimes working alongside one another and sometimes against one another. The most powerful of these were Assyria and Babylon.

Ishtar and Utu

Usually despotic, theocratic regimes governed the whole of Mesopotamia. At the center of the religious philosophy was Ishtar, the goddess of love and fertility. Then a sun god, Utu, god of wisdom, and an important god of the city of Babylon, Marduk – as well as a multitude of local deities whose names, functions and importance vary according to the times, the regions and the ruling elite.

The art created between the Tigris and the Euphrates served either religious or political purposes. Numerous artifacts have survived, all of which show evidence of a high degree of skill. They are recognizable by their often monumental style. The Iraq Museum keeps parts of its total of 100,000 items on two extensive floors, arranged according to the sites where they were found. Such sites were mostly the center of government at the time, each with its own significant culture.

Some of these objects are world famous – such as the Nimrud treasure, which escaped the plunderers, and the late Sumerian seated figure of King Gudea of Lagash.

The statuettes of people praying are Sumerian sculptures dating from the 3rd century B.C. (above left).

Lexical entries in cuneiform script – the characters were impressed in moist clay (above right).

The bull's head from the 3rd century B.C. is part of the decoration on a harp-like instrument from Sumerian times. It was probably a burial object (below left).

The Iraq Museum in Baghdad has the advantage of complete authenticity (below right).

The Treasures of Persia

From Persepolis to **TEHERAN** – the Iranian
NATIONAL MUSEUM displays seven centuries of art

Teheran
IRAN

Red Sea

INDIAN
OCEAN

ADDRESS:
Eman Khomeini Eman
Khomeini Avenue,
Si-e-Tir Corner, Teheran

OPENING HOURS:
Wed.- Mon. 9 am to
1 pm and 2 pm to 5 pm

INTERNET:
Address not available

PUBLIC TRANSPORT:
Bus or minibus

OTHER ATTRACTIONS:
Shahid Motahari
Mosque, Golestan
Palace, Carpet Museum

Of the two dozen or so museums to be found in the Iranian capital of Teheran today, the National Museum is one of the oldest and also the most important. It opened in 1937 under the name, Iran-e Bastan. The proposal to build it came from a Frenchman, archeologist André Godard who, from 1931, was head of the Iranian Antiquities Authority for almost thirty years.

The monumental building has two floors and striking tower-like extensions at the corners. The ground plan includes two internal quadrangular courtyards to provide sufficient light for the exhibition rooms. It is built of dark red brick. The entrance is in the south wall and is slightly recessed in the center. The courtyards are reached via a long, vaulted corridor walk characteristic of Arab and oriental architecture and known as an iwan, or liwan. The origins of this style of building date back to the time of the Sassanids, the last dynasty to rule Persia before its conquest by Islam. The National Museum is modeled on the magnificent Sassanid palace in Firuzabad, erected by the founder of the dynasty, King Ardashir I.

The Sassanid rule began in the third century A.D. It was not the first time that the upland regions of Iran had attained a dominant position in politics and culture. The history of the settlement of the area stretches back to the Neolithic age. The first great kingdom came into being in the sixth century B.C. It was ruled by monarchs with such famous names as Cyrus, Cambyses, Darius and Xerxes, who came into armed conflict with the neighboring countries, including ancient Greece.

Break with tradition due to Islam

Archeological and cultural relics from all periods are on show in the Iranian National Museum, along with important works of art from more recent times. The most significant turning point occurred in the seventh century A.D., when Arab tribes invaded the country and conquered the last Sassanid king, forcing the previous state religion of Zoroastrianism to give way to Islam. From then on, Persia was part of the great Arab Empire. Not until the Renaissance was the country again ruled by its original inhabitants, Iranian princes with the title of Shah. The other part of the Iranian National Museum is stocked with relics from various periods of Islamic rule.

The first advanced civilization in ancient Iran coincides with the great kingdoms of the Archemid Kings, Darius and Xerxes. Their summer residence, Persepolis, which lies close to the southwest Iranian city of Shiraz and whose historic center remained a field of ruins after its destruction by Alexander the Great, was a monument of considerable beauty and status. Artifacts from this site are also to be found in the National Museum. They include what is known as the *Audience Relief of Darius*, originally mounted on the steps of the Apadana, which was the reception hall in Persepolis. Xerxes had the work removed and taken to his treasure house. Darius can be seen seated on his throne, with the crown princes standing behind him, all in profile. In front of them, separated from them by two incense burners, waits the court chamberlain,

Farnaka, who is announcing the representatives of the various peoples of the kingdom. Stylistically, there is a visible affinity with the reliefs of Assyria and Babylon, but it is equally clear that the art of ancient Iran has a highly individual and characteristic style, which can also be seen in the many other exhibits from that time: sculpture in the round, reliefs and architectural ornamentation. The seated figure of a Persian princess and the bronze sculpture of a Parthian prince are well known. Both figures reveal Hellenistic influ-

ences while the extensive mosaic floors draw their inspiration from Rome.

Hellenistic influences

A new three-story building was erected to house the exhibits from the Islamic period. The showpiece is the very richly decorated marble prayer niche, or mihrab, which stands on a platform on the first floor. It comes from the Friday Mosque in the small central Iranian town of Abarkuh. As we know, like the Jewish faith, Islam is a religion without images. The figu-

rative has always been and is still forbidden in Islamic art, a prohibition which led to the development of a religious art consisting of an extraordinary variety of ornamentation, in earthenware, glass, wood, stone, metal and textiles.

Ceramics are on display in various rooms in the National Museum, as are friezes with inscriptions, stucco work and mosaics. Calligraphic texts, especially magnificent editions of the Koran, are exhibited around the *mihrab*.

From the 14th century, Persia became the center of miniature, sometimes figurative, painting on paper, which soon became highly prized even in Christian countries.

One of the showpieces of the National Museum is the *Audience Relief of Darius* (above left).

The *Golden Lion Rhyton* dates from the Achemenid period. This ancient Iranian drinking vessel was made in the 5th century B.C. (above right).

The Parthians were feared warriors in ancient times. This bronze head of a warrior (detail, below left) was made in the 1st century B.C.

The National Museum building, an impressive brick edifice, was completed in 1937 (below right).

Japan's gallery of emperors

The KYOTO NATIONAL MUSEUM contains an outstanding selection of art ranging from the Heian to the Edo dynasty

ADDRESS:
527 Chayamachi,
Higashiyama-ku, Kyoto

OPENING HOURS:
Tues.–Sun. 9:30 am
to 5 pm

INTERNET:
www.kyohaku.go.jp

PUBLIC TRANSPORT:
Bus, Routes 206 or 208
to Hakubutsukan
Sanjusangendo-mae

OTHER ATTRACTIONS:
National Museum
of Modern Art

Kyoto, on the island of Honshu, was the capital of Japan for nine centuries. Tokyo did not assume this status until 1868. With its 2,000 historic palaces, temples and shrines, Kyoto has remained the country's treasure house.

Japan is a country of ancient civilizations. It is not the oldest in eastern Asia, since Korean and Chinese cultures are even older. Both of those have always had an influence on the development of Japanese art. These foreign influences became absorbed into the national culture and were coined "Japanisation." As a result, an esthetic approach developed which is fundamentally different from that of either of the two other countries.

What has been characteristic for Japan throughout all the centuries of change is its consistent love of the expression of all that is beautiful in sensory terms, an outward harmonization, harmony itself, expressed in Japanese as *wa*. An important factor is the aesthetics of omission, whereby the incomplete is regarded as beautiful since empty space invites imagination to fill the gap. The aesthetic appreciation derived from this is generally accepted as a fundamental part of Japanese culture.

Affinity with nature
The country's three different religions, Zen Buddhism, Confucianism and Shintoism, have been significant in the country's artistic development. They co-exist, each producing a unique artistic style. Shintoism is the oldest and still the most widely practiced. It is based on animism and polytheism. The nation's strong fascination with nature – even in its artificially produced form such as garden landscaping – can largely be traced back to the influences of this religion.

The sacred essence of Japanese art gradually found itself competing with growing secularization. Calligraphy and pottery developed into disciplines of considerable diversity. Along with calligraphy – artistically scripted texts – came illustrations. Japanese ceramics developed a degree of sophistication and individuality matched only by those of the Chinese. As a general principle, it can be said that the boundaries between free and applied art in Japan are much more fluid than in Western Europe. The history of art in Japan is divided, like its political development, into several epochs: the Heian period, which coincided with Kyoto's role as Japan's capital city, followed by the Kamakura, Muromachi, Momyama and Edo dynasties. The Meiji reforms in the mid-19th century mark the beginning of modernism in Japan and signaled a general opening up toward the West, a development which has endured to this day.

During the Muromachi period from 1333 to 1573, Japan went through a period of intensive painting activity, largely due to Chinese influence. Some of the names of artists from that period are known to us, for instance, the artistic genius and Zen priest, Sesshu, who reproduced natural subjects with unsurpassed delicacy. Other famous names from this period are Kao, Kensu and Shubun. Some of their landscapes were intended for murals, once again demonstrating the blurred boundaries between free and applied art. The custom of decorating wall panels or sliding doors with paintings was also typical of the Momyama period, with its occasional forays into the monumental. The Kano School of Art played an influential role at that time.

All these developments are amply illustrated in the Kyoto National Museum, situated east of the city. The largest and most beautiful of a total of 24 museums in this ancient imperial city, the Kyoto National Museum was opened in 1897 as an imperial museum. Some of its exhibits originally came from Shinto shrines and Buddhist temples while others were donated by the imperial finance ministry.

The collection of artifacts grew and it acquired the status of a national museum in 1952, which resulted in a complete reorganization of the exhibits. Today, the collection numbers approximately 10,000 items, 230 of which were formerly classed as national treasures. The exhibits are arranged into three sections: visual arts, handicrafts and archeological exhibits.

Ceramics and lacquer work
The pieces, including stone tombs and bronze mirrors dating from the country's early history, are impressive. The arts and crafts section contains, in addition to ceramics, traditional Japanese lacquer works, as well as metal items and textiles. The visual arts department houses significant examples of Chinese painting and calligraphy, together with wooden sculptures dating from the Kamakura period (1185–1333), regarded as an important period for sculpture in early Japan. The figures were fashioned from wood – the ideal was from a single piece. The finished carvings were then coated with chalk and painted.

This procedure permitted a division of labor so that more and more people could be involved in the work. Various schools of this particular art form existed, led by well-known masters. The ink drawings by Sesshu, for example, are one of the Kyoto National Museum's unrivaled highlights.

This praying figure of a servant of the water spirit is taken from an illustrated scroll dating from 1127 (left).

These graceful cranes were painted in the 17th century by Tawaraya Sotatsu. The calligraphy drawings are by Hon'ami Koetsu (above center).

Pheasants and Flowers **is the title of this 16th century drawing by Kano Motonobu (center right).**

The main entrance to the National Museum, which opened its doors in 1897 (below right).

Tradition and modernity

The **TOKYO MUSEUM OF ART** gathers contemporary Japanese art

ADDRESS:
3-1 Kitomaku Koen,
Chiyoda-ku, Tokyo

OPENING TIMES:
Tues.-Sun. 10 am
to 5 pm, Fri. to 8 pm

INTERNET:
www.momat.go.jp

PUBLIC TRANSPORT: U-
Bahn, Tozai-Linie bis
Station Takebashi

OTHER ATTRACTIONS:
Tokyo Metropolitan
Museum, Museum
of Western Art

Art on four floors: the main building of the Museum of Modern Art (below left).

Trees cast their shadows in the light. The trunks are silvery and the leaves are colored in fall hues. Some leaves are still on the branches, but most have fallen and cover the ground. The trees are widely spaced against the background of a pale sky. The picture is entitled *Dead Leaves* and exhibits all the characteristics of Impressionism – pastel colors, effects of light and shade, nature devoid of human presence. The wood could be that at Fontainebleau and the artist one of Théodore Rousseau's companions, perhaps Jules Dupré. The painting was, in fact, created at the height of the Impressionist period, 1891 to be precise, but the artist, Kuroda Seiki, is Japanese.

At the end of the 19th century European artists, notably Henri de Toulouse-Lautrec, were clearly influenced by traditional Japanese art. Yet an artist from the land of the rising sun turned to contemporary Western art for his subject matter and style.

He was not alone. Japan's strenuous rejection of Western influence, true of earlier periods, (but even then not continuously), ended with the onset of the 19th century. Portuguese and Dutch merchants of the Baroque period brought their illustrated books to Japan. The native artists took note of the printed graphics they contained and henceforth started to use central perspective, which was previously uncommon.

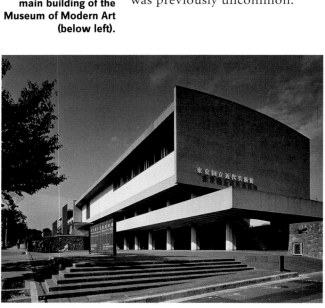

Japanese isolation ended irrevocably after 1868 with what are known as the Meiji reforms. The absolutist feudal state was transformed into a constitutional monarchy; industrial advances were made and determined developments that would elevate Japan to one of the world's leading economic powers. Nowadays, Japanese cities have all the technology and insignia of a globalized world along North American lines.

Like the salons of Paris

Fine arts were not exempt. Japanese artists studied in Europe, mainly in Paris. In return, Tokyo introduced Western European artists to the country so they could teach at domestic educational institutions. Every new development in Western art was noted attentively and adopted by domestic artists.

Corresponding groups and associations formed, each with their own art magazine. Annual exhibitions, where the results could be viewed, were organized along the lines of the Paris salons and received considerable public attention. The Japanese participated in every avant-garde art trend in the Western world, despite the country's internal political developments between the wars, which were highly nationalistic, ultimately resulting in an authoritarian fascist regime. Even after the Meiji reforms, there were always influential defenders of traditional Japanese art, but

they were unable to fully assert themselves. The Expressionist and Surrealist movements took place in Japan, as well as Suprematism, Abstraction and Action Painting. The directions existed side by side, not always without conflict, but to the advantage of both sides, because the coexistence of traditionalism and modernity created the charm of modern Japan, particularly in the arts.

From the Meiji period to the present day

In 1952, the government decided to create a separate museum in Tokyo for the considerable collection of modern Japanese art. A former office building close to the imperial palace was converted. The architect responsible was Kunio Maekawa. The Museum opened in December 1952.

It has since been expanded several times. A wealthy patron, Shojiro Ishibashi, financed the construction of a complete new wing in 1969, designed by Yoshiro Taniguchi. Later, in 1977, a gallery for arts, crafts and design opened in an already existing building, the former headquarters of the imperial palace guard. The Western-style brick buil-

ding, one of Tokyo's first buildings in this architectural style, is a UNESCO-listed building.

The main Museum building is on four floors. The permanent exhibition is divided into five sections that cover the Meiji period to the present. In the second department, city art between 1926 and 1989, there is a picture entitled, *Sea*. It is a surreal collage of a variety of of civilized and natural objects, from a sailing

ship, via the Zeppelin, to a machine plant; from seagulls and fish to a woman in a dark bathing suit. Stylistically, the picture is somewhere between Max Ernst and Giorgio de Chirico, but the painter is Harue Koga.

The striking thing about Japan's modern artists is how they relate to traditional art forms. *Autumn among Trees* by Kanzan Shimomura is painted on paper. The pen and ink drawing with two pictures was created in 1907 (above).

The double picture *Serving Girl at a Spa*, 1918, by Bakusen Tsuchida is also a pen and ink drawing. In this case, the artwork is done on silk (center).

The influence of contemporary European art on Japanese painting is documented by the 1929 painting, *Sea*, by the Japanese artist Harue Koga (below right).

Japan's classic art

During the Edo period, woodcuts reached the peak
of perfection: the **NATIONAL MUSEUM** in **TOKYO**

ADDRESS:
13-9 Ueno Park,
Tokyo

OPENING TIMES:
Mon.-Sun. 9:30 am
to 5 pm

INTERNET:
www.tnm.go.jp

PUBLIC TRANSPORT:
Subway, JR line,
Hibiya Tokyo-Metro
to Ueno station

OTHER ATTRACTIONS:
Meiji Shrine, Asakusa
Kannon Temple, Kabuki
Theater

The historic center of Tokyo is called Edo. The whole city was once so named, when it became the imperial residence. The Edo or Tokugawa period, from around 1600 to 1868, is one of the most important periods in Japanese fine art. It is particularly regarded as the great era of Japanese woodcuts.

The Japanese had known how to print books for a long time, but now artists set about producing prints. Blocks were mostly carved from cherry wood. It was customary to produce several blocks so they could be used for different colors; two or three were common, but some prints used 20 to 30 plates. Multicolored calendars appeared from 1765, commissioned by well-to-do poets' societies. They frequently had erotic designs. The name for these was *nishiki-e*, 'brocade pictures,' and the art form as a whole was known as *ukiyo-e*.

Master Hokusai

The word means "pictures of the floating world" (everyday life). The term is a reminder of Buddhist concepts of the transitory nature of happiness, but this art was concerned with the fleeting fashions and unstable lives of actors, courtesans and other inhabitants of the amusements quarter rather than strict piety. *Ukiyo-e* was dominated by portraits of these people.

The art of woodcuts during the Edo period produced some extremely famous masters, such as Suzuki Harunobu, Kitagawa Utamaro and Katsushika Hokusai (1760-1849), who was known far beyond the borders of Japan. His works appeared in world expositions in Paris and Vienna in the 19th century and had an extraordinary impact on Europe. Western European contemporary art became a slave to all things Japanese, in-

fluencing such varied artists as Henri de Toulouse-Lautrec, Vincent Van Gogh, Aubrey Beardsley and Gustav Klimt. Even European Art Nouveau owed a lot to Hokusai and others.

Hokusai created numerous landscapes, including views of the holy mountain, Fuji. His picture *Kanagawa-oki namiura*, or "Great wave off the coast of Kanagawa," has also become famous. He illustrated books, fairy tales and adventure novels, his total works numbering some 30,000. He led an unsettled life and taught a succession of gifted pupils.

Art from the Edo period is the focal point of exhibitions in the National Museum which, together with the Kyoto National Museum, is the most important in the country. It dates back to 1872, when the Ministry of Culture organized a public exhibition of Japanese art in a former temple. Three years later, the project, with the addition of a library, came under the aegis of the Ministry of the Interior.

An imperial museum from 1886, a new main exhibition building opened in 1909, but suffered severe damage in an earthquake in 1923. The present main gallery dates from 1938 and is in the conservative imperialist teikan style, which dominated the period immediately before the Second World War. It has been the National Museum since 1947.

Courtesans and actors

The Museum comprises five separate pavilions. They stand on the Uenokoen site, where other important museums are also located. There is a research center, shops and restaurants. A Japanese garden exemplifies the ancient and highly developed Japanese art of shaping nature. The Heiseikan Pavilion exhibits archeological finds; the Toyokan Pavilion displays Asian art, mainly from Korea, China and India. The Horyu-ji Treasury contains 319 exhibits from a former temple that were previously owned by the emperor: lacquer work, paintings, textiles and masks. The Hyokeikan building is used for special exhibitions.

The main building, Honkan, documents 12,000 years of Japanese art over two floors in chronological order, commencing with earthenware of remarkable skill from times when the natives of the archipelago still lived as hunter-

gatherers. The collection progresses through ceramics of various shapes and metal grave goods to the start of the Haniwa period, when the cities of Nara and Kyoto rose to be centers of political and cultural importance, and Buddhism made its entrance. Portraits are characteristic of Edo period art. Many of the sitters are courtesans and kabuki players and there

Twelve thousand years worth of art are exhibited in Honkan, the main National Museum building (below left).

are depictions of warriors and priests. The art of portraiture did not begin in the Edo period, but dates back to the Momoyama period and was gradually refined over the centuries until it achieved its peak in the work of artists such as Watanabe Kazan (1793–1841).

娘日時計 巳ノ刻

Hokusai's woodcut, *View through Waves off the Coast of Kanagawa* (above), is regarded as a masterpiece of the Edo period and was created in the 19th century. The holy mountain Fujiyama can be seen in the background.

The picture by Utamaro entitled *Hour of the Snake*, from the *Women at various Hours of the Day* series also dates from the Edo period and was painted in the 18th century (below right).

Expulsion of the Ruling Family to Rokuhara was painted during the Heiji civil war in the 13th century (below center).

203

The Taipei Palace houses ancient Chinese art

The NATIONAL PALACE MUSEUM in TAIWAN exhibits art from Beijing

ADDRESS:
221 Chi-shan Road, Taipei

OPENING TIMES:
Daily 9 am to 5 pm

INTERNET:
www.npm.gov.tw

PUBLIC TRANSPORT:
Subway to Shilin, from there bus route 30

OTHER ATTRACTIONS:
Taipei Fine Art Museum

At first glance, you could imagine that you are in China. Although it is a little smaller and painted pale yellow instead of crimson, the curved roofs and high wall protecting the building complex of the National Palace Museum in the Taipei, opened in 1965, are reminiscent of the Forbidden City, Beijing's ancient imperial residence. The similarity is intentional since the important ancient Chinese art displayed in Taipei once lay in the Forbidden City's treasuries, before they reached Formosa, now Taiwan, during the turmoil of 20th century wars.

As long ago as the first millennium before Christ, rulers of the empire beautified their palaces with valuable antiques, laying the foundation for one of the most splendid art collections in the world. Emperor Wu-ti, who ruled China from 140 to 87 B.C., built a great hall to display many ancient bronzes, paintings and scrolls. His successor, Yuan-ti, is said to have been so obsessed with collecting that he neglected his rule. An inventory ordered by Emperor Hui-tsung in the 12th century A.D. recorded more than 7,000 individual items in a "Catalogue of Antiquities," the first volume of which is exhibited in Taipei.

Fifteen thousand masterpieces

Later, large sections of the treasure fell into the hands of Mongols. Under Mongolian rule, the considerable remains reached Beijing for the first time, where they were preserved and added to the Forbidden City by the succeeding Ming dynasty. In the 19th century, invading French and British troops were "accompanied" by imperial art treasures when they withdrew. Further losses were sustained during fires and secret sales. After the last emperor was driven out, the collection still comprised around 800,000 separate items. When the Japanese marched into China in 1931, the Chinese nationalist government, under Marshal Chiang Kai-shek (1887–1975) packed the palace treasure into more than 19,000 crates and spirited them away to various parts of China. Almost 3,000 of the crates ended up in Taiwan in 1949.

Around 15,000 masterpieces from the massive collection saved now form part of a permanent exhibition in Taipei. One of the oldest exhibits is a jade pendant in the form of a stylized bird from 3,000 B.C. Richly decorated bronze vessels used for sacrificial rituals when burying the dead and incantations to the ancestors, are more than 3,000 years old. There are a striking number of representations of dragons in semiprecious stones, silver, gold and bronze. This fantastic creature was prized by the Chinese as a bringer of luck and simultaneously symbolized the power of the imperial "Son of Heaven" on the Dragon Throne.

Folding screens and scrolls

Paintings on scrolls and screens predominantly reflect court scenes from the China of the Middle Ages, together with portraits and landscapes. A portrait by an unknown artist of the Emperor T'ai-Tsung, who ruled in the 10th century, is particularly impressive. Wrapped in a white robe, the heavy-set man sits on a red-painted throne, his feet resting on a footstool. A scroll which has been lent out to foreign museums shows a delicate watercolor painting of the flowering apricot tree in whose bark the Emperor Kao-Tsung is said to have carved his poems for 37 years.

In the ceramics department, valuable old Chinese porcelain catches the eye. Some of the most beautiful pieces, fired for the first time in the 14th century, are decorated with cobalt blue on a white background. Blue is also the color of the decorative dragon on a spherical vase from the Ming era. Other pieces are decorated with oxblood glaze or have a multicolored floral pattern. The commonest shapes are bellied vases, pumpkin-shape vases and dishes with or without round feet. Some preserved pieces of porcelain also have a monochrome color scheme using the color preferred by the ruling dynasty at that time, such as red or imperial yellow.

A department particularly arresting for students of Chinese is devoted to antique writing scrolls, letters and literary texts, including the "Erh-Ya" (Near to Correctness) dictionary, first recorded around 200 B.C. It is considered the oldest dictionary in the world.

To this day, heated controversy surrounds the rightful ownership of the 15,000 exhibits and 650,000 safely stored works of art. Until the end of the last dynasty, the collection was regarded as the legitimate possession of the imperial "Son of Heaven." Since the new political order emerged, China feels it is the rightful heir and accuses Taiwan of art theft.

Genghis Khan (1206- 27), founder of the Yuan dynasty who made China the center of the Mongol Empire (left).

Hunting scene from the 13th century, painted on silk. A work of art from the time of the Yuan dynasty (below center).

Banqueting scene from the 10th century with musical entertainment (below right).

The Palace Museum in Taipei is a new building opened in 1965.

Australia's young art

The NATIONAL GALLERY OF AUSTRALIA in CANBERRA exhibits Australia's most important artists

ADDRESS:
Parkes Place,
Canberra

OPENING TIMES:
Mon. -Sun. 10 am
to 5 pm

INTERNET:
www.nga.gov.au

PUBLIC TRANSPORT:
Bus, Route 30 or 34

OTHER ATTRACTIONS:
National Portrait
Gallery, Canberra
Museum and Gallery,
National Museum of
Australia

Technology penetrating the expanse of nature? Sidney Nolan called his 1946 painting, *Ned Kelly* (below left).

Two eagles circle a sky laced with threadlike clouds floating against pale blue. Below, sheep graze under a watchful eye. The scenery is gently undulating, the leaves on the trees are beginning to turn and the grass is largely dried out. In the background that shades to dark blue, the Yarra River lazily flows along. The painting, *Golden Summer, Eaglemont*, was painted by Arthur Streeton in 1889.

He was born in 1867 in Duneed, a township in the Australian state of Victoria. The teacher's son first worked for a wine and spirits firm in Melbourne, taking painting and drawing courses in his spare time. His heroes were Camille Corot and the Barbizon School, J.M.W. Turner and the French Impressionists.

Massive formats

He had his first one-person exhibition in 1885. From 1888, he lived for a time in Eaglemont, near Heidelberg, a town to the north of Melbourne. Later, he undertook numerous journeys and lived in London before returning to Australia. Knighted in 1937, he died in 1943. His landscape paintings are among the most important works in Australian fine art. *Golden Summer, Eaglemont* is one of the star exhibits in the National Gallery Canberra.

Painter and photographer Sean Scully was born in Dublin in 1945 and grew up in London. His paintings can be seen in many exhibitions and are hung in many museums, from Chicago to Madrid, Düsseldorf to Tokyo. They are often on a massive scale and they are always purely abstract: brilliantly colored bands meet at right angles or overlap, reminiscent of fabric patchwork or a greatly enlarged weave, an impression intensified by the visible brushstrokes.

Scully falls between Kasimir Malewitsch, Piet Mondrian and Mark Rothko; his works display moods between cheerfulness and depression. The National Gallery Canberra possesses his *Wall of Light Desert Day* of 2003, acquired, amongst others, by Brian Kennedy, its director from 1997 to 2004, and a great admirer of Scully.

Heidelberg School

The Gallery is a young institution, Australia is a young country and Canberra is its young capital. Parliament and government moved here from Melbourne in 1927. The Gallery building was constructed from 1974 and was opened in 1982 by Queen Elizabeth II, Australia's head of state. Paintings by artists Arthur Streeton and Sean Scully represent two of the Gallery's main collecting and exhibiting activities: concern for the domestic artistic tradition and striving to maintain contact with the international art scene. There are a couple of Baroque Italian

works and modern artists such as Anselm Kiefer as well as Scully, of course. Australian artists represent a particular focus which, together with Arthur Streeton, includes the remaining representatives of what is known as the Heidelberg School: Tom Roberts and Frederick McCubbin.

They all represent just one aspect, European-inspired, fine art in Australia. Because of Australia's geographic proximity to Asia, the National Gallery contains a comprehensive collection of Asiatic art, including pieces from Thailand, Japan, Bangladesh and Iran, Chinese porcelain and woodcuts as well as works by modern Chinese artists.

Aboriginal Memorial

But Australia itself is not only represented by European immigrant artists. The indigenous peoples of Australia, the Aboriginals, persecuted and neglected by white colonists, have managed to preserve a distinct culture which has since been recognized outside Australia. Modern artists have admired and attempted to decipher

its symbols. Works by Paul Klee, Keith Harring and A.R. Penck draw inspiration from them.

The National Gallery Canberra devotes a lot of space to these artists. Between 1987 and 1988, a total of 43 artists created the *Aboriginal Memorial*, an installation for the Gallery's sculpture garden. The artists came from Arnhemland, the Aboriginal reservation in the northeast, in the Northern Territory. They erected 200 painted sculptures in tree trunks that have been hollowed out, mostly as a result of being eaten away by termites. The Aboriginals place the bones of the dead in the empty spaces. They are coffins that are not covered with earth, but are planted in the ground, decorated with the totems and insignia of the clans from which the dead originated. The National Gallery Canberra's sculpture garden brings together 200 poles, standing close together, reminiscent of a forest of death. Strange and magical, it stands as a memorial to the nameless victims of a colonization policy whose horrors are only now

surfacing in the consciousness of Australian society.

Arthur Streeton's painting, *Golden Summer,* Eaglemont (above), painted in 1889, is one of the Gallery's attractions.

The present National Gallery building was opened in 1982 (below right).

PHOTO CREDITS (reproduction rights, artwork & photo)